Gesture and Film

Gesture has held a crucial role in cinema since its inception. In the absence of spoken words, early cinema frequently exploited the communicative potential of the gestures of actors. As this book demonstrates, gesture has continued to assume immense importance in film to the present day. This innovative book features essays by leading international scholars working in the fields of cinema, cultural and gender studies, examining modern and contemporary films from a variety of theoretical perspectives. This volume also includes contributions from an esteemed actor, and a world-renowned psychologist working in the field of gesture, enabling a pioneering interdisciplinary dialogue around this exciting, emerging field of study. Drawing on philosophy, psychoanalysis and psychology, the chapters think through gesture in film from a range of new angles, pointing out both its literal and abstract manifestations. Gesture is analysed in relation to animal/human relations, trauma and testimony, sexual difference, ethics and communitarian politics, through examples from both narrative and documentary cinema. This book was originally published as a special issue of the *Journal for Cultural Research*.

Nicholas Chare is Associate Professor of Modern Art in the Department of History of Art and Film Studies at the Université de Montréal, Canada. His most recent book is *Sportswomen in Cinema: Film and the Frailty Myth*.

Liz Watkins is a Lecturer in the History of Art at the University of Leeds, UK. Her research interests include the significance of colour for film theories of subjectivity, perception and sexual difference. She has published on feminism, film/philosophy, the materiality of film and archive in *parallax, Paragraph, British Journal of Cinema and Television* and *NECSUS European Journal of Media Studies*. She is co-editor, with Simon Brown and Sarah Street, of *Color and the Moving Image: History, Theory, Aesthetics, Archive* (2013) and *British Colour Cinema: Practices and Theories* (2013).

Gesture and Film

Signalling New Critical Perspectives

Edited by
Nicholas Chare and Liz Watkins

Routledge
Taylor & Francis Group

LONDON AND NEW YORK

First published 2017
by Routledge
2 Park Square, Milton Park, Abingdon, Oxon, OX14 4RN, UK

and by Routledge
711 Third Avenue, New York, NY 10017, USA

Routledge is an imprint of the Taylor & Francis Group, an informa business

British Library Cataloguing in Publication Data
A catalogue record for this book is available from the British Library

ISBN 13: 978-1-138-90019-6

Typeset in TimesNewRomanPS
by diacriTech, Chennai

Publisher's Note
The publisher accepts responsibility for any inconsistencies that may have arisen during the conversion of this book from journal articles to book chapters, namely the possible inclusion of journal terminology.

Disclaimer
Every effort has been made to contact copyright holders for their permission to reprint material in this book. The publishers would be grateful to hear from any copyright holder who is not here acknowledged and will undertake to rectify any errors or omissions in future editions of this book.

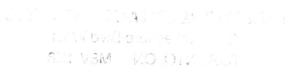

Contents

CONTENTS

Citation Information

The following chapters were originally published in the *Journal for Cultural Research*, volume 19, issue 1 (March 2015). When citing this material, please use the original page numbering for each article, as follows:

Chapter 1

Cinematic gesture: The ghost in the machine
Laura Mulvey
Journal for Cultural Research, volume 19, issue 1 (March 2015) pp. 6–14

Chapter 2

Speech-gesture mimicry in performance: an actor → audience, author → actor, audience → actor triangle
David McNeill
Journal for Cultural Research, volume 19, issue 1 (March 2015) pp. 15–29

Chapter 3

Films, gestures, species
Barbara Creed
Journal for Cultural Research, volume 19, issue 1 (March 2015) pp. 43–55

Chapter 4

Gesture in Shoah
Nicholas Chare
Journal for Cultural Research, volume 19, issue 1 (March 2015) pp. 30–42

Chapter 6

The disquiet of the everyday: gesture and Bad Timing
Liz Watkins
Journal for Cultural Research, volume 19, issue 1 (March 2015) pp. 56–68

Chapter 7

Image as gesture: notes on Aernout Mik's Communitas *and the modern political film*
Patricia Pisters
Journal for Cultural Research, volume 19, issue 1 (March 2015) pp. 69–81

Chapter 9
The time of gesture in cinema and its ethics
Elizabeth Cowie
Journal for Cultural Research, volume 19, issue 1 (March 2015) pp. 82–95

Chapter 10
'The exchange of two fantasies and the contact of two epidermises': gestures of touch in Gattaca *(1997),* The Talented Mr. Ripley *(1999) and* The Piano *(1993)*
Naomi Segal
Journal for Cultural Research, volume 19, issue 1 (March 2015) pp. 96–109

Chapter 11
A mark on the Canvas
Carol Mayo Jenkins
Journal for Cultural Research, volume 19, issue 1 (March 2015) pp. 110–113

For any permission-related enquiries please visit:
http://www.tandfonline.com/page/help/permissions

Notes on Contributors

Paul Bowman is Professor of Cultural Studies, Director of the Race, Representation and Cultural Politics Research Group, and founder of the Centre for Interdisciplinary Film & Visual Culture Research, Cardiff University, UK. His publications include *Beyond Bruce Lee: Chasing the Dragon through Film, Philosophy, and Popular Culture* (2013), *Reading Rey Chow: Visuality, Ethnicity, Sexuality* (2013), *Culture and Media* (2012) and *Deconstructing Popular Culture* (2008).

Nicholas Chare is Associate Professor of Modern Art in the Department of History of Art and Film Studies at the Université de Montréal, Canada. His most recent book is *Sportswomen in Cinema: Film and the Frailty Myth*.

Elizabeth Cowie is Emeritus Professor of Film Studies at the University of Kent, Canterbury, UK. She is the co-founder of *m/f a journal of feminist theory*, and the author of *Representing the Woman: Cinema and Psychoanalysis* (1997) and *Recording Reality, Desiring the Real* (2011). She has subsequently written on film noir, on the horror of the horror film, and on the cinematic dreamwork. Her work has also recently appeared in both *Screen* and the online journal *Media Fields*.

Barbara Creed is Redmond Barry Distinguished Professor Emeritus in the School of Culture and Communication at the University of Melbourne, Australia. She has spoken and published widely in the area of film and visual cultures. Her books include *The Monstrous-feminine: Film, Feminism, Psychoanalysis* (1993), *Phallic Panic: Film, Horror and the Primal Uncanny* (2005) and *Darwin's Screens: Evolutionary Aesthetics, Time and Sexual Display in the Cinema* (2009). She is currently carrying out research in two related areas: animals and the emotions and the cinema of human rights. She is the Director of the Human Rights and Animal Ethics Research Network.

Carol Mayo Jenkins is Artist in Residence – Acting in the Department of Theatre at the University of Tennessee, Knoxville, TN, USA. She made her Broadway debut as Natasha in William Ball's production of *Chekhov's Three Sisters*. She has appeared on Broadway in *Oedipus Rex*, *First Monday in October* and *The Suicide*. Off-Broadway she appeared in *The Lady's Not for Burning*, *Little Eyolf* and *The Old Ones*, among many others. She also appeared in the television series, *Fame*, in which she played an English teacher, Elizabeth Sherwood, for five years. She has worked extensively in Regional Theatre since her years in television.

David McNeill is Emeritus Professor of Psychology and Linguistics at the University of Chicago, IL, USA. He has worked in the area of gesture and language since 1980, playing a founder's role in establishing gesture studies as a modern intellectual field, and was part of the discussions leading to the foundation of the International Society for Gesture Studies and the journal *Gesture*. He has published or edited nine books, four of which focus specifically on gesture and language: *Hand and Mind* (1992), *Language and Gesture* (2000), *Gesture and Thought* (2005) and *How Language Began* (2012).

Laura Mulvey is Professor of Film and Media Studies, and Director of the Birkbeck Institute for the Moving Image, at Birkbeck College, University of London, UK. She is the author of *Visual and Other Pleasures* (1989, 2009), *Fetishism and Curiosity* (1996, 2013), *Citizen Kane* (1996, 2012) and *Death 24 × a Second: Stillness and the Moving Image* (2006). She is the co-director (with Peter Wollen) of *Riddles of the Sphinx* (1977) and (with Mark Lewis) *Disgraced Monuments* (1994) and *23 August 2008* (2013).

Patricia Pisters is Professor of Film Studies in the Department of Media Studies of the University of Amsterdam, The Netherlands. She is one of the founding editors of *Necsus: European Journal of Media Studies*. Her publications include *The Matrix of Visual Culture: Working with Deleuze in Film Theory* (2003) and *Mind the Screen: Media Concepts According to Thomas Elsaesser* (ed. with Jaap Kooijman and Wanda Strauven, 2008). Her latest book is *The Neuro-Image: A Deleuzian Film-Philosophy of Digital Screen Culture* (2012).

Griselda Pollock is Professor of the Social and Critical Histories of Art, and the Director of Research in the School of Fine Art, History of Art and Cultural Studies at the University of Leeds, UK. Her most recent publications include *Concentrationary Memories: Totalitarian Terror and Cultural Resistance* (with Silverman, 2013), *Visual Politics and Psychoanalysis: Art and the Image in Post-traumatic Cultures* (2013) and *After-Affects I After-Images: Trauma and Aesthetic Transformation in the Virtual Feminist Museum* (2013).

Naomi Segal is Professorial Fellow in French and German Studies at Birkbeck, University of London, UK. She has served on or chaired numerous inter/national committees including within ESF, HERA and the AHRB/C. Her recent work includes *Vicissitudes: Histories and Destinies of Psychoanalysis* (2013), '*When familiar meanings dissolve…': Essays in memory of Malcolm Bowie* (2011), *Consensuality: Didier Anzieu, Gender and the Sense of Touch* (2009), *Indeterminate Bodies* (2003) and *André Gide: Pederasty and Pedagogy* (1998).

Liz Watkins is a Lecturer in the History of Art at the University of Leeds, UK. Her research interests include the significance of colour for film theories of subjectivity, perception and sexual difference. She has published on feminism, film/philosophy, the materiality of film and archive in *parallax, Paragraph, British Journal of Cinema and Television* and *NECSUS European Journal of Media Studies*. She is co-editor, with Simon Brown and Sarah Street, of *Color and the Moving Image: History, Theory, Aesthetics, Archive* (2013) and *British Colour Cinema: Practices and Theories* (2013).

Introduction: Gesture in film

Nicholas Chare and Liz Watkins

In his classic study, *Gesture*, Adam Kendon describes the visible actions that comprise utterances (Kendon, 2004, pp. 1–2). These visible utterances can occur in conjunction with, or independently to, speech. Kendon's definition of gesture draws attention to it as a deed and a doing. Gesture is an activity, a product of energy and motion. Human gestures occur as a result of movements of the body, of the face (such as rolling the eyes, winking), the neck (nodding, shaking the head), the hands (the V sign, waving), the shoulders (shrugging), the knees (genuflecting), the torso (bowing, turning your back on someone), the buttocks (mooning, twerking) or combinations thereof. Many gestures form pictures through specific motions: outlining an absent object's dimensions or mimicking exploits. David McNeill distinguishes between imagistic and non-imagistic gestures. For him, as Kendon summarises, '*imagistic* gestures are those in which movements are made that are interpreted as depicting the shape of an object, displaying an action of some kind, or representing some pattern of movement' (Kendon, 2004, pp. 99–100). These kinds of gestures are moving representations of acts or of artefacts: motion pictures of a kind. Given that gestures are often imagistic, connecting gesture and film, as this collection of essays proposes to do, is an evident, if not unproblematic, move to make.

It is common to examine gestures made by actors in films. Recently, André Habib has movingly explored his enduring memories of the gestural power and influence of the actor Jean-Pierre Léaud's left hand, particularly in Jean-Luc Godard's *Masculin Féminin* (Dir. Jean-Luc Godard, France, 1966), but also in other films (Habib, 2015). Gesture forms a key means by which an actor can establish the personality of a character. In films such as *Cruising Bar* (Dir. Robert Ménard, Québec, 1989), in which one actor assumes multiple parts, gesture works alongside make-up and voice to establish character differentiation. The actor Michel Côté plays four different roles in *Cruising Bar*, four aspiring Lotharios whose temperaments are each associated with a specific animal. Côté is Jean-Jacques (the peacock), Gerard (the bull), Patrice (the lion) and Serge (the earthworm). Each possesses distinctive gestural traits: Jean-Jacques is upright, elegant and strutting, Gerard lumbers and ruts, Patrice is touchy feely and extravagant with his movements, while Serge is uptight, gesturally repressed, repeatedly baring his teeth in a nervous smile. *Cruising Bar* amplifies how gesture is used by an actor as a tool to create and detail a given demeanour.

Gesture frequently forms an integral dimension to a film's mise en scène, a bodily contribution to mood. In *12 Angry Men* (Dir. Sidney Lumet, USA, 1957), for example, the gestures of each of the jurors play a major role in establishing their personalities and their shifting positions within the evolving power dynamic in the jury room. The thoughtfulness

1

an actor and director dedicate to gesture is eloquently attested to by Carol Mayo Jenkins's coda to the book. Jenkins writes insightfully about the different gestural demands roles in theatre and film place upon an actor. She points towards ways in which even the slightest of deliberate, deliberated motions can assume intense significance or, as she calls it, 'define a moment' in film. In a beautiful exploration of the actor's approach to gesture in their craft, Jenkins draws attention to how gestures move beyond words. Visible utterances are frequently carefully choreographed to lend emotional weight to a part. They can imbue a sense of human warmth, poignancy or tragedy to a scene.

Gesture can also be used by an actor as a means by which to signal a lack of humanity. In the television series *Äkta människor* [*Real Humans*] (Dirs. Harald Hamrell and Levan Akin, Sweden, 2012–2013), for example, the alterity of the hubots (humanoid robots) is communicated by way of a certain gestural stiffness and an occasional motional stuttering. The physical movements of the homicidal cyborg played by Arnold Schwarzenegger in *The Terminator* (Dir. James Cameron, 1984, USA) prefigure this gestural otherness. In a studied strategy to indicate his character's otherworldliness, Schwarzenegger slowly swivels his head when looking at things. He scans his surroundings, receiving and processing data, in a gesture that signals that he is a product of the Digital Age. The low speed of the gesture and its tightness marks out the cyborg as a simulation of a human rather than the real thing. Constantin Stanislavski commented on how an actor exhibiting 'muscular tautness' would be unable to communicate 'inner emotional experience' (Stanislavski, 1981, p. 97). In *The Terminator*, intractability is exploited to portray a literally heartless character. The force of the gesture resides in its failure to mirror common human motion. Schwarzenegger's staged inhumanity augments the drama.

The dramatic power of gesture is obvious in *Festen* (Dir. Thomas Vinterberg, Denmark, 1998), in which the central character, Christian, a child abuse survivor, repeatedly, nervously rubs his hands together as if endeavouring to remove a stain. Here the actor playing Christian, Ulrich Thomsen, consciously cultivates a physical symptom of trauma, a bodily manifestation of the memory of unspeakable events to communicate psychic distress to the spectator. The gesture, however, is obviously meant to be viewed as an unconscious one. Gestures, as utterances, are not always the product of conscious intent. Some gesticulations emerge unbidden, indexing the agency of the unconscious in bodily communication. Gestures, chattering fingers in Christian's circumstance, betray repressed memories.

The capacity for bodies to suggest psychic trauma is considered in Nicholas Chare's 'Gesture in *Shoah*' which, developing his earlier work regarding how gesture points towards aspects of psychic life beyond signification (Chare, 2012, pp. 131–176), argues that an analysis of the film that is attentive to its gestural economies enriches understanding. The essay draws on the ideas of David Efron, Edith Stein and Charlotte Wolff as a means to consider gesture in *Shoah* at the level of the interviewees and also in relation to cinematography and editing. The study explores the potential, through becoming absorbed in the gestures of another, of sharing another's mental state.

In his essay 'speech-gesture mimicry in performance', David McNeill also examines how gesture links bodies on screen with the bodies of spectators. Building on his earlier ground-breaking work on gesture, McNeill develops his ideas on the relationship of hand gestures and thought processes, addressing their usefulness in a film and theatre context (McNeill, 1992, 2005). With poise, McNeill traces the dynamic role of mimicry of gestures in ideation and communication across writing, acting and reception, suggesting a triangle that links the author, the actor and the audience. On set, in the absence of a live audience, McNeill suggests that actors imbue the camera with personality, ensuring that the triangle is maintained.

The camera in such instances becomes personified. It becomes a pseudo-human. Gestures, however, are not restricted to humans. The gestures that are employed by Côté in *Cruising Bar*, for instance, are intended to reflect the 'animal' qualities of the four characters. In *Cruising Bar*, these gestures reveal Western culture's anthropocentric tendencies. The vanity of the peacock, for example, is the product of projecting a human quality onto an animal. Animals do, nevertheless, gesture. Michael Argyle has discussed how they use non-verbal communication (Argyle, 1988, pp. 27–48). He describes the role of gestures in a chimpanzee society (pp. 42–43). Barbara Creed examines the visible utterances of chimpanzees in the film *Project Nim* (Dir. James Marsh, USA, 2011) as part of her essay 'Films, gestures, species', an inspiring analysis of how the continuity between animal and human gestures has been registered in cinema. Creed views gesture as figuring the animal in the human and the human in the animal. At times gestures are neither human nor animal; they are both animal and human, unfixing longstanding beliefs regarding oppositions between species. Creed's deconstructive manoeuvres permit the free play of gesture as a signifier. Previous scholarship related to animal gestures, in particular, has suggested that visible utterances possess singular meaning. Creed, however, through drawing attention to the role of reception in sense-making in the animal world, queries such notions.

A crisis at the level of visible utterance's articulation and interpretation undergirds what is currently one of the most influential texts on gesture in relation to cinema, Giorgio Agamben's 'Notes on gesture' (2000, pp. 49–60).[1] In this idiosyncratic essay, Agamben argues that since the end of the nineteenth century, the Western bourgeoisie have lost their gestures. As part of this thesis, Agamben discusses Gilles de la Tourette's research suggesting that the shocks suffered by patients with Tourette's syndrome prevent their being able to gesture: 'if they are able to start a movement, this is interrupted and broken up by shocks lacking any coordination and by tremors that give the impression that the whole musculature is engaged in a dance (*chorea*) that is completely independent of any ambulatory end' (p. 51).

If a gesture is interrupted, it remains unfinished, open ended. Agamben states: 'patients can neither start nor complete the simplest of gestures' (p. 51). Here Tourette's comes to stand for a situation that impacts on the bourgeoisie as a whole, as is evident from the films of Étienne-Jules Marey and the Lumière brothers, namely that in modernity, 'everybody had lost control of their gestures and was walking and gesticulating frantically' (Agamben, 2000, p. 52). Gesture, as figured by Agamben, signals an inessential communal action of which Western society has lost sight (Chare, 2015, pp. 69–70). Cinema, however, remembers this gesture, a means without ends, pure means. Agamben's gesture is not a visible utterance, not a specific physical action, but an abstract idea, a trope pointing towards a coming politics that is non-identitarian.

Agamben's 'Notes on gesture' suggest that what is ineluctably cinematic of gesture is not determined by an image, but timeliness in the transience of communication. Gestures constitute a temporality of movement that transforms the photographic into the cinematic, an alteration that demands to be deciphered and yet does not bind the meanings that are to be formed to the content of the image. As Elizabeth Cowie's insightful reading of *Exotica* (Dir. Atom Egoyan, Canada, 1994) explains, although abstract gestures entice interpretation, they are not germane to meaning. The mediality of such gestures, rather, instantiates an ethical stance: recognition of the potential of an exchange communicates communicability, the possibility of which is invoked and then thwarted, questioning the positionality of each subject. Cowie's analysis of Egoyan's film finds that gestures are staged as invitations, which signal the spectre of meaning whilst confounding the spectator's attempt to read them as expressive. The ambiguities of sanctioned and improper desire are figured in the actions and expressions of characters through a gestural performance. Cowie argues that the undecided gestures of the film present an ethics of desire.

The political qualities of cinematic gestures, which are considered of Agamben's work by Janet Harbord in her essay on psychology and ethics (2015), are explored in another register by Patricia Pisters through reference to Deleuze in a reading of the video installations in Aernout Mik's exhibition *Communitas*. Pisters explores Robert Bresson's 'Notes on the cinematographer' and Gilles Deleuze's work on the modern political film to formulate a reading that reaches out to the temporality and movement that unfolds as people visiting the exhibition space encounter the positioning and repetition of bodies and movements on screen. Here, the mediality of gestures registers discontent with a language or law that is not sufficient to the instance of need. Pisters's analysis of *Touch, Rise and Fall* focuses on the 'non-place' of airport security that is evoked of its officers' gestures as they cut and search bags. The moments in which the alarms are activated, as visitors move through the exhibition, marks the endless gestures of control which leave the officers mesmerised by the repetition of their task. The mechanical movement of these disciplined bodies is reminiscent of the cinematographic animation of gestures in silent film and yet is encountered in a new medium. Pisters finds that the silence of Mik's video works pervades the collective space of their exhibition. Thus, the gestures that are operative between viewer and screen emphasise the potential of the video image itself as a gesture.

The interrelations of performance and the cinematographic can be traced in the segmentation and animation of bodily movement that are integral to filmic representation. Mobilised by Agamben's note on dance as gesture, Laura Mulvey offers new insight on the interactions of performance and the cinematographic as she examines stillness and repetition in Marilyn Monroe's dance in *Gentlemen Prefer Blondes* (Dir. Howard Hawks, USA, 1953). Mulvey's use of slow motion as a process of reduplication finds the mediality of gesture between a pause in the fluidity of Monroe's performance, which calls to both the poise of her star image and the stasis of the 24 frames per second that belie the cinematic illusion of movement. In this and her analysis of *Imitation of Life* (Dir. Douglas Sirk, USA, 1959) (2006, pp.149–151), Mulvey is attentive to the nuances of performance which intersect with the motion of the camera and the film medium itself, that is, between the multiple registers of stillness and movement from which cinematic representation is formed (2006, pp. 67–68). Thus, the connections between film technologies, performance and the illusionary worlds that unfold on the cinema screen are explored to consider gesture as medial of these intersecting strands.

Mulvey's approach evokes the readings that were made of the filmic system in the 1970s (Willemen, 1971) for the potential of abstract gestures to become a form of distanciation that distances the viewer from the process of reading (Mulvey, 2006, pp. 149–150) and yet indicates a new direction through an exploration of the intermediality of stills photography, performance and the cinematographic. Gesture, as a form of distanciation, was theorised as a disturbance in the film text which solicited the spectator's attention to indicate broader issues of social and political discontent. The refraction of ideologically complicit forms of representation registers a pervasive disquiet in the social order otherwise expressed by the melodramas directed by Douglas Sirk under the stipulations of the Hollywood studio system (Willemen, 1971; Mulvey 1989, 1996). The interplay of performance and the cinematographic can become emphatic of certain aspects of the text or signal the failure of that system of representation to signify the specific desires of displaced and effaced subjectivities beyond a demarcation as *other*. This precedent can be tracked back to figure of the mute in the 1940s melodrama as the enactment of a site of social praxis. In the melodrama *The Spiral Staircase* (Dir. Robert Siodmak, USA, 1946), trauma is marked in the deflection of signifying material on to other non-verbal registers such as gesture, music and mise en scène (Doane, 1988, p. 85). The film's heroine, Helen Capel, stands before her reflection in a mirror, her hand clasped over her mouth in a gesture that embodies the silencing of her voice. The effect of Capel's gestures – from the demarcation of her absence from speech, to the desired invisibility of her labour which is an integral aspect of the class system of the house, to the expressive movements through which she implores assistance under the pursuit of a murderer – mark the ethical and moral complexities that are staged in melodrama through emotional and psychological fortitude in relation to other characters.

The excessive gestures of Monroe's dance, like those of the mute in melodrama are operative between movement and image as the cinematographic articulation of her body leads into the close-up of the female star. Mulvey's analysis of Monroe's performance finds a moment of stasis which underpins as a signifier the gesture's relation to meaning, 'sometimes excessive or sometimes ineffable'. Mulvey refers to Peter Brooks' *The Melodramatic Imagination* (1975) to suggest that such gestures can form a supplement to language or signal imminent meaning. This cinema of delay – the slowing of the film speed and the latent details that it allows the viewer to discern – highlights the ways in which both the gestural quality of Monroe's performance and her use of the cosmetic as mask and masquerade emphasise artifice and embody the cinematic. Between stillness and movement, performance and the cinematic, Mulvey formulates a compelling analysis of the way in which gestures intimate the close-up as tinged with the mortality of a Bazinian death mask and sexual excess. Monroe's performance exhibits the materiality and rhythm of the cinema machine as it dismantles the naturalised erotic image of woman to reveal the artifice of cinema.

Gesture can be discerned of a movement that is taken up by the motility of the camera, a force that can disrupt the formation of meaning as it signals a deviation in an ideologically complicit system of representation. Gesture can underscore or undermine the representation of socially acceptable and gendered bodies. The organisation and disruption of the filmic system in classic Hollywood cinema is entwined with the construction of the image of woman: 'sexuality, its prohibition' (Heath, 1975, p. 107). Watkins' analysis of gesture in *Bad Timing* (Dir. Nicolas Roeg, Great Britain, 1980) examines the ways in which the fragmentary form of the film's narrative draws the spectator into a process of reading for connections between otherwise disparate images and characters. The work of memory can be traced in the desire to make sense of a disassembled narrative form of associative editing echoes a fascination with parapraxis – of a misplaced objects or of miswriting – and their potential to disturb the 'history behind things being kept in place in "order"' (Freud, [1901] 1991, p. 190). Roeg plays with the concept of parapraxis. Watkins focuses on the transience of gesture and the interrelations of body and language, through which the disquiet of miswriting in narrative, as sequences are repeated and stories altered as they are retold, betrays the historical allocation of a disarticulated image of woman as a fate. The film's heroine, Milena, eludes the incoherence of this dissembled image of woman as her desire, which is silenced in film dialogue, is sublimated into her gaze, a displacement of the senses which can be read as a gesture of discontent.

The potential of cinematic gestures to mediate other non-verbal senses in the visual field is explored by Naomi Segal through a specifically filmic figure of a caress. Read through Jean-Paul Sartre and Maurice Merleau-Ponty, the caress diverges from the haptic and is constituted by optical effects such as the blending of two faces, the reflection or refraction of a detail in the composition of a frame. Such images, although figured in the visual field, signify a kind of 'touch' that is medial. The non-haptic caress differs in using the back of the hand to touch the other, marking a desire to *be* rather than *have*. In *The Piano* (Dir. Jane Campion, Australia, France, 1993), movements such as the brush of Ada's hand across her beloved piano and as she sweeps her daughter's hair from her forehead, find touch to be medial of the mute heroine's voice. Such gestures are evocative of desire in relation to the other as they make visible a caress in the effaced image of surfaces which touch and trace a network of connections between characters and actors who are materially present in a fictive world where the figure of a caress incites the viewer's imagination.

Through an analysis of recent Chinese language martial arts films, Paul Bowman's essay explores how gesture in the fictive world of mainstream narrative cinema is sometimes interpreted as a sign of fidelity to the real. Bowman highlights that in many martial arts films, the gestural choreography is so practiced and seamless that fight sequences exhibit an impossible perfection. He suggests that in this context, the messy brawl between Daniel Cleaver (Hugh Grant) and Mark Darcy (Colin Firth) in a film such as *Bridget Jones's Diary* (Dir. Sharon Maguire, UK, 2001), with its flawed gestures, its stumbling and miskicks, attains a veracity to which flawless bouts in films such as *Ip Man* (Dir. Wilson Yip, Hong Kong, 2008) and *The Grandmaster* (Dir. Wong Kar-wai, Hong Kong and China, 2013) cannot aspire. Studied imperfections at the level of gesture generate a sense of realism. For Bowman, however, debate about which fight in what film is the most realistic is ultimately wrongheaded. He suggests that gesture forms a hinge between reality and representation, articulating and disarticulating these seemingly opposed realms. In his 'Letter to a Japanese Friend', Derrida describes the event of deconstruction as both a structuralist and anti-structuralist gesture and therefore as vitally ambiguous (Derrida, 1985 [1983], p. 2). Bowman draws attention to gesture as undecidable to argue that the separation of the domains of the filmic and lived daily life is a needless metaphysical convention. In reality, the two domains supplement each other and gesture forms a crucial means by which to trace their co-implication.

The brevity and transience of gestures have been recognised as a form of intimation by Elsaesser, signalling the intimacy of the 'borders and edges' where contradicting forces meet (2014, p. 18). Referring to the work of Laura Berlant, Elsaesser notes the sparse gestures that intimate what is between things. It is in this sense that the 'exhibition of mediality' (Agamben, 2000, p. 54) which orientates Griselda Pollock's analysis of cinematic and photographic images of 'Marilyn Monroe' might form its antonym. Pollock's compelling analysis, however, traces the nuances of the actor's performance of 'Marilyn Monroe' across this combination of visual sources as constituting a gesture that disrupts the sexualised iconic image of woman. Pollock moves beyond socio-cultural, semiotic and ideologically inspired readings of Monroe, identifying an excess, an affective dimension to images of the star that inflects our reception of them.

Utilising images from photo shoots and stilled frames from films including *Niagara* (Dir. Henry Hathaway, USA, January 1953), *Gentlemen Prefer Blondes* (Dir. Howard Hawks, USA, July 1953) and *How to Marry a Millionaire* (Dir. Jean Negulesco, USA, December 1953), Pollock reads for aspects of the actors' performance of 'Marilyn Monroe' as disruptive of the sexualised image of woman produced by the 1950s Hollywood cinema machine. Pollock combines these images in a *Mnemosyne Bilderatlas*, a wordless picture atlas such as that created by Aby Warburg between 1926 and 1929. In an insightful approach inspired by Warburg and Agamben, Pollock indicates a 'virtual movement of Western humanities' gestures' (Agamben, 2000, p. 54) within the figure of 'Marilyn Monroe'; a movement that operates at the intersections of the cinematic and gestural performance. This gesture, between images and film, typifies the contradictory discourses of female sexuality in 1950s culture and yet disturbs the gravity of the film away from its masculinised Hollywood narrative and the phallocentric psycho-semiotics of sexuality it embodies and toward instances of affective intensity that are, instead, in the feminine.

Cumulatively, the varied approaches to reading and understanding gesture provided in this book demonstrate the rich potential for film analysis that this topic provides. Gestures frequently inform narrative without being bound to it, thereby indicating valuable ways to move beyond traditional modes of interpretation. Gesture can possess affective qualities that resist, or fall outside, semiotically informed approaches to the study of film. Even at the level of the sign delimiting gesture can often be difficult, as evidenced by *The Remains of the Day* (Dir. James Ivory, UK, 1993). One scene at a bus stop in this film depicts a last goodbye between the housekeeper Mrs. Benn and the butler Mr. Stevens, two people in love yet unable to verbally express or physically act on their feelings.

As Mrs. Benn's bus leaves, their clasped hands are pulled apart. A shared gesture of physical affection rapidly transformed into one of heartfelt loss for the now solitary Stevens. The fingers of his empty hand straighten as the object of his affection moves out of reach. This action would be read as nothing more than a reflex was it not for the subtle, yet certain, retention of this pose. The bare hand becomes gestural *in time* yet fixing the moment at which the hand transforms into an utterance is not easy. This example demonstrates that the beginnings and ends of gestures are always subject to slippage. Jean Epstein recognised this refusal to be limited suggesting that 'on the screen, the essential quality of a gesture is that it does not come to an end' (Epstein, 2012 [1921], p. 273). As the essays that follow each demonstrate, gestures continually provoke new thoughts and point towards fresh directions of enquiry.

Note

1. We are grateful to Nicholas Heron for sharing his thoughts on how Agamben's ideas about messianism relate to 'Notes on gesture'.

References

Agamben, G. (2000) Notes on gesture, trans. Vincenzo Binetti and Cesare Casarino, in *Means Without Ends: Notes on Politics*, Minneapolis: University of Minnesota Press, pp. 49–60.

Argyle, M. (1988) *Bodily Communication*, 2nd Edition, London: Methuen & Co.

Brooks, P. ([1975] 1995) *The Melodramatic Imagination, Balzac, Henry James, Melodrama, and the Mode of Excess*, New Haven: Yale University Press.

Chare, N. (2012) *After Francis Bacon: Synaesthesia and Sex in Paint*, Farnham: Ashgate.

Chare, N. (2015) *Sportswomen in Cinema: Film and the Frailty Myth*, London: IB Tauris.

Derrida, J. ([1983] 1985) Letter to a Japanese friend (Prof. Izutsu), trans. David Wood and Andrew Benjamin, in *Derrida and Différance*, eds. David Wood and Robert Bernasconi, Coventry: Parousia Press, pp. 1–5.

Doane, M.A. (1988) *The Desire to Desire: The Woman's film of the 1940s*, Basingstoke: Macmillan.

Elsaesser, T. (2014) Touch and gesture, on the borders of intimacy, in *Intimacy in Cinema: Critical Essays on English Language Films*, eds. D. Roche and I. Schmitt-Pittiot, Jefferson, NC: McFarland & Company, pp. 17–33.

Epstein, J. (2012) Cinema and modern literature [1921], trans. Audrey Brunetaux and Sarah Keller, in *Jean Epstein: Critical Essays and New Translations*, eds. Sarah Keller and Jason N. Paul, Amsterdam: Amsterdam University Press, pp. 271–276.

Freud, S. (1991) *The Psychopathology of Everyday Life* [1901], ed. James Strachey, trans. Alan Tyson [1966]. London: Penguin.

Habib, A. (2015) *La main gauche de Jean-Pierre Léaud*, Montréal: Éditions du Boréal.

Harbord, J. (2015) Agamben's cinema: psychology versus an ethical form of life, *NECSUS, European Journal of Media Studies*, Autumn. Available online at www.necsus-ejms.org/agambens-cinema-psychology-versus-ethical-form-life/ (accessed 7 February 2016).

Heath, S. (1975) Film and system: terms of analysis Part II, *Screen* 16, 2, pp. 91–113.

Kendon, A. (2004) *Gesture: Visible Action as Utterance*, Cambridge: Cambridge University Press.

McNeill, D. (1992) *Hand and Mind: What Gestures Reveal about Thought*, Chicago: University of Chicago Press.

McNeill, D. (2005) *Gesture and Thought*, Chicago: University of Chicago Press.

Mulvey, L. (1989) Notes on Sirk and Melodrama in *Visual and Other Pleasures*, London: Macmillan, pp. 39–45.

Mulvey, L. (1996) Social hieroglyphics in two films by Douglas Sirk, in *Fetishism and Curiosity*, London: British Film Institute, pp. 29–39.

Mulvey, L. (2006) *Death 24 x a Second*, London: Reaktion Books.

Stanislavski, C. ([1961] 1981) *Creating a Role*, trans. Elizabeth Reynolds Hapgood, London: Methuen.

Willemen, P. (1971) Distanciation and Douglas Sirk, *Screen* 12, 2, pp. 63–67.

Cinematic gesture: The ghost in the machine

Laura Mulvey

Department of Film, Media and Cultural Studies, School of Arts, Birkbeck, University of London, London, UK

My essay considers the relationship between a gesture and the emotion it conveys as a moment of narrative halt that has an analogical relation to the halt enabled by new forms of spectatorship. It explores this halt as the pause of emotion and the pause for thought. I will also examine how the star system produces an intrinsically "gestural" and "emotive" performance style.

I would like to use the opportunity offered by this essay to return to my visual analysis of a fragment of *Gentlemen Prefer Blondes* (Dir. Howard Hawks, USA, 1953). In the song and dance duet, "Two Little Girls from Little Rock", performed by Jane Russell and Marilyn Monroe, Marilyn moves towards the camera with four distinct gestures, finally nearly filling the screen with her trademark close-up. The movement takes thirty seconds, which I then re-edited, stretching it into three minutes, pausing on Marilyn's gestures and repeating the sequence, twice slowed down and silent, but beginning and ending with normal speed. In *Death Twenty-four Times a Second*, I mention this "re-mix" briefly as an experiment in the kind of delayed cinema that I was discussing in the book. Before I had ever thought of re-editing the sequence, I had watched it many times, fascinated by Marilyn's ability to hover between movement and stillness and the way that the pauses, slow motion and repetitions of delayed cinema simply, in this case, materialised something that was already there. I realised that my attention had been literally caught as the figure moved into a fleeting moment of stasis; and that I paused the film to catch the high point within this unfolding of a gesture. It seemed that digitally derived "delayed cinema" had a special, privileged relationship to cinematic gesture. In the end, I decided to turn these moments of casual analysis (always partly trying to possess and hold on to the body, partly reflecting on and analysing its cinematic nature) into a re-mix. If the piece has continued to interest me, it is due to the way that Marilyn Monroe's qualities as film star and performer lead further towards a more abstract consideration of the aesthetics of cinematic gesture as such.

Delayed cinema creates fragments that exist in limbo, extracted from their larger filmic continuum but residually tied to it; similarly, a frozen frame is always part of a series and differs essentially from the temporal self-sufficiency of the still photograph. This "in between-ness" that characterises the fragment or the freeze-frame has a parallel in the aesthetics and significance of gesture. In his essay, "Notes on Gesture", Giorgio Agamben suggests that gesture is characterised by a state of suspension, of being in a time linked neither to beginning nor to completion, neither goal directed nor an end in itself. Gesture exists in between desire and fulfilment in "a sphere of pure and endless mediality" (Agamben, 2000, pp. 58–59). He points out, for instance:

> If dance is a gesture, it is so, rather because it is nothing more than the endurance and the exhibition of the media character of corporeal movements. *The gesture is the exhibition of mediality: it is the process of making a means visible as such.* (Agamben, 2000, pp. 57–58)

In this sense, the act of delaying cinema reduplicates, and makes visible (as such), the exhibition of mediality with which Agamben defines gesture. The two intertwine when cinematic gesture is the subject of the fragment: the body caught in gesture occupies a space and time of its own just as the fragment is detached from narrative linearity or the logic of cause and effect. This aesthetic of "in between-ness" underpins as a signifier the gesture's relation to meaning, sometimes excessive or sometimes ineffable. At its most literal, gesture is mime-like, a recognisable signal proffering a supplement to the verbal, reducing the abstraction of language to bodily, material expressiveness. On the other hand, gesture hovers on the brink of meaning, suggesting but resisting and remaining closer to the ineffable than the fullness of language. Peter Brooks draws on both kinds of gesture in his analysis of melodramatic performance and summarises its second form:

> Mute gesture is an expressionistic means – precisely the means of the melodrama – to render meanings which are ineffable, but none the less operative in the sphere of human ethical relationships. Gesture could perhaps then be typed as the nature of catachresis, the figure used when there is no "proper" name for something … Yet of course it is the fullness, the pregnancy of the blank that is significant: meaning-full though unspeakable. (Brooks, 1984, pp. 72–73)

And:

> Gesture appears as a way to make available certain occulted perceptions and relationships, to render, with the audacity of an as-if proposition, a world of significant shadows. (Brooks, 1984, p. 77)

Both of these forms of gesture are to be found in the *Gentlemen Prefer Blondes* sequence: the readable and the mime-like lead into the close-up, in which meaning is excessive, elusive and ultimately ineffable.

The sequence begins with both stars on screen. Marilyn takes up the song and, at first, she seems to address Jane Russell, with the words: "I learned an awful lot in Little Rock". Her hand gestures to her head with "learned" as she turns, confidentially, to Jane; then her right hand reaches to her left shoulder, raising it and tugging at her dress, as though it were about to slip off (Figure 1). The gesture is a pronounced and integrated into the choreography of the dance, and she simultaneously gives an erotic twist to her body. But the pseudo modesty and extreme artificiality of the gesture draws attention immediately to Marilyn's sexual excess and the suggestion of the slipped dress is a gesture of "suggestiveness". She then pauses with her hand on her heart, still looking at Jane, (Figure 2) before turning towards the camera. She moves forward and beckons, looking slightly to one side of the camera (just avoiding the taboo of the lens) but implicitly addressing the spectator (words: "here's some advice …") (Figure 3).

Figure 1. The gesture of stopping her dress from slipping is integrated into the choreography of the dance.

Figure 2. Marilyn pauses with her hand on her heart.

She moves further forward and pauses again (words: "I'd like to give") before throwing herself forward into the final pose of the close-up (Figure 4). With her wide mouth, half closed eyes and head thrown back, the gesture signifies sex, as desiring and as desirable, ineffable and fleeting, infinitely resonant but without meaning. As she moves fractionally away from the stasis of the pose, her expression mutates very slightly (Figure 5). The initial gestures, such as the beckon, belong to a recognisable vocabulary and work as expressive "add-ons", in which the body claims, through this physical supplement to language, its own material form of meaning. But all four gestures are distinctively cinematic in their mode of performance, combining the stillness of pose and the movement of dance.

Figure 3.   Marilyn moves forward and beckons to the spectator, just avoiding a direct address of the camera.

Figure 4.   Marilyn in close-up.

Pasi Valiaho (using Agamben) argues that " … the moving image is gestural by nature. It takes not immovable and rigid forms but material, bodily dynamisms as its subjects" (Valiaho, 2010, p. 17). Going back to the early days of cinema, he points out that in the trick films of the period, those of George Méliès in particular, the cinema takes hold of the animate body: "The moving image does not simply re-present bodily gestures, poses and movements but, instead, harnesses gestures into its into its techno-logical positivity by becoming immanent to them in terms of dynamically modulating the body" (Valiaho, 2010, p. 31). Gradually, across film history, this relationship becomes less flamboyant. Although star performance, particularly female star perfor-mance, revolves around pose, the subordination of the animate body to the machine is smoothed out and narrative naturalises cinema's fundamental unnaturalness. But the

Figure 5. Marilyn in close-up as she moves slightly away from the stasis of the previous pose (Figure 4).

mediality of Marilyn's gestures enhances the medium of cinema itself as process and material texture. The filmic body on display also exhibits the cinematic machine in a fusion of the human and the mechanical. Marilyn's gestures denaturalise the erotic through exaggeration and excess and give a particular edge to her screen appearance. Her gestures are not simply bodily *re-presented* but visibly technologically *harnessed* and mechanically *modulated*. At moments like this, cinema materialises, gesturing to its own being through its privileged relation to the gestures of the figure embodied within it.

While Marilyn quite obviously embodies "attraction" in its sexual sense, her screen presence also conjures up Tom Gunning's use of the term for a cinema that exhibits itself. Furthermore, while any song and dance number puts pressure on the continuities of a narrative, the choreography of the *Gentlemen Prefer Blondes* sequence exaggerates exhibition and direct address. As Gunning puts it:

> It is the direct address of the audience, in which an attraction is offered to the spectator by the cinema showman, that defines this approach to filmmaking. Theatrical display dominates over narrative absorption, emphasising the direct stimulation of shock or surprise, at the expense of unfolding of a story or creating a diegetic universe. (Gunning, 2006, p. 384)

Marilyn's gestural performance creates, as it were, an attraction within the wider attraction of the Russell/Monroe number. When she throws back her head and takes up the "Marilyn pose", her look seems to travel through the camera and down the years to future audiences and spectators who will continue to feel as though she has transcended time and space to bestow her desiring gaze on them. The "now" set in motion by that cinematic moment continues to reverberate.

As Marilyn slides from one gesture through to the next, she embodies the paradoxical characteristics of the cinema: its fusion of the stillness of the filmstrip and the illusion of movement produced by the projector, as well as its play on the animation of the inanimate. Watching and working on Marilyn's series of gestures in the *Gentlemen*

Prefer Blondes sequence, I came to see her as emblematic of the cinematic paradox and as an exemplary figure of "photogenie".[1] It seemed as though an analysis that simply theorised Marilyn Monroe in terms of the relationship between body and the medium would overlook the intelligence that she brings to film (which goes beyond, however essential they may be, physical presence and glamour), that is, her "photogenic sensibility". As though in some way cognisant of the tension between stillness and movement in the cinema, as well as the tension between film and the photograph, she could take up and hold a pose either within the flow of film or the instant of the photograph. In either case, the pose appears to be fleeting, suggesting continuum of movement in the context of the still image or denaturalised stasis within the moving image. Marilyn's photogenic sensibility inhabits an uncertain space, somewhere between the paradoxical relationship between still and moving images that her "photogenie" touches on.

Of course, Monroe's performance style changed over the course of her career. My points relate primarily to *Gentlemen Prefer Blondes*, in which she achieved her supremely iconic status as *the* figure of Hollywood, and thus American, glamour. So many of her later parts were bound to be variations, satiric or otherwise, on this image. Quite understandably, Monroe, the person, came to baulk at the constraints built into this kind of gestural performance. Jacqueline Rose has pointed out, in an elegant and perceptive analysis, not only that Marilyn Monroe lived out the contradictions demanded by US at a time of national ideological and social contradiction, but also that she lived them with extreme self-awareness. She comments on Monroe's personal aspirations for her acting career: "She wanted to play the part of a woman who told the world, told men, the truth" (Rose, 2012). Rose evokes Monroe's conscious attempt to reconcile her own personal awareness of injustice and social oppression with her professional voice. With her turn towards the Actors' Studio, for instance, she rebelled against her earlier, gestural, mode of performance. In her desire to become an actress rather than a movie star, she aspired to a flesh and blood presence on the screen that would convey interiority, not only of a character, but also of the human, and particularly, the female, body. As Rose points out, Roslyn in *The Misfits* (apart from *The Seven Year Itch*, the only film of the seven since *Gentlemen Prefer Blondes* in which she was not cast as a showgirl) seemed to offer the opportunity she needed. And this film (directed by John Huston) would be in the tradition of the Lumière brothers, shot on location with an aesthetic of verisimilitude, rather than that of Méliès and the Hollywood studio system.

However, it was during the filming of *The Misfits* (John Huston, 1961), that Monroe posed for Magnum photographer Eve Arnold in a series of sessions that encapsulate the paradox of Marilyn as still image. If the artifice of her performance in *Gentlemen Prefer Blondes* seems to take her beyond the movement of life that is usually associated with the cinema, the Eve Arnold photographs search out and capture the contingent moment in which Marilyn produces a fluidity of actual movement for the instantaneity of the shutter. Both modes foreground the photographic mechanism, embodied, in turn, by the photogenic sensibility of the star: in the medium of movement, her pose suggests stillness and in the medium of stillness her pose suggests flow. Eve Arnold noticed Marilyn's affinity with the photographic process. After their last photo session, a reporter waylaid her and asked "What is it like to photograph Marilyn?" She comments:

I waved him off and went on my way. But the question would not be denied. What was it like to photograph her? It was like watching a print come up in the developer. The latent image was there – it needed just her time and temperature controls to bring it into being. It was a stroboscopic display, and all the photographer had to do was stop time at any given instant and Marilyn would bring forth a new image (Arnold, 1992, p. 137).

There are three aspects to the thirty seconds of the *Gentlemen Prefer Blondes* sequence that I hoped to highlight in the re-mix and all contribute not only to its gestural quality but also illuminate Marilyn's "photogenic sensibility". The first is artifice and her use of cosmetics as mask and masquerade; the second is pose, the way she dismantles her movement into distinct gestures which combines with her ability to embody the cinematic, fusing the animate and the inanimate; and finally, the resonances of the close-up in which intimations of mortality tinge this image of sexual excess.

It took Monroe some time to emerge with the style and appearance that came to connote "Marilyn" and which could be recognised diagrammatically in a few quick marks of a pencil. Her made-up "look" developed gradually in collaboration with Whitey Snyder, her make-up man since her early days at Twentieth Century Fox. Without that distinctive look, she could (and did) move around the streets of say, New York or Los Angeles, without being noticed. Eve Arnold noted

> Her make-up was a total mystery. According to Whitey Snyder, her veteran make-up man, she knew more about shadowing her eyes and using special lipstick to keep her mouth glossy than anyone else in the business. These secrets were kept even from him. (Arnold, 1992, p. 27)

While all stars tend to have a recognisable stamp of their own, a look, stance and style, Marilyn's image was flamboyantly "cosmetic". In addition to her artificial blondeness, the features painted onto her face have a glamour of surface reminiscent of a reverse, but equally highly stylised, mask of a clown. While her "painted" features necessarily restrict her range of facial expressions, her blondeness and her use of cosmetics keep vitally alive the luminosity that produced her special rapport with the photographic medium. Without even slowing down the flow of film or freezing a frame, the graphic nature of Marilyn's "mask" creates its own slowness, absorbing the camera's attention as though into a slowness of its own so that her close-ups create a point comparative repose or stasis. A director would be conscious of this effect and one reason, no doubt, for the particular power invested in the *Gentlemen Prefer Blondes* sequence is that Howard Hawks is, in the very opening number of the movie, highlighting Marilyn as "attraction" (in both senses of the word), using the artifice of the dance to give her close-up maximum impact.

Marilyn's movements share something of the graphic quality of her make-up and facial expressions. This is, in the first instance, an attribute of costume and the choreography of the dance, itself highly stylised as a showgirl set piece and thus distinguished from other, more informal, numbers later in the film (such as "Bye bye baby" and "When love goes wrong"), in which the sets have a certain depth and a sketchy dramatic verisimilitude. The red shiny costumes in "Two Little Girls from Little Rock" cling to the bodies of both stars and thus exaggerate movements already choreographed by the dance; but in this sequence Marilyn is literally foregrounded by a particularly denaturalised eroticism. To evoke the, perhaps useful, cliché of the opposition between Méliès and the Lumières: on the one hand, a cinema of contingency, nature (the wind in the trees, a casual and unrehearsed gesture) and bodily coherence; on the other, a cinema of abstraction and the elimination of chance in favour of bodily disintegration and distance from nature. One flourishes as an analogical and indexical cinema, the other foregrounds cinema as the mechanical and phantasmatic. Pasi Valiaho traces the cinema of illusion and the transformation of the animate into the inanimate to the legacy of eighteenth-century automata. These mechanisms were distinguished precisely by their ability to perform distinct and specific gestures, which, while limited, were marvellous in their imitation of the human. With my delay of "Two Little Girls from Little Rock" sequence, I tried to play on this lineage and to bring out, through Marilyn's gestural performance, the fact that the beauty of the cinematic illusion is an effect of its mechanisation of the human. While the digitally delayed cinema can exaggerate and reflect on these effects, its technology is at a far remove from cogs and wheels, which, with an intermittent motion, turn the reels of celluloid in a camera or a projector. While so much of cinema has been dedicated to repressing this jerkiness (essential for creating the illusion of movement) it might be the now archaic, automaton-like nature of the mechanical figure that seems so beautiful.

I suggested earlier that final gesture of the sequence, Marilyn's close-up, evades meaning due to the ineffableness of sex and desire. Her pose is elongated and held still for a second, unaccompanied by a phrase of the song. But in the last few frames she turns slightly aside and, as though her luminosity had been crossed by an almost invisible shadow, her features lose something of the distinctive, iconic Marilyn "look" as though mortality had tinged the of celebration of sexuality. Now, with the benefit of hindsight, the spectator who delays and reflects on this image can easily superimpose the close-up "Marilyns" that Andy Warhol silk-screened as a tribute to her during the four months following her death in August 1962. In these works, he makes the mask of beauty and the death mask uncannily close and the superimposition of the Warhol images onto the then living Marilyn has a sense of deferred meaning, as though the pose prefigured the stillness of death, enhanced, of course, by the spectator's knowledge of the death that was to come. The shock of her untimely death is now so much part of her mystique and her legacy that the artifice and cosmetic nature of her image seems to be already simultaneously defending against and prefiguring it. This kind of additional knowledge, combined with the passing of time, brings the "shudder at the catastrophe that has already occurred" mentioned by Roland Barthes in relation to Lewis Payne, the young man photographed before his execution. "I read at the same time: This will be and this has been; I observe with horror an anterior future of which death was the stake" (Barthes, 1981, p. 96). Here, the other cinematic paradox emerges: not only do its machines (camera and projector) animate the inanimate still frames of the film strip and give the illusion of movement to the images of its human players, but the illusion also keeps the dead alive, as they perfectly perform and re-perform their once upon a time living gestures.

Coda

Whitey Snyder tells this story about Marilyn Monroe. While *Gentlemen Prefer Blondes* was shooting, she had to go into hospital. When she was preparing to leave, she called Whitey to do her make-up "so when she met the public or the press or anybody, she'd look alright". She asked: "Will you promise me that if something happens to me in this world, when I die, promise me you'll do my make-up so I look good when I leave." He answered "If I get you while you're warm, Marilyn". She gave him a money-clip that said: Whitey Dear While I'm still warm Marilyn. When she died, Joe DiMaggio called him and said "Whitey, you promised". So he went to the mortuary and did her make-up for the last time (Crown, 1987, p. 210).

This anecdote, to my mind, gives a poignant verisimilitude to Marilyn's "photogenic sensibility", almost as though she grasped the relationship between the cosmetic mask, the photographic image and the mask of death. But it also extends the idea of gesture to this "exchange of gestures" between the two people who collaborated to create the Marilyn close-up, the emblematic summation of Hollywood glamour. Ironically, this globally recognised image of Hollywood might have helped to conceal the decline of the studio system that was taking place precipitously during the 1950s. It may be due to her awareness of these changing times, and the demands of a "new" cinema, that Monroe worked hard to change her sex symbol status, associated with the studio system, for the naturalised gestures and expressive interiority associated with the Actors' Studio.

Note

1. "Photogenie" was the term used by certain French avant-garde filmmakers of the 1920s to describe the way that the camera could use its mechanical properties and its relation with light, shade and the materiality of celluloid to transform ordinary things or, indeed, people into something specifically cinematic.

References

Agamben, G. (2000). *Notes on gesture. Means without ends*. Minneapolis: University of Minnesota Press.

Arnold, E. (1992). *Marilyn*. London: Heinemann.

Barthes, R. (1981). *Camera Lucida*. New York, NY: Hill and Wang.

Brooks, P. (1984). *The Melodramatic imagination: Balzac, Henry James, Melodrama and the mode of excess*. New Haven, CT: Yale University Press.

Crown, L. (1987). *Marilyn at Twentieth Century Fox*. London: W. H. Allen.

Gentlemen Prefer Blondes. (1953). Film directed by Howard Hawks. USA: 20th Century Fox Film Co. Ltd.

Gunning, T. (2006). Cinema of attraction(s): Early film its spectators and the avant-garde. In W. Strauven (Ed.), *The cinema of attractions reloaded*. Amsterdam: Amsterdam University Press.

Rose, J. (2012). A rumbling of things unknown: Marilyn Monroe. *London Review of Books, 34*, 24–34.

Seven Year Itch. (1955). Film directed by Billy Wilder. USA: Twentieth Century-Fox Film Corporation.

The Misfits. (1961). Film. directed by John Huston. USA: United Artists Corp. Ltd.

Väliaho, P. (2010). *Mapping the moving image: Gesture, thought and cinema 1900*. Amsterdam: Amsterdam University Press.

Speech-gesture mimicry in performance: an actor → audience, author → actor, audience → actor triangle

David McNeill

Department of Psychology, The University of Chicago, Chicago, IL, USA

In this paper, I put forth the idea that a process in the production of speech can also be found, on an entirely different scale, in theatrical and film performance. Not simply that actors speak, but the semiotics of language, as a dynamic system, also appear, on their own, in the semiotics of theater. It forms a kind of "triangle" of gesture mimicry: actor → audience, audience → actor, and author → actor. Each leg has its own realization. Many reactions take place and are part of the performance triangle. The actor to audience portion is similar to what gesture coders do – spontaneously mimic the gesture and speech of a subject on video made even decades before. The author to actor leg is more surprising. Carefully written 'scanable' prose contains gesture-like imagery. Part of writing is building in gesture, not describing it but placing it as a pattern on which the written text is orchestrated. Actors can recover the author's built-in gestures. Finally, the audience to actor leg arises when the actor mimics what have been termed 'phantom' gestures and bodily attitudes sensed in the audience. The triangle exists in film acting with the actor conjuring an audience of his or her own to complete it, and explains why in fact film actors do this (even endowing the camera with personal properties). The audience is active on its leg of the triangle. The audience is more complex and participatory than just watching. Overall, theatre and film have the same dialectic of semiotic opposites as gesture and language. As actors speak and gesture the performance itself, too, is a process of imagery and codified form, and they are in a dialectic unity. In this sense, in heightened and public form, theatre is a continuation (and not just an exploiter) of language, which perhaps partly explains its appeal and universality.

Introduction

The theme of this paper is that spontaneous, unconscious mimicry of another person's gestures and bodily attitude, together with mimicry of their speech, is a force in theatrical performance. It creates an actor → audience, audience → actor, author → actor gesture triangle. Mimicry is a natural social response, sometimes overt but often unnoticed and unwitting, and need not be conspicuous. It is more prominent, the more identified the participants, the mimicked and the mimic. The same triangle appears in film acting but with interesting and necessary modifications. I will take up film at the end, after explaining the triangle and what takes place around it in theatre.

Speech-gesture mimicry appears on each triangle leg. One theory concerning language is that, with gesture, its semiosis – the signs it uses or, better, that it inhabits

– is doubled: two kinds of signs, gesture and linguistic form, simultaneously embodying the same idea units. All utterances are like this. At bottom, speech resolves into units that are both gesture and codified form. This is true even if an overt gesture is lacking. A gesture is still present as imagery. Imagery is gesture's most important aspect; the outward movement is its material embodiment but since less newsworthiness summons less material, the absence of gesture is just the endpoint of this newsworthiness continuum. A dual semiosis of imagery and form still is present (Vygotsky 1987 introduced the concept of a material carrier; for a diagram of the continuum in both gesture and speech, see McNeill, 2012, p. 127).

Imagery and linguistic form however do not reduce one to the other. They retain their semiotic identities in an imagery-language dialectic. One idea in two modes at the same time is unstable. This instability seeks resolution and drives thought and speech forward. I have argued for this dynamic system in many places, most recently in connection with the origin of language (McNeill, 2012). My contribution now is that theatre also seems to embody a dialectic of semiotic opposites. There is in theatre, too, codified form and imagery, and they are in a dialectic. In this sense theatre, in heightened and public form, is a language. It is a language in a deeper sense than one might suppose; it gives substance to the hackneyed phrase, "the language of theatre". Michael Chekhov, in his advice to actors, wrote about Atmosphere in a way that suggests this dual semiotic. It is, he says, "dynamic" not static and arises out of an intersection of what are semiotic opposites, the Atmosphere, which is global and synthetic, like a gesture image, and the actor's motions and speech, which are necessarily linear and with training codified (Chekhov, 1991, p. 34)

The parallel of theatre to language is naturally not complete. This is hardly surprising. Theatre raises and lowers conceptualizations to extremes. Lecoq (1997, p. 35) comments on this in connection with theatrical speech. He is especially interested in how speech in the theatre includes silences, both before speaking and after, a build-up and then "nothing more to say". Speech is presented as a circumscribed block, and this is purely theatrical. Daily speech does not come in blocks separated by silences. Interlocutors struggle to avoid them.

The triangle, then, is a consequence of a mode of cognition deeply built into the human psyche. Not surprisingly, the long history of theatre and rhetoric has absorbed this – how could it be otherwise? It is a natural form of thought and a theatre that contradicts or just ignores it would not long survive (although theatrical experiments, some of which I describe later, can exploit it). This cognitive mode is not unique to theatre, although it takes its own form there. The very dynamics of how the audience experiences the actor and he or she experiences the audience, and through the actor the audience experiences the author, revolve around the essence of language as a dynamic whole. I do not mean simply that actors and authors use language and gesture. Of course they do, but theatre relies on a mode of semiosis that while often exaggerated is not fundamentally different from that of gesture as an integral part of language. We begin, accordingly with this semiosis. To understand the role of dual semiosis in theatre, it is best to start with it in gesture and language itself.

What are gestures? How they shed light on thinking-for-(and while)-speaking

Among the many manifestations of the embodiment of human language and thought gestures are outstanding – natural and universal. Most basically, gesture is not an "add-on" (as Kendon, 2008 once dubbed this contrary view, arguing against it as well).

Gesture is an integral part of language, a fact that because gesture is not written tradition has overlooked (although I shall argue later that written language also includes it). Gesture imagery is an integral component of speaking, not an accompaniment but actually is part of it. Much evidence supports this idea but its full significance has not always been recognized.

When I speak of gestures, I am not referring to stylized gestures; also I do not attempt to recapture the gestures of a historical period; nor do I mean a gesture like pulling down the eyelid that people who compile dictionaries of "French gestures", "Italian gestures", etc. often cite. A definition for our purposes is this: a "gesture" is an expressive action that enacts imagery (not necessarily by the hands or hands alone) *that is an integral part of the process of speaking*. The italicized part is important. Gestures are as much part of speaking as are the sounds of speech. Speech itself is in part gesture. We shall see some of the implications of this important fact.

The growth point

The psycholinguistic model we are following

When gesture and speech synchronize (as they do in more than 90% of utterances, Nobe, 2000), one idea – in Figure 1, Sylvester's ascent via a drainpipe – is simultaneously in two opposite semiotic modes, imagery and language. The result is an idea unit in which imagery and words co-exist, and this is an inherently dynamic situation. The smallest unit of this dialectic is called a *growth point*, or GP.

- A growth point or GP is the minimal unit of the imagery-language dialectic. It is called a growth point because it is meant to be the initial pulse of thinking-for- (and while)-speaking, out of which a dynamic process of organization emerges.
- A GP absorbs its context – its field of meaningful oppositions – adding to language's dynamic dimension. The GP exists as a point of differentiation within this context, which is constructed in part to make the differentiation meaningful.

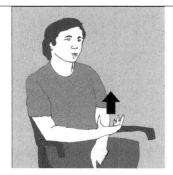

(a) Storytelling gesture contrasting interiority to previous exteriority, accompanying "he goes up th[**rOUgh** the pipe] this time.

(b) Storytelling gesture for same event but with no contrast to exteriority, accompanying [he tries **clImb**ing up the rai]n barrel."

Figure 1.   Gestures by two speakers recounting the same event (ascent on the inside) but differing in contexts. Computer art in this and the following figures by Fey Parrill, who is now on the faculty of Case Western University. Used with permission of University of Chicago Press.

- The GP is an empirical concept. It is a hypothesis concerning observed speech-gesture data inferred from the totality of communicative events, with special focus on speech-gesture synchrony and co-expressivity.

These concepts are illustrated with the examples from a storytelling experiment that are shown in Figure 1. Small differences tell a large story. Each speaker is recounting to a (naïve) listener the story of a cartoon that she has just watched. The cartoon genre, a Tweety and Sylvester adventure, was familiar to the speakers but the specific cartoon *Canary Row* (Dir. Isadore "Friz" Freleng, USA, c1950) was new. In the cartoon, Tweety is perched in his cage on a window ledge, high above the street. Sylvester's problem is how to reach him. The narrator in (a) has already described how Sylvester had just previously used a conveniently situated drainpipe to reach Tweety's window by climbing it, only to be thrown back to the street by the fearsome Granny. The narrator is now describing Sylvester's second attempt, this time a stealth approach, climbing the pipe on the inside. She says, "he goes up th[rough the pipe] this time" – brackets indicating the gesture phrase, the whole "expressive action"; boldface the gesture stroke, the part with meaning; underlining a gesture hold, preserving the stroke's posture and position but without motion; and larger font the point of prosodic speech emphasis. The gesture stroke and its synchronous emphasized speech jointly contain the idea that Sylvester's approach included interiority, and that this was the newsworthy information. The (b) narrator is also describing the inside ascent but, for her, this is Sylvester's first attempt to climb the pipe (she had forgotten the first outside ascent). And as we see, her gesture and speech lack the interiority feature. Without contrast to exteriority, interiority even though noticed is not newsworthy. We know it was noticed, because she went on to describe how Tweety dropped an improbably large bowling ball into the pipe, "[he tries climbing up the rai]n barrel and Tweety Bird uh sees him coming and *drops a bowling ball down the rain barrel*", which makes narrative sense only if she had observed and remembered that Sylvester was inside. Speakers 1(a) and (b) respond in exactly the same way – their GPs built around what is newsworthy – but because of different contexts have different ideas of what it is: 1(a) featuring interiority, 1(b) just climbing.

Opposite modes

Even when the denotative information in gesture and speech is the same, as it is in Figure 1(a) and (b), it is in *opposite semiotic modes*. By this I mean:

- The gesture is *global*, the significance of its parts (hands, motion, space, etc.) depends on the meaning of the whole. Meaning determination is *top-down*. In Figure 1(a), the hand is Sylvester climbing, the open space is the interior of the drainpipe, the direction is his upward ascent. These meanings do not exist outside this gesture, but knowing the whole, we can see the meanings of the parts.
- And it is *synthetic*, meaning that the one gesture contains information that, in speech, is distributed over different constituents. The gesture combines these meanings into one symbolic form.
- Language is the opposite on each point. It is *analytic and combinatoric*. The event is broken into components ("goes" + "up" + "through" + "the pipe") which then are combined according to patterns (syntax) to make a whole, a different mode of semiosis altogether. The words have meanings independent of the episode being recounted. Meaning determination here is *bottom-up*.

- Thus, when gesture and speech contain the same idea, at the same time, they create conditions of an imagery-language dialectic.

Context

A further source of dynamism is that a GP and its gesture do not exist without a context. This is dynamic because contexts, especially the immediate contexts of speaking, constantly change. A GP is a point of differentiation within such a context. It is what Vygotsky called a *psychological predicate*. In Figure 1(a), where the form and motion of the gesture highlighted the interiority of the ascent, presenting it as the newsworthy contrast to exteriority, the context was something like WAYS OF CATCHING TWEETY VIA THE PIPE, and the psychological predicate, the newsworthy point of differentiation, ON THE INSIDE. Differentiation and context cannot be separated. It is not unlike the perceptual concept of a gestalt, a "figure" which exists only in contrast to a "background". A gesture is a gestalt of action, acting as a point of differentiation in a background of possibilities. Such a figure-ground meaning differs from theories in which content is piled up, for example, as reference and association, traditional concepts of meaning in linguistics, philosophy and psychology. The Figure 1(b) speaker, who did not mention the outside ascent, had a different context or background, even though describing the same scene, something like WAYS OF CATCHING TWEETY, and the psychological predicate, her point of newsworthy differentiation, was CLIMB THE PIPE (her first mention of it). This point – meaning is inseparable from context – will be important later when we consider mimicry in theatre.

How the GP sheds light on the actor → audience, audience → actor, author → actor gesture triangle

We can apply the logic of the GP model to the theatre and to the legs of our triangle. First of all, it is important to note that the same logic has been repeatedly noticed by theoreticians of performance from Quintilian on. Again, it is not just that actors speak and gesture, but that theatre and performance in general embody the same dual semiosis as language.

Mind-merging

Quintilian, as described by Roach (1993), saw transmigration of *anima* or soul from one body to another. This is not unlike the 'mind-merging' of growth points. In mind-merging, two (or more) people jointly build a shared growth point. For example, one person provides the gesture and the other the speech synchronized with it. Then, both have the same GP. An unexpected form of mind-merging is tip-of-the-tongue contagion, when someone unexpectedly cannot recall an ordinary word whose meaning is clear to everyone, and suddenly her interlocutor is also unable to recall it. If the interaction includes mind-merging, it could also include "tip-of-the-tongue merging" through spontaneous mimicry.[1]

Roach describes Quintilian as seeing the actor's art endowed with three "potencies" that we can see promote mind-merging with the audience (Roach, 1993, p. 27). Our triangle has similar "potencies". The actor mimics the author, which corresponds to Quintilian's first power – the power to act on his own body. He in turn is mimicked by the audience, aligning with the third power – to act on the bodies of the spectators. Acting on the space around him – the second power – seems to be gesture itself but could also be our third leg, the actor mimicking the audience (the audience's reactions the actors picking up). By mimicking another's gestures and speech, on any leg, the psychological predicate and field of meaningful oppositions it differentiates come to life. There is a progression of mind-merging all around. The triangle is the key, and its key is mimicry.

Mimicry

Mimicry gives access to the GPs and the fields of oppositions of other speakers and makes mind-merging possible. Gesture coders often spontaneously mimic, as a way of understanding what they code – they code by encoding, via mimicry. Doing so brings the idea unit of the gesture as well as the context it differentiates into the cognitive being of the mimic/coder.

Applying this idea to an imaginary conversation between two people, we imagine contexts accessible to each via mimicry and incorporated into their own mode of being. This includes both the GPs and the fields of meaningful oppositions of each other. And applying it to the audience and actor, we can imagine the activation of joint contexts and meanings during performance.

Theatres were once laid out to make mimicry easy. In the modern Globe, built to the specifications of the original, the audience stands close to the stage. Given Renaissance audiences – active, to say the least – there was plenty of room for the audience to mimic the actors and for the actors the audience, all spontaneously. Daylight through the open roof would make even subtle gestures and other movements visible, combined with both the actor's and (apparently often) the audience's speech.

I will summarize a few points concerning mimicry inside and outside of theatre. It is not preposterous to imagine mimicry of actors by audience (as well as of authors by actors, but of this later):

- In round-table meetings, we have observed mind-merging – participants creating joint GPs and fields of oppositions when one speaker takes over from another (McNeill et al., 2009).
- The mechanism of mind-merging is mimicry (McNeill, 2010).
- Through mimicry, GPs, and discourse segments can be coordinated and synchronized between individuals.
- This leads Person C to Person Y's fields of oppositions, and vice versa
- By their nature, GPs are not independent of the context they differentiate. This means that if a speaker generates a context, the very process of mimicking the gesture can activate, for the mimic, a GP and a new field of oppositions that matches GP and field of meaningful oppositions of the speaker.
- The triangle thus enables mind-merging along each leg. Human bodies offer identical possibilities for embodiment of sense and meaning. Mimicry is a kind of *borrowed embodiment* – borrowing the significant actions of the other.

Is there spontaneous mimicry? Yes, in many cases

Irene Kimbara (2006) studied gestural mimicry as an interactive phenomenon. The example in Figure 2 is from her research. Mimicry is a process of "interpersonal synchrony," as Kimbara terms it, which creates a sense of solidarity and is prominent when

Figure 2.   Interpersonal mimicry. From Kimbara (2006). Used with Permission of University of Chicago Press.
Panels 1 and 2. Speaker on right: describing the line as 'irregular'; her gesture depicts lines of waiting passengers; the separation of her hands may depict the density of the crowding. Speaker on left, in (b), hands entering the gesture space and preparing to perform gesture in panels 3 and 4. Panels 3 and 4. Continuous with panels 1 and 2. Speaker on left mimics right speaker's two-lines gesture as she emphatically agrees ('yes, yes, yes, yes'), including absolute direction (in both figures, the hands are moving toward camera). Meanwhile, in (4), right speaker is preparing her next gesture.

the interlocutors are personally close. Figure 2 presents such a case. Two friends are having a conversation. The example begins with a gesture by the friend on the right. She is describing the chaotic scene that develops on Tokyo subway platforms during rush hour, where multiple lines of waiting passengers take form but disintegrate when the train arrives into an elbow-swinging crowd. Panel 1 depicts the lines; panel 2 is their thickness and leftward direction vis-à-vis the speaker. The listener is commencing her gesture preparation during panel 2 as well, and panels 3 and 4 are her mimicry. The imagery is the same as the original: the same two lines, the same thickness and even the same absolute direction. From a psychological predicate viewpoint, the second speaker's idea unit included imagery from the first speaker's psychological predicate.

Kimbara's subjects were close friends but gesture and speech mimicry with appropriation takes place, as well between strangers, and this is closer to the theatrical context. An experiment devised by Furuyama (2000) had one person teach a second person, a stranger, how to create an *origami* box. In Figure 3, panel 1, the learner on the left mimics the teacher's gesture. It occurred without the learner speaking but was synchronized with the *tutor's* speech. As the tutor said, "[pull down] the corner", the learner performed the gesture during the bracketed portion. The learner appropriated the other's *speech,* combining it with *her gesture*, as if they were jointly creating a single psychological predicate. The similarities to what Gill (2007) calls entrainment are notable.

The reverse mimicry also occurs. The learner mimics *the tutor's gesture* by combining it with *her speech*. Again, there is inhabitance, this time of gesture, and there is again a kind of joint psychological predicate. In Panel 2 the learner takes manual control of the tutor's gesture and combines it with her speech. She says, "[you bend this down?]," and during the bracketed speech moves the tutor's hand down. As Furuyama observes, the tutor had turned in his chair so that the same left-right gesture space was available to him and the learner, a maneuver that invited the learner to enter his gesture space. It is striking that the American cultural taboo normally prohibiting strangers from non-accidental physical contact was overridden (a split second after Figure 3), possibly because the hands had become symbols and were no longer "hands", actual body-parts, belonging to another person.

Do-it-yourself mimicry

The ultimate in mind-merging is perhaps a coder's mimicry of a stranger who is visible and can be heard only in a video. The result is to bring a point of differentiation and its context into the coder's own momentary state of cognitive being; the coder now inhabits the gesture and speech and gains her own grasp of it. An exercise in McNeill (2012, pp. 150–154) replicates the experience. Three speakers are represented who created different fields of oppositions for the same cartoon event. By mimicking their gestures and speech, provided in the exercise, a reader can experience the original fields of meaningful oppositions arising as if by magic (but it is not "magic"; it is mind-merging through mimicry).

	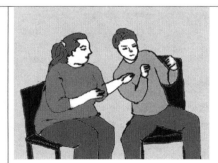
Panel 1. Mimicry by learner (on left)	Panel 2. Appropriation by learner (left)

Figure 3.   Embodiment in two bodies. From McNeill (2005). Used with permission of University of Chicago Press.

Performance and audience

Having described how gesture and speech form minimal units of thinking, GPs, and how mimicry is mind-merging, the mimic recovering the original speaker's GPs and fields of meaningful oppositions, we can now see how this applies in theatre performance.

The three legs

Mimicry of actor by audience

This is the most straightforward – it is what gesture coders do. The audience, through mimicry, mind-merges with the performer. Minimal movements, even just body tension, could be the materialization of the audience's mimicry. By attentively watching and mimicking the gestures of the actor, the GPs, and fields of oppositions embedded in the performance come to life, and shared being becomes possible. Ravid (2013) describes a phenomenon known in the theatre world as "dilation" – the actor as he stands on the stage seeming to the audience to expand in size before their eyes. Dilation would be a prime case of mimicry and embodiment – small tendencies on the actor's part, engendered by his own sensations of dilation, are mimicked by the audience, which recreates the sensation in them. They refer it back to the actor, who seems to expand.

Mimicry of author by actor

Does writing include hidden gestures? Written prose does not necessarily mean that imagery is lacking; rather it is possible that we write in such a way that gestures – orchestrating language in GPs through imagery – are incorporated into the written text. A reader, reading out loud, will restore the gestures that are a part of these GPs in the text implicitly. Writing is traditionally described as decontextualized, as standing on its own. However, tradition may have missed something. If the origin of language was in fact the origin of language and *gesture*, a unified system, there may be gestures hidden in written prose as a matter of its own history. Writing systems that engage the sounds of speech would encounter the gesture imagery that orchestrates speech actions, the moment the writing goes beyond a mere phoneme notation to actual prose.

We cannot tell if the gestures we produce reproduce the author's own gestures, but the imagery was placed there by the author as part of her writing and their realizations in gesture are readily evoked. Even without overt gestures imagery is present, and can be mimicked. Hence, the second leg. Much of what we sense as the rhythm of written prose, descriptive, as well as dialog, seems gestural. And so the actor can recover the gestures the author – even one from the past – has placed in the written text he is delivering. And through mimicry the actor can recover the author's GPs and fields of meaningful oppositions. We of course do not know that Jane Austen's own gestures, if she ever recited a passage aloud, were as our own, but we know that the gestures we find for ourselves were placed there by her. If you read this small bit from a letter by the character Jane in *Pride and Prejudice* aloud with hand movements, you readily spatialize the text gesturally: "[…] something has occurred of a most unexpected and serious nature; but I am afraid of alarming you – be assured that we are all well. What I have to say relates to poor Lydia […]" (Austen, 1852, p. 204). An actor, reciting these lines, could reactivate the gestures built into them, and in this way recover Austen's original GPs and fields of meaningful oppositions.

On the other hand, a verbatim transcript of actual spoken speech, its original gestures lost, strikes one as distinctly unrhythmic and nearly unintelligible (if you read such a transcript and form gestures, the gestures seem to be repeated beats, hitting each stress peak, which alone remains of the original gestures).

> Haldeman: Pat does want to. He doesn't know how to, and he doesn't have, he doesn't have any basis for doing it. Given this, he will then have the basis. He'll call Mark Felt in, and the two of them ... and Mark Felt wants to cooperate because ...

Since this leg of the triangle is possibly the least expected by the reader, I will take a bit of time to illustrate it in an actual performance. Taking *Pride and Prejudice* again, at one point Lizzie, touring Pemberley and believing that no one of the family is at home, suddenly finds herself face-to-face with Darcy. For both characters it is a moment of surprise and awkwardness. But it is also a moment of importance for the story. Austen describes Darcy's reaction as one of being "absolutely started" (p. 187).

I first tried a gesture that would go with just this line, without considering the preceding context of Lizzie's dawning new relation with Darcy. It was a sharp upward jerk of one hand (described by an observer as looking like a seizure) – to be sure an "absolute start" that was tied to the text. However, considering Austen's likely own field of meaningful oppositions, this gesture would not be what she had built into the narrative as part of her GP. An altogether different gesture appears when the immediate context is considered (in which the Pemberley Housekeeper, to Lizzie's astonishment, has given an enthusiastic recommendation of Darcy's character – generous, amiable, fair, "the best master" (p. 186)).

My two hands now form an open sphere and rock forward and upward. This fits a field of meaningful oppositions in which the Lizzie–Darcy relationship is in focus and transforming. The gesture "presents" this image of the dawning relationship and moves it forward, in a future direction. Austen's own GP as she wrote would plausibly have had some such meaning, this opening up (and beyond, in the following narrative, Darcy's own transformed demeanor).

The scene has been played in filmed versions of *Pride and Prejudice*. An actor fits his performance into this sort of dynamic context. Unlike his character, the actor also knows the preceding and following context of Darcy's absolute start. In one performance, a start is certainly present but the expression of surprise was briefly anticipated by a smile as well and also possibly a forward lean (not unlike the motion of my metaphoric gesture) – both conceivably reflecting the dawn of the new affiliation of Darcy with Lizzie (it does not matter if this scene was filmed before or after the full start scene – it is the actor's mimicry of the author's gesture we seek). So perhaps something like Jane Austen's GPs, fields of meaningful oppositions, and momentary states of cognitive being were present after all.[2]

Mimicry of audience by actor (thanks to Cornford, 2011)

A Shakespearean audience was fully accessible to the actors. But modern audiences are subdued and in darkness. Chekhov provides a theoretical basis for (modern or former) audience mimicry by actors. The means is what Cornford, inspired by Ramachandran and Blakeslee's (1998) description of phantom limbs, terms Chekhov's "phantom" gestures, the body expressing inner energy with minimal movement. Phantom gestures are a source of acting technique, but also can be an avenue for the actor to mimic the audience. A theatre audience is like a musical performance audience from the standpoint of materialization/mimicry. Movements in musical audiences are typical and acceptable within limits (limits varying widely by genre) but even in the most decorous classical audiences discrete foot-tapping, handwaving, bobbing, back and forth torso movements are acceptable, and provide bodily carriers of the performance. To even the untrained listener, one who is attentive, music can be a form of being, absorbing the person who, for the moment, is shaped by the music, the performer and composer. Theatrical audiences can do the same and they also have speech to guide them.

And the performer can sense these audience phantom gestures of posture shifts, tensions, and head and foot movements (curiously, using opposite extremities). Mind-merging with the audience is possible via mimicry of its phantom gestures and will create shared moments of being all along our triangle – author to actor, actor to audience, and back again. Even a large audience can occupy its leg.

Hence, the third leg of our actor–audience, audience–actor, and author–actor gesture triangle is complete. Together, these reveal a kind of three-way communication during a performance, actor to audience, audience to actor, with the absent and possibly long-dead author also taking part.

Breakdowns, offshoots, and film acting

To summarize: the author–actor–audience triangle is the dual semiotic of language in an unusual setting, a theatrical performance, where one participant (the actor) acts alone, another (the audience) acts as a mass in the dark, and the third (the author) may not be present at all and be even long since departed. Mimicry, a natural part of language dynamics, is the heart of the triangle:

- Mimicry is a lodestone, attracting mind-merging.
- Mimicry regenerates GPs and fields of oppositions of speakers.
- The same applies to performance and audience, working in all directions, from author to actor, actor to audience, and back again.

Breakdowns – failing to complete the triangle

A failure to complete the triangle can lead to breakdowns. These failures may be some of the characteristic failures of performance. Not establishing the actor → audience link is simply a failure to connect; not having the audience → actor link may be a source of stage fright (and establishing the link a way to combat it). Finally, a failure to find the author → actor link may be one meaning of what it is to be a ham.

Offshoots – minimizing imagery or form

The concept of dual semiotics as the foundation of performance also opens the possibility of offshoots, wherein one semiotic mode is emphasized over the other. Such attempted single semiotics would lack the dynamism Chekhov sought, but may have other features that lend themselves to experiments on performance and theatrical form. Emphasizing imagery in motion one immediately thinks of mime, but this is yet another form of systematic encoding, not speech but the mime's art, and is still a dual semiotic. Perhaps the closest approach to pure imagery is the Alexander Technique for actors. It does not appear to be a full acting method as Chekhov or Lecoq envisioned, but it does highlight the significance of action imagery – a tension that pulls back the head and puts downward pressure on the spine (while not a gesture in the normal sense) is linked to a global effect of suppression, choking, and diminishment; problems the actor needs to overcome. The Technique identifies and labels them (the tension being called a "downward pull"[3]). Kalb (2011) describes certain modern plays "treating language as pure gesture …," which may also be an effort to diminish dual semiosis. Voiceovers and live radio do not exclude embodiment, including gesture, and are not good examples. Some immobile plays may qualify, but I can suppose that actors, although static, supply their own gesture and body movements, and these too have dual semiosis. Some demanding experiment in which gestures and all other body movements are suppressed and the entire performance is only speech could be an example (perhaps in the form of a Watergate transcript, if this has not already been tried), but the actor must work against the self-defeating urge to tap the audience's "phantom" gestures. Ofer Ravid (pers. comm.) points out immobile plays by Samuel Beckett where verbal form is highlighted at the expense of imagery (for example, a character buried up to her neck in sand). The "fourth wall" deliberately blocks off the audience–actor leg and makes the stage into a self-contained universe of its own. I am told, again by Ofer Ravid (pers. comm.), that the fourth wall was introduced to ward off stage fright, but has evolved into an established acting practice without that in mind. He adds that it is often coupled with an introspective acting style, and this perhaps is the secret: introspection is what you are drawn to if there is lessened actor–audience mimicry.

Film acting – the actor conjures an audience

How does all this work for film? From what we have seen, an audience is an essential component of the performance triangle. A film actor has the same access to the author as does a stage actor, and the audience, absent but watching the film, has access to the actor and through her the author, but for the actor, an audience is absent during the performance itself, and this means that one must be invented. Again we turn to Chekhov. According to Mala Powers (in her Afterword to Chekhov, 1991), his word for acting in film was producing little pieces of art. And of course the actor, in contact with each of the nodes of our triangle, feels a need for an audience. It is only in this way the triangle can be completed. Her need is deeper than just wanting to have eyes focused on one. It is a matter of completing the triangle. Mala Powers described how Chekhov emphasized the importance for a film actor of *simulating an audience*. Even the camera can become *audience*. Powers apparently did this regularly, giving this device its own personality and so completing her triangle. The director, the other actors, and crew also play a role.

Kappelhoff and Müller (2011) analyze Wyler's 1938 *Jezebel* (Dir. William Wyler, USA, 1938) visually as (among other things) a metaphor of energy-stasis, the realization of which scenes and the actors' movements structure. Wyler, the audience of one, could have guided this with instruction and discussion but also, since he was right there, through his own movements mimicked by the actors. Bette Davis almost literally flies into the film (a wild horseback ride), herself a volcano of energy. At film's end she is transformed, utterly still, her beloved retrieved but dying on her lap (horses figure in both scenes, violent in one, funereal in the other, and this heightens the

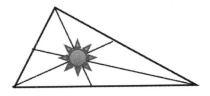

Figure 4.   Gesture triangle.

contrast, following Roman Jakobson's, 1960 "equivalence principle" of a contrast within an equivalence). The transformation is more than movement-to-stasis; it is of character, the movement-stasis dimension metaphorizing this.

Using mimicry (of her bodily attitudes – gestures are stylized and few), we can try to recover something of Davis' modes of differentiation and contexts as she instantiated Jezebel's transformation. Is the metaphor recoverable? To a film actor, I can imagine that each "little piece of art" transects the centre of the actor–audience, audience–actor, author–actor triangle, which is then recreated over and over, shot-by-shot in the making of a film. Was Davis transecting the triangle with a sense of energy passing into stasis? I believe she was. A context of frantic energy at the start becomes serene by the end, and this transition is palpable with mimicry. So we complete our own triangle as well (Figure 4).

Conclusions

(1) Theatrical performance includes a dialectic of semiotic opposites like that of gesture and language. I do not mean simply that actors speak and gesture – of course they must – but that in theatre, too, there is a dual semiosis of imagery and codified form, and they are a dialectic unity.

Chekhov wrote of "Atmosphere" – a kind of global-synthetic imagery of the scene that the actor has to combine with codified movements and speech to create the dynamism of performance, just as we can say that speakers combine gesture with speech to fuel speaking and thinking. Quintilian wrote of three "potencies" that align (more or less) with our triangle. In this sense, in heightened and public form, theatre is a continuation (not just a user) of language. It is, conceivably, even the culmination of language, conceptualized as a specialized dual mode of semiosis, and this is, I believe, a secret of its appeal. Any theatre that violates fundamental modes of human experience could not have survived so long.

(2) And the triangle is a constant. We have seen how there is a triangle and each leg is traversed by mimicry. Many reactions take place and are part of the performance involving all participants, author, actor, and audience. For most of us – the audience seated in the dark – the experience is far from passive. It is more than just watching. If actor and director are skilled, it is mind-merging with the actor and ultimately with the author, as we may have done watching a growth point and field of meaningful oppositions that may have originally been alive in Jane Austen more than 200 years ago.

Acknowledgements

I am grateful to the editors, Nicholas Chare and Liz Watkins, and two friends from the theatre world, Ofer Ravid and Tom Cornfield, for precious advice.

Notes

1. Discovered by Liesbet Quaeghebeur.
2. It would have been interesting to see how Lawrence Olivier, playing Darcy, handled the absolute start, but his 1940 film does not include any scenes with Pemberley, let alone this one with the absolute start.
3. This term and description derives from an online article, Andrews and Bartner, alexandertech nique.com/articles/acting (accessed 04/05/12).

References

Austen, J. (1852). *Pride and prejudice: A novel*. London: Routledge.
Chekhov, M. (1991). *On the technique of acting: The first complete edition of Chekhov's classic to the actor*. New York, NY: Harper.
Cornford, T. (2011, July 2). *Michael Chekhov and the phantom limb*. Retrieved June 1, 2012, from http://www.tomcornford.com/sitefiles/24/8/6/248608/CONF010.pdf
Furuyama, N. (2000). Gestural interaction between the instructor and the learner in origami instruction. In D. McNeill (Ed.), *Language and gesture* (pp. 99–117). Cambridge: Cambridge University Press.
Gill, S. (2007). Entrainment and musicality in the human system interface. *AI & Society, 21*, 567–605.
Jakobson, R. (1960). Concluding statement: Linguistics and poetics. In T. Sebeok (Ed.), *Style in language* (pp. 350–377). Cambridge, MA: MIT Press.
Kalb, J. (2011). *Great lengths*. Ann Arbor: University of Michigan Press.
Kappelhoff, H., & Müller, C. (2011). Embodied meaning construction: Multimodal metaphor and expressive movement in speech, gesture, and in feature film. *Metaphor and the Social World, 1*, 121–153.
Kendon, A. (2008). Some reflections on the relationship between 'gesture' and 'sign'. *Gesture, 8*, 348–366.
Kimbara, I. (2006). On gestural mimicry. *Gesture, 6*, 39–61.
Lecoq, J. (1997). *The moving body: Teaching creative theatre*. New York, NY: Routledge.
McNeill, D. (2005). *Gesture and thought*. Chicago, IL: University of Chicago Press.
McNeill, D. (2010). Gesten der Macht und die Macht der Gesten' [Gestures of power and the power of gestures]. In E. Fischer-Lichte & C. Wulf (Eds.), *Gesten* (pp. 42–57). Munich: Fink Publishers. Retrieved from mcneilllab.uchicago.edu
McNeill, D. (2012). *How language began: Gesture and speech in human evolution*. Cambridge: Cambridge University Press.
McNeill, D., Duncan, S., Franklin, A., Goss, J., Kimbara, I., Parrill, F., … Tuttle, R. (2009). Mind merging. In E. Morsella (Ed.), *Expressing oneself/expressing one's self: Communication,*

language, cognition, and identity: essays in honor of Robert Krauss (pp. 143–164). London: Taylor and Francis.

Nobe, S. (2000). Where do *most* spontaneous representational gestures actually occur with respect to speech? In D. McNeill (Ed.), *Language and gesture* (pp. 186–198). Cambridge: Cambridge University Press.

Ramachandran, V. S., & Blakeslee, S. (1998). *Phantoms in the brain: Probing the mysteries of the human mind*. New York, NY: William Morrow.

Ravid, O. (2013). *Presentness: Presence in practice* (Unpublished PhD). Toronto: York University.

Roach, J. (1993). *The Player's passion: Studies in the science of acting*. Ann Arbor: University of Michigan Press.

Films, gestures, species

Barbara Creed

School of Culture and Communication, University of Melbourne, Parkville, Australia

As non-verbal communication, gestures are central to the cinematic representation of the animal. How has the cinema constructed creaturely gestures? How do animals enunciate? Charles Darwin argued in *The Expression of the Emotions in Man and Animals* (1872) that there is an evolutionary continuity between human and animal expressions and gestures. In his book, he drew on photography to provide visual evidence of his theory that the emotions evolved in human and animal, and that animals also experienced a range of emotions similar to those experienced by the human animal. To what extent has the cinema represented a gestural continuity between species? This paper explores these questions in relation to a range of films. It focuses on the extent to which the cinema deploys human and animal gestures to reinforce and/or undermine an anthropocentric discourse and point of view.

Project Nim (Dir. James Marsh, UK, 2011) is a fascinating and disturbing documentary directed by James Marsh that explores sign language as a form of animal gesture. Nim Chimpsky, a newborn chimpanzee, was the subject of a scientific experiment to see how effectively an ape might learn sign language if adopted into a human family from a very young age. His name was intended as a punning reference to Noam Chomsky who believed only humans could use language fully. Dr Herb Terrace, a Professor of behavioural psychology at Columbia University, organised for Nim to be taken from his mother when only a few days old to live with a colleague, Stephanie LaFarge and her family of seven children and her husband. He stayed with the LaFarge family for five years. Stephanie brought Nim up as one of her own children even to the point of breastfeeding the infant chimpanzee. This was the 1970s, when American society was experimenting with freer lifestyles and exploring a range of different moral values. Director James Marsh tells Nim's story in documentary form, combining archival film footage, photographs, dramatic recreations and interviews with all of those who taught and worked with Nim. Although Terrace concluded that the experiment was a failure, there is no doubt that Nim not only learnt the meaning of over 125 hand gestures, which signified specific concepts, but that he also communicated his feelings to members of the LeFarge family and his teachers. In addition, Nim also used other gestures, as distinct from hand signs, to express his needs and desires.

A disturbing episode occurs in Marsh's film when Nim is taken from his human family to be relocated at Lemsip, an experimental medical centre at New York University.

Nim is introduced to another chimpanzee, Mack, for the first time. Up to this point, Nim has not encountered another ape. He appears to identify completely with Stephanie and his human teachers and companions – wearing clothes, eating at the table, sleeping in a bed, brushing his teeth and using the toilet. He also accompanies them on walks, plays games, smokes pot, asks to be held and cuddled, and generally takes part in a wide range of human activities. During his encounter with Mack, Nim's immediate response is one of fear. He casts his eyes in different directions, then points at the newcomer and finally backs away. He does not appear to recognise a member of his own species although we have seen Nim before the mirror where he recognises himself as he brushes his teeth and puffs out his chest in pleasure. Next in a fairly universal gesture that signifies fear mingled with shock, Nim places both hands over his eyes and shrinks into the background. The gesture appears instinctive. Humans similarly cover their eyes to shield themselves from frightening or abject sights. As Nim's future is uncertain, this gesture occurs at a significant moment in the narrative. There is a possibility that Nim might become the victim of medical experimentation at Lemsip.

Charles Darwin argued in *The Expression of the Emotions in Man and Animals* (1872) that there is an evolutionary continuity between the ways in which humans and animals express emotions. In addressing this new area of non-verbal communication, he asked the question: Why do facial expressions adopt the forms that they do? Why do human and non-human animals curl their lips and bare their teeth when enraged, and stare with their eyes open wide when overcome with fear? He drew on photography to provide visual evidence for his theory. Darwin concluded that animals also experience a range of emotions similar to those experienced by the human animal and that the ability to express emotions evolved in human and animal alike. The reason why these particular expressions have persisted is that in evolutionary terms they have acquired a certain communicative significance.

In the silent film period, when cinema communicated its narratives without dialogue, the form relied heavily on gestures and expressions. According to the French film critic Pascal Bonitzer, gesture was its essential form of communication (Bonitzer, 1981). In referring to the writings of Bonitzer and Agamben on film and gesture, Pasi Väliaho writes that "[b]ased on these conceptualizations, one could say that the moving image is gestural by nature. It takes not immovable and rigid forms but material, bodily dynamism as its subjects" (2010, p. 17) The absence of dialogue meant that film had the power to communicate to all peoples regardless of their specific spoken language. As a result, during the silent era film became popularly known through Hollywood marketing as "a universal language" or an "Esperanto of the eye". Film directors such as D. W. Griffith believed that the power of film was so great it might help to unite peoples of the world, giving them a common purpose such as bringing about world peace. Another area of universal appeal lies in the ability of film to represent the shared gestural expressions of human and animal.

The cinema has drawn on various techniques to encourage the spectator's identification with animals and animality. It has represented animals as "human" through the techniques of anthropomorphic representation, particularly the use of visual gesture and human voice-over, which are central to the Disney animal cartoon and animated children's feature films such as *Babe* (Dir. Chris Noonan, Australia, 1995) and *Happy Feet* (Dir. George Miller, USA, 2006). Conversely, film has represented humans as animals through the techniques of cinematic zoomorphism, such as gesture, which are particularly evident in jungle adventure films such as the universally popular *Tarzan* series and horror films such as *Dr Jekyll and Mr Hyde* (Dir. Rouben Mamoulian,

USA, 1931) *The Wolf Man* (Dir. George Waggner, USA, 1941) and more recently *The Fly* (Dir. David Cronenberg, USA, 1986). In these films, the human protagonist metamorphoses through special effects into a creature. Essential to zoomorphism is the adoption of animal gestures as part of the transition from one species to another. Films also represent animals as animals – creatures able to express themselves as the animals that they are through gesture as in the documentaries *Project Nim* and *Nénette* (Dir. Nicolas Philibert, France, 2010).

If the role of human gestures in the cinematic experience has received little theoretical attention, the role of animal gestures has attracted even less. Yet as a form of non-verbal communication, gestures lend themselves to the domain of animal communication. As with human gestures, animal gestures can also take many forms including those that are conscious, unconscious, involuntary, rhythmic, repetitive, facial, manual and somatic. The study of gestures enjoys a long history stretching back into antiquity with the writings of Cicero and Quintilian and forward to contemporary studies, which include a range of disciplines such as literature, history, sculpture, theatre, painting and film. In his writings on gesture, Herman Roodenburg notes that recently there have been attempts to advance an interdisciplinary approach[1] one which would:

> integrate more fully the insights of anthropologists and sociolinguists with a historical approach, and also to follow the history of gestures as embedded in everyday life and in their "recoded" quality in painting, sculpture, stagecraft, literature, and so on. (1991, p. 399)

Herman Roodenburg points out that although most theorists concur that some measure of volition is usually involved, there are no clear cut definitions:

> Most scholars agree that a degree of volition should be implied. They also acknowledge that there are no watertight divisions between posture and gesture, or between voluntary (or "conventional") and involuntary (or "natural") gestures; indeed, these divisions have a history of their own. (2001, p. 1)

A study of animal gestures in film offers not only a fuller appreciation of the shared gestural behaviours of human and non-human animals but it also enhances our appreciation of the specificity and nuances of gesture in film as represented in *Project Nim*. In its power to emphasise the continuity between human and animal, film also points to the ancient and evolutionary origin of gesture as discussed by Darwin. This is clearly evidenced through the "Animal Exercise" of method acting techniques, which I shall discuss later in this essay. A study of animal gesture also asks us to explore the ways in which the spectator understands screen performances. There is clearly a willing engagement on the part of the spectator to make sense of gestures performed by non-human animals in order to construct, or at least help to shape, the text's wider narrative meaning. In this context, the cinema reveals that one of its most important aesthetic achievements is its power to speak – through gesture – to the human spectator about the emotional lives of animals. Similarly, film has the power to speak to the viewer about the animal *in* the human.

Sequences in which gesture is central to the representation of animals occur in documentary and fiction films. Here, I discuss the significance of creaturely gestures in relation to *Au hasard Balthazar* (Dir. Robert Bresson, France, 1966), *Sang des Bêtes* (Dir. Georges Franju, France, 1949), *Maîtresse* (Dir. Barbet Schroeder, France, 1976), *The Story of the Weeping Camel* (Dirs. Byambasuren Davaa & Luigi Faloma, Mongolia,

2003), *Attenborough in Paradise* (Dir. Paul Reddish, UK, 2006), and *Nénette* (2010). Drawing on a zoomorphic aesthetic, these films raise a series of important issues in relation to the representation of creaturely gestures. Some explore the issue of intentionality in relation to animal gestures. In other words, does the animal need to produce the gesture itself – as in Nim's covering of his eyes – for the act to signify a particular emotion? What difference does it make if editing is utilised in the production of an animal gesture, as it frequently is with a human protagonist? To what extent does the spectator "produce" the emotional effect of gesture imaginatively in relation to the animal protagonist? To what extent does the cinema deploy gesture as a means of questioning the anthropocentric nature of human discourse? The films selected cover a range of gestural forms: hand gestures and hand signing, the act of looking as gesture and the gaze, involuntary bodily gestures, courtship displays and the shedding of tears.

Au hasard Balthazar (1966)

Directed by Robert Bresson, *Au hasard Balthazar* represents the animal's gaze as a gesture created through montage. Bresson tells the story of Marie, a young girl, and her donkey, Balthazar, whom she has raised from infancy on her parent's farm. The narrative follows their lives, which mirror each other in relation to their respective mistreatment and suffering at the hands of others. It ends with Balthazar's death. Throughout the film, Bresson depicts Balthazar's sufferings, moments of happiness, and endless hours of labour demanded by his various masters. Bresson's approach to film-making is to direct his actors in such a way that they rarely express their feelings in terms of visible emotion or gesture. Although Balthazar suffers, Bresson gives no sign of what the donkey is feeling. Apart from an occasional cry, Balthazar's performance is impenetrable. The spectator however does "read" emotions into Balthazar's actions – particularly in the zoo sequence where Bresson uses montage to encourage the spectator to interpret Balthazar's act of looking as a gesture. Bresson's aim, in presenting events from Balthazar's point of view, is to undermine the conventional anthropocentric or human-centred discourse.

Having escaped from the clutches of Arnold, his cruel master, Balthazar finds himself in a circus. In a series of cross-cuts, Balthazar stares at a number of animals held captive in cages: a tiger, polar bear, elephant and a chimpanzee (in chains) all of whom are inside their own prisons. Balthazar stops before each one and looks intently at the captive animal. We are encouraged also to stare at the caged animals as if through the eyes of Balthazar. The donkey's stare, and the way his gaze directs us to look at the various captive animals seems to declare – "See, the misery of the animal!" There is no dialogue or music – only sounds made by the animals. Bresson does not offer any guidance as to how we should look or what we should feel. It is not difficult, however, to imagine that Balthazar is experiencing empathy for his fellow creatures whose lives are even more wretched than his own. The spectator is encouraged to empathise with Balthazar – although some critics have argued that empathy with the emotions of other species is impossible. J.M. Coetzee has considered this issue in his novel, *Elizabeth Costello*. Here, the eponymous heroine states that if she can identify with fictional characters in novels, such as those of James Joyce, then she can similarly identity with other living beings. "I can think my way into the existence of a bat or a chimpanzee or an oyster, any being with whom I share the substrate of life", the heroine suggests. Furthermore, Elizabeth argues that there are "no bounds to the sympathetic imagination" (Coetzee, 2004, p. 80).

In the zoo sequence, Bresson comments on the famous experiment by Lev Kuleshov, the soviet film theorist of the 1910s and 1920s, who set out to understand the workings of the sympathetic imagination in film. There is no reason why Kuleshov's experiment could not equally apply to the non-human animal protagonist in film. Kuleshov designed an experiment in which he took a shot of an actor's blank face and intercut it with a bowl of soup, a woman reclining on a divan and a dead child in a coffin. The film was shown to an audience who said that the expression on the actor's face changed depending on the object of his gaze. The audience expressed great enthusiasm for the actor's powers – his ability to express hunger for the soup, passion for the reclining woman and grief over the dead child. Kuleshov concluded that it is the spectator who creates meaning by projecting an emotional connection between the shot of the actor's blank face and the object he is observing – the soup, the woman and the child. Bresson uses the zoo sequence to demonstrate that it is the spectator's "sympathetic imagination", which projects an interpretation onto Balthazar's actions. Bresson has said that he never required that his actors express themselves in a dramatic manner. Mirella Affron suggests that Bresson asks his actors instead "to wipe away non-existent tears, to find not the gesture through feeling, but the feeling through the simplest and most stylized of gestures" (Naremore, 1988, p. 67). Balthazar's gaze acts as a simple, stylised but low-key gesture pointing out each animal while telling us what we already know – that there can be no justification for the captivity and suffering of other creatures. In making Balthazar the main protagonist of his film, instead of a human actor, Bresson demonstrates that it is possible to utilise cinematic techniques to encourage the spectator to empathise with other creatures through gesture.

Sang des Bêtes (1949), Maîtresse (1976)

Georges Franju's documentary *Blood of Beasts* (*Sang des Bêtes*) demonstrates how an animal gesture can take an unconscious, involuntary form. *Blood of Beasts* documents the daily workings of an abattoir located in the outskirts of suburban Paris. Franju documents the horrific scenes in a cool, detached, often poetic style. Although he presents the view that the workers carry out their bloody tasks dispassionately, Franju himself says his concern is to ask whether or not such slaughter can be justified. To elicit spectator sympathy, Franju uses an ageing white cart-horse who trustingly lets itself be led to the slaughter yard. The horse stands quietly in the dawn light. A man appears and stands in front of the horse while aiming a fatal blow to the horse's forehead with a Behr-gun. As the sound of a loud crack fills the air, the horse jumps then falls to the ground. As the horse falls, each of its forelegs fold underneath its body so that it appears to adopt a kneeling position. This act communicates itself as if this were the horse's final gesture in life – a kind of bowing out of life into death. The animal's gesture is clearly involuntary but it is even more eloquent for being so. This moment sends uncanny reverberations through the following scenes, undercutting the jaunty whistles of the workers and infusing them with a sober, chilling undertone.

There is a similar scene in Barbet Schroeder's fiction film *Maîtresse*. The male protagonist Olivier, played by Gerard Depardieu, visits an abattoir when he is feeling depressed and abandoned. Here, Schroeder inserts a documentary sequence, in which Olivier watches one of the workers slaughter a horse. After the animal has been killed, it is hung upside down by hooks. In a lyrical but strange moment, the horse's legs move in an involuntary gesture. It is as if the animal were alive and cantering across an imaginary field. The animal's bodily gesture starkly emphasises the sudden and brutal nature of death, which drains the animal of life before it is ready to die. Shortly afterwards Olivier visits a butcher's shop where he buys a slab of horsemeat, and later cooks and eats it. Schroeder has explained that he wanted to include a scene of Oliver identifying with and then eating the animal in order that he might think about the cruel side of human nature. Oliver's gestural act signifies what Schroeder describes as a "primitive unconscious ritual" (Smith, 1995, p. 12). In both films the horses' involuntary gestures, performed as each one dies, emphasise the fragile line between life and death.

Attenborough in Paradise (2006)

David Attenborough's nature documentary, *Attenborough in Paradise*, explores the issue of sexual display, intentionality and gesture in the world of birds. The documentary is filmed in the forests of Papua New Guinea, which is home to 38 of the 42 varieties of these remarkable creatures. Attenborough's crew have captured on film the mating rituals, which include elaborate dances, of the male birds. The male makes a clearing in the forest to construct a dance floor on which he performs highly complex dances in order to attract a mate. Attenborough's film captures a scene in which Wilson's Bird of Paradise appears and begins to clear a stage as well as pick leaves from tree branches so the light will show his brilliant colours to their full advantage. The male bird has a blue cap, yellow and red feather and two white quills which spiral out from his tail to form circles. The colours of his costume are incandescent. When a female appears he dances, sings and spreads his feathers. In another sequence, a male carefully clears all fallen leaves from his stage. An audience of females assembles to watch. The male puffs out his body feathers to form a wide skirt and begins his performance – prancing from side to side as he swishes the feather in his top knot. Suddenly he flies above one of the females, pounces on her and begins to mate. In some courtship scenarios, if the female is not impressed she will turn her back on the performing male and walk away. In addition, as Darwin demonstrated, the males have developed, through evolutionary processes of sexual selection, amazingly beautiful masses of plumage, of all colours, to enhance their display. Their dances involve elaborate gestural displays designed purely to attract the female. Darwin's discussion of the display of the male peacock points to a similar gestural performance:

> Ornaments of all kinds ... are sedulously displayed by the males, and apparently serve to excite, or attract, or charm the females. All naturalists who have closely attended to the habits of birds ... are unanimously of opinion that the males delight to display their beauty. (Crist, 1999, p. 113)

Darwin discusses the unusual fact that male peacocks will sometimes show off their beauty to other species including poultry and pigs. In Darwin's view, the male is so desirous of displaying himself he will perform for other species simply in order to show off "his finery". Crist argues that this is a clear instance of the peacock's conscious intention and as such is a gesture:

> As a consequence of being performed, his action comes through as a *gesture*. In virtue of being initiated and directed by the peacock himself, the gesture emerges as immanently meaningful, despite the fact that it is out of proper context. (1999, p. 114)

In her view, animal courtship clearly "involves the design and presentation of gestures" which can be seen perhaps more "than any other type of action" as "subjectively expressive, both loaded with import and intentionally addressed" (1999, p. 167). It is tempting to argue that the representation of acts of human courtship in classical ballet and the Hollywood musical have much in common with the gestures of bird courtship in the real world. In the musical, human performances similarly erect a stage on which to sing and dance as well as dress up in elaborately designed costumes often decorated with feathers and topknots. Think of the final scene of Busby Berkeley's *The Gang's All Here* (Dir. Busby Berkeley, USA, 1943) in which Carmen Miranda appears bedecked in her famous *tutti-frutti* hat. Here, the actress performs all of the mating gestures necessary to attract a mate: singing, dancing, evocative gestures and parted, smiling lips.

The Story of the Weeping Camel (2003)

There are various species of animals, such as elephants and camels, who weep when deeply upset. This happens, for instance, when mothers are separated from their young. *The Story of the Weeping Camel* is a documentary which records an unusual event that takes place between a female camel and her newborn colt. Directed by Luigi Falorni and Byambasuren Davaa, it documents the daily lives of a group of nomadic shepherds who live in the Gobi region of Mongolia. The family live in yurts in close-knit companionship with their herds of camels – human and animal rely on each other for survival. The family are confronted with an unusual crisis when one of the female Bactrian camels, that is, two-humped camels, undergoes a very difficult birth eventually producing a rare white infant. Having struggled bravely to give birth, with assistance from the shepherd family, the mother then adamantly rejects her newborn calf refusing to bond with the infant or to allow him to drink her milk. This is her first calving. Every time he approaches she either kicks out at him or chases him away. The situation where a mother camel rejects her infant is rare but does occur. After a prolonged search, at the time of filming, the film-makers discovered a camel who had rejected her newborn infant. All efforts by the family, including the performance of a special ritual, fail to unite mother and son. In desperation, the family send their two young sons to the nearest township where they search for a well-known musician whom they believe might be able to assist by performing the traditional *Hoos* ceremony in the hope that the mother camel will accept her infant colt. The Gobi desert dwellers have created this ancient musical ritual designed to move the female camel emotionally and reunite her with her rejected offspring. The boys return with the musician who plays a Mongolian violin known as a *morin khuur*.

The group assemble sitting on tussocks in a semi-circle. The mother is led over to the musician and the colt tethered nearby. The ceremony commences. A young woman begins to sing and stroke the mother camel's fur. She responds with utterances, which sound like a lament. The film cuts between close-ups of the girl's hand stroking the camel's fur, and the camel looking at the scene before her and at her offspring. Her lips appear to quiver. As the baby suckles, and the musician plays his haunting melody we see tears trickle from the camel's eyes. As the music gently rises the mother camel appears visibly moved and continues to weep. Tears stream from her eyes as she accepts her calf allowing him to drink from her teat. The shepherds are also emotionally moved. Camels, like elephants, possess tear ducts and female camels are known to weep when separated from their young or depressed. When weeping, camels also utter sounds, which indicate sadness. Crying is a particularly expressive gesture which, when it occurs in human and animal, suggests a close parallel between the emotional lives of human and animal alike. Throughout *The Story of the Weeping Camel,* the film-makers present scenes in which we see the shepherds and their camels engaged in parallel activities: eating, sleeping, mothering, suckling and weeping. The performance of the weeping ritual, and its combination of human and animal gestures, also creates a sense of interspecies reciprocity. Various reviewers reported that the sight of the weeping mother also caused them to shed tears.

Recent scientific research indicates that humans and various species of animals, such as dogs, apes and dolphins, not only have the ability to express empathy but also that one species can experience empathy on behalf of another. In *The Empathic Civilisation*, Jeremy Rifkin discusses recent research into the relationship between the experience of empathy, facial expressions and gestures. Scientists have discovered that some animals and humans experience empathy when they see another being express their emotional state by giving a specific facial expression or gesture. The observer's brain will mirror this expression or gesture thus enabling the observer to feel what the other is feeling, to place themselves literally in the place of the other. As Rifkin notes:

> While scientists have noted that visual gestures and expressions, as well as auditory reso-nances, activate mirror neurons, they are also finding that touch does so as well, creating still another sensory path for empathic extension. (2009, p. 84)

Current research indicates that gestural expression is central to the experience of empa-thy in humans and some non-human animals. While this research is in its infancy, it is clear that the cinema has always represented narratives, which depict the expression of empathy between human and non-human animals through gestures. This research may also help to explain why the film spectator is able to identify so directly with screen characters, human and animal, to the point where they feel themselves swept away by the plight of another, emoting along with them.

Nénette (2010)

Nicholas Philibert's documentary *Nénette*[2] explores the daily life of an orangutan as well as focusing the spectator's attention on the minutiae of her bodily gestures. *Nénette* is a female orangutan from Borneo who was taken captive and sent to the menagerie of the Jardine des Plantes in Paris 40 years previously. Philibert filmed Nénette's many visitors as they watch her but we only hear their conversations. Described as an "unknowable celebrity" she appears fully aware of performing for her visitors. She frequently looks directly into the lens as if she intended to communicate with the spectator. The image track depicts the orangutans going about their daily activities while the sound track con-sists of comments made by the zoo visitors and the trainers. The disjuncture between sound and image draws attention to the degree to which the human spectator projects his/her own emotions onto the animals. They tell Nénette she is lonely, that she must miss her homeland and that she needs a husband. The dominant viewpoint projected by Nénette's trainers is about her boredom. One keeper says:

> There are marks too on the wall, of scratches of annoyance or in any case, of a surge of energy. There must be times when she can no longer stand this state, her condition. It's the realm of "doing nothing". She spends her life doing nothing.

Nénette communicates her boredom through her bodily gestures – she is shown staring at the camera, lying in the straw, sleeping, eating and basically doing nothing. In one sequence, she raises her blanket and pulls it around her head as if she wanted to shut out the world. It is a simple but eloquent gesture, which the spectator fully understands. Her keeper sees her as a consummate actor:

> And then the quality of her idleness makes me think of an exercise in an acting class ... You can follow her inch by inch in her acts that are all linked to each other by idleness and inaction ... She is fully there, that's all.

The keeper's comments on Nénette's performance recall Stanislavski's theory of method acting. James Naremore argues that Stanislavsky's writings on acting have been the most influential in the history of Hollywood. He defines the hallmark of Stanislavskian aesthetics as follows:

> ... the belief that good acting is "true to life" and at the same time expressive of the actor's authentic, "organic" self ... All varieties of teaching derived from his work try to inculcate spontaneity, improvisation, and low-key psychological introspection; they devalue anything that looks stagy ... (1988, p. 2)

Nénette's daily "performance" of living with boredom is clearly "true to life". She is both performing and not performing. Her performance largely consists of what Stanislavsky called "gestureless moments", which he believed were best created through the close-up shot in order to construct the desired sense of naturalism. Meaning is created by other methods such as editing, framing and the close-up. This does not mean, however, that certain minimalist gestures are not important in creating a sense of naturalism. According to Naremore, Pudovkin was right when he described acting "as a relatively passive phenomenon" (1988, p. 40). The rationale for this statement is as following:

> [This is] not only because the meaning of expressions can be determined by editing, but because the camera takes on a rhetorical function when it selects details or changes the scale of an image ... The camera's mobility and tight framing of faces, its ability to "give" the focus of the screen to any player at any moment, also means that films tend to favour reactions ... As a result some of the most memorable Hollywood performances have consisted largely of players isolated in close-up, responding nonverbally to offscreen events. (1988, p. 40)

Naremore's description of a memorable performance describes Nénette's performance throughout the film. Philibert has chosen to frame Nénette in tight close-ups carrying out her daily activities without any recourse to off-screen events, not even shots of the visitors who speak to the orangutan through the glass. The keeper states that Nénette performs with "astounding virtuosity". Her gestures which include staring, rearranging the straw bedding, sleeping and draping a shawl over her head are small and inconsequential. Yet her performance is riveting.

The topic of animal gestures in film raises the issue of anthropomorphisation. To what extent does the spectator read human intentions into animal gestures? In her book on anthropomorphism and the animal mind, Eileen Crist calls for "the suspension of the sweeping indictment of anthropomorphism as a distorted perspective on the reality of animal being" (1999, p. 12). Crist argues that much of this unjustifiable indictment arose in prejudiced response to Darwin's work, whereas Darwin's approach resulted from "a resounding affirmation of the evolutionary continuity between animals and humans" (1999, p. 13). Anat Pick observes that Andre Bazin, the French film theorist, distinguishes between positive and negative forms of anthropomorphisation. The latter occurs when a film "anthropomorphises the animals in a negative sense of the word, removing what is animal about them and obscuring their nature" (2011, p. 111). Positive anthropomorphisation does not deny or obscure what it is that is animal. A study of the representation of animal gestures in film also affirms a Darwinian continuity between human and animal and the expression of emotions. From an opposite perspective, there are films that adopt a zoomorphic perspective, that is, they represent human protagonists who express through gesture the animal in the human. The representation of the animal in the human occurs across genres and includes fiction films such as *Tarzan the Ape Man* (Dir. W.S. Van Dyke, USA, 1932) and *Cat People* (Dir. Jacques Tourneur, USA, 1942), the biopic *Gorillas in the Mist* (Dir. Michael Apted, USA, 1988), the film of the Peter Shaffer's stage play *Equus* (Dir. Sidney Lumet, UK, 1977) and the documentary *Grizzly Man* (Dir. Werner Herzog, USA, 2005). It is primarily through a study of gesture that these connections concerning the shared gestures of human and animal, as represented on the screen, become clear.

Although diverse, all of these films include scenes in which the main protagonist adopts animal gestures, or animal "behaviour", in order to express his/her alignment with the animal as well as a strongly felt inner sense of being an animal. These gestural moments undermined an anthropocentric point of view: Tarzan beats his chest and emits his famous ape cry; the heroine of *Cat People* imagines she has metamorphosed into the panther she watches it intently in its cage at the zoo; Sigourney Weaver in her role as Dian Fossey moves and grunts as if she were a gorilla in order to signal that she is "one" of the group; the boy in *Equus* wears a bridle in his mouth and whips his flanks as if he were a stable horse and Timothy Treadwell the protagonist of *Grizzly Man* believes he is closer to being a grizzly bear, than a human animal. In one scene, he joyously reaches out to touch repeatedly a pile of warm bear excrement in order to feel closer to Wendy, the bear in question, just as a bear might sniff another bear's excrement to gather information through close contact. He says "I know it might seem weird that I touched her poop that was inside of her but its her life, its her. And she's so precious to me". As the director, Werner Herzog, explains Treadwell only felt truly at home in "primordial nature". Ecologist Marnie Gaede, who is interviewed in the film, explains that Treadwell did not simply want to imitate the bears, rather he desired to become a bear.[3] He felt such a strong connection to the bears it engulfed his entire being; living with the bears was a deep, mystical, even religious experience. Treadwell films himself telling God: "I am one of them. I will die for these animals". For Treadwell the gesture of touching, reaching out to the bears, which he does repeatedly, signifies the deepest intimacy.

Further consideration of *Project Nim* reveals ways in which Nim was able to use gesture not just to communicate but also to manipulate his teachers and charm them into doing as he wished. Although Nim learns over 125 signs, Dr Herbert Terrace in the end concludes that Nim has not learnt to communicate as a human being. This is relatively obvious comment – Nim is not a human being. He does, however, learn to communicate with human beings *as* a chimp who has learnt to sign. Nim is able to make requests, express his needs and desires and display his emotions. When Nim wants to be forgiven for misbehaving, he kisses the hand of his teacher: when he wants comfort he will ask for a full body hug. Terrace, however, states in a television interview that Nim is simply a "brilliant beggar". Nim, he argues, cannot actually express his desires in grammatical sentences as would a human. Terrace uses this argument, combined with the fact that Nim is becoming difficult to control, to send him to an experimental facility, Lemsip. Nim's teachers are distraught. They disagree with

Terrace, arguing that as far as they were concerned Nim had learnt many, many signs and that he was able to communicate in quite complex ways with them. In their view, the experiment was a success. Nim, they all agree, was treated appallingly.

In one episode, we see Nim use sign language in a particularly astute way. After his idyllic infancy, Nim is sent to School with his teachers; he works with them in a fifteen-feet square, cement room which one teacher describes as a "dungeon". Nim clearly dislikes his new environment as much as his teachers. We see him throwing his arms around Joyce in an intimate gesture signifying a "hug". Joyce explains how she taught Nim the sign for "dirty", which is to hold his hand up under his chin. During the lesson, Nim signs the word "dirty" so that Joyce will take him out of the cell and to the toilet. Marsh the director, inserts archival photographs of Nim signing "dirty" along with film footage in which he both signs and takes Joyce by the hand to lead her out of the room. Joyce says in interview: "And that's when I knew. You little bugger! You used that sign because you knew it would make us leave there and get us out of there". Nim did not need to know about grammatical constructions. In combining sign language with body language, Nim was able to express his desire with perfect clarity through gesture.

This episode emphasises the bodily nature of gestures. The role of animal work in method acting is relevant here. Lee Strasberg, who created method acting, based on the teachings of Constantin Stanislavski, influenced generations of film actors in Hollywood. Strasberg argued for the importance of actors drawing on animal behaviours to make themselves more aware of their bodies and ways in which to express emotions through physical characterisation. Lee J. Cobb, for instance, studied the behaviour and physical gestures of elephants in order to portray Willy Loman from Arthur Miller's *Death of A Salesman* as an old man weighed down by the burdens of daily living. Actors were asked to study animal postures, movements and to try and imagine the animal's thoughts. They were then instructed to make the animal human. This approach, known as the "Animal Exercise" was central to method acting, which valued a low-key, naturalistic approach. In so far as gesture is a bodily form of communication, it bridges the gap between human and animal and is central to method acting.

Some have argued that gesture makes language redundant allowing for universal communication between different races of the human species. Desmond Morris, for instance, holds that survival is tied to our ability to communicate non-verbally (1994). Ray Birdwhistell who founded kinesics believed that bodily movements, including facial expressions and postures, convey up to 70% of information in acts of conversational communication (1970). Birdwhistell, however, rejected the view that body language might have set universal meanings insisting that every situation should be analysed in relation to its own context. Birdwhistell also argued that unlike animal gestures, human gestures are polysemic, that is, they are open to different meanings. In my view, meaning is dependent on interpretation and this may be very nuanced in relation to the interpretation of animal as well as human–animal gestures. Many animals are also very skilled at reading human and non-human body language. Gesture also allows for communication between human and non-human species, thus, extending the possibilities for communication across the species divide.

The representation of animal gestures in film, regardless of whether the gestures are intentional or unintentional, in general serves to bring together the domains of animal and human. This move towards unification endorses what Crist sees in her discussion of sociobiology as the "Darwinian idea of continuity", which has been central to my discussion of gesture:

> The move to unify the animal and human realms is an affirmation of the Darwinian idea of continuity, which extends, if only indirectly to mental life … the present time is marked by the dawning intent to bring down the human-animal barrier, or at least to make it more diaphanous and yielding. (1999, p. 165)

A study of gestures in film focuses attention on the details and nuances of animal gestures, which have been largely ignored in critical discussion. The deployment of gesture in film through the human and animal body, that is, through the expressive potential of physicality is an important feature of modernity in that it questions an anthropocentric view of human and animal. With its focus on gesture as such a significant mode of communication for human and animal alike, the cinema is the aesthetic form par excellence that is ideally suited to bringing about an erosion of the human–animal boundary. This is achieved through the zoomorphic nature of cinematic representation and the powerful manner in which film gives agency to all creatures, human and animal, through the cinematic construction of subjectivity, intentionality, empathy and most significantly – gesture. The difference between the representation of human and animal gestures in film is that the latter are almost always naturalistic, rather than stylised (unless the animal is a trained performer) and as such they ask the spectator to attend closely to the image in order to apprehend the organic yet expressionistic nature of animal gestures as represented on the screen.

Notes

1. A number of theorists discuss gesture from an interdisciplinary perspective. In addition, many disciplinary areas now study gesture. See Algazi (2008); Bremmer and Roodenburg (1991); Godøy, and Leman (2010); Kappelhoff and Müller (2011); McElhaney (2006).
2. For a fuller discussion of *Nénette* in relation to the human/animal boundary see Creed (2013).
3. Astrida Neimanis analyses *Grizzly Man* in relation to Deleuze and Guattari's theory of "becoming animal". See Neimanis (2007).

References

Algazi, G. (2008). Norbert Elias's motion pictures: History, cinema and gestures in the process of civilization. *Studies in History and Philosophy of Science Part A, 39*, 444–458.

Birdwhistell, R. (1970). *Kinesics and context: Essays on body motions communication*. Philadelphia: University of Pennsylvania Press.

Bonitzer, P. (1981). It's only a movie. *Framework: The Journal of Cinema and Media, 14*, 22–24.

Bremmer, J., & Roodenburg, H. (Eds.). (1991). *A cultural history of gesture from antiquity to the present day*. Ithaca, NY: Cornell University Press.

Coetzee, J. M. (2004). *Elizabeth Costello*. London: Vintage.

Creed, B. (2013). Nénette: Film theory, animals, and boredom. *NECSUS European Journal of Media Studies*. http://www.necsus-ejms.org/nenette-film-theory-animals-and-boredom/

Crist, E. (1999). *Images of animals: Anthropomorphism and animal mind*. Philadelphia, PA: Temple University Press.

Darwin, C. (1999). *The expression of the emotions in man and animals*. London: Fontana Press.

Godøy, R. I., & Leman, M. (2010). *Musical gestures: Sound, movement, and meaning*. New York, NY: Routledge.

Kappelhoff, H., & Müller, C. (2011). Embodied meaning construction: Multimodal metaphor and expressive movement in speech, gesture, and feature film. *Metaphor and the Social World, 1*, 121–153.

McElhaney, J. (2006). Howard Hawks: American gesture. *Journal of Film and Video, 58*, 31–45.

Morris, D. (1994). *Bodytalk: A world guide to gestures*. London: Jonathan Cape.

Naremore, J. (1988). *Acting in the cinema*. Berkeley: University of California Press.

Neimanis, A. (2007). Becoming-grizzly: Bodily molecularity and the animal that becomes. *PhaenEx, 2*, 279–308.

Pick, A. (2011). *Creaturely poetics: Animality and vulnerability in literature and film*. New York, NY: Columbia University Press.

Rifkin, J. (2009). *The empathic civilization: The race to global consciousness in a world in crisis*. London: Penguin.

Roodenburg, H. (1991). Gestures. In P. N. Stearns (Ed.), *Encyclopaedia of social history* (pp. 398–399). New York, NY: Charles Scribner's Sons.

Roodenburg, H. (2001). Gestures. In C. Blakemore & S. Jennett (Eds.), *The Oxford companion to the body* (pp. 315–316). London: Oxford University Press.

Smith, G. (1995). The joyous pessimism of Barbet Schroeder. *Film Comment, 31*(2), 1–20.

Väliaho, P. (2010). *Mapping the moving image: Gesture, thought and cinema ca. 1900*. Amsterdam: Amsterdam University Press.

Gesture in *Shoah*

Nicholas Chare

Department of History of Art and Film Studies, Université de Montréal, Canada

This essay analyses gesture as embodied history in Claude Lanzmann's film *Shoah*. It explores how gestures can serve as vital indicators of traumatic experience and also potentially assist in working through traumas. Gestures in *Shoah* are examined for the referential meaning they hold which can provide insights as valuable as those contained within the oral histories scholars have previously tended to focus on in their readings of the film. Gesture, cannot, however be divorced from those spoken histories. The essay will show that if gesture is accompanied by speech in a film it must be interpreted in tandem with it rather than in isolation from it. The essay concludes by analysing the gestural significance of camerawork employed in *Shoah*.

Notes on gesture

In 1941, David Efron, a researcher working with Franz Boas at Columbia University, published *Gesture and Environment* (Efron, 1972).[1] In the same year, the first extermination of prisoners took place at Auschwitz. Efron was born and educated in Argentina, raised in an orthodox Jewish home (Efron, 1972, p. 157). *Gesture and Environment* compared the gestures of groups of immigrant Italians and Jews in the USA and also of their first-generation offspring. Efron discovered that that the gestural vocabularies of the groups were markedly different. He also determined that among the first-generation children, those who maintained their cultural traditions in diaspora communities continued to exhibit the distinct gestural style of their parentages whereas those who assimilated into American culture did not manifest the distinguishing non-verbal behaviour of their progenitors.

Using these findings, *Gesture and Environment* explicitly set out to challenge the scholarship of political anthropologists and biological racialists working in the Third Reich who claimed that "the amount and the manner of gesticulation of an individual are basically determined by racial descent" (Efron, 1972, p. 21).[2] The book refused the idea that gesture was biologically determined. Efron's opening chapter exposed the empirical failings of research conducted into gesture by scholars such as Wilhelm Böhle, Ludwig Clauss, Hans Günther, and Fritz Lenz. He suggested that the racial explanations of gestural behaviour propounded by these men were "more indicative of [their] poetical gifts [...] than of their fitness to engage in factual research" (Efron, 1972, p. 37). *Gesture and Environment,* therefore, formed a valuable counterpoint to the pseudo-science promulgated by the Third Reich, debunking racial theories of the origins of gesture.

In 1945, the year after the extermination of prisoners at Auschwitz had ceased, the German doctor Charlotte Wolff's *A Psychology of Gesture* was published in London. It was the first major English-language intervention in the study of gesture authored by a woman. Wolff uses numerous clinical case studies of the gesticulations of mental patients to form arguments which, contra Efron, suggest gestures are constitutional not environmental in origin. There are traces of race science in her discussion of gesture differentials between African, Latin and Nordic races (Wolff, 1945, p. 62). She appears to view gesture as biological rather than cultural whilst acknowledging that education can contribute to obscuring innate gestural tendencies (Wolff, 1945, p. 62). Subsequently, Wolff would summarise her position at the time as being that "the basic structure of the individual could only be understood through biological functions" (Wolff, 1971, p. 43). In her later work on sexuality, however, she embraced psychological approaches that recognised the impact of environment on behaviour alongside biological factors.

Like Efron's work, Wolff's is marked by the National Socialism in terms of its content. There are, however, also others ways in which her book registers the effects of Nazism. Wolff was a lesbian and a Jew. In her classic study of lesbianism, *Love between Women*, when she writes that homosexuals in Germany, "like the Jews, were dumped in concentration camps and classed as outcasts" there is a poignant element of personal experience underlying the observation (Wolff, 1971, p. 13). Her Aryan lover, Katherine, left her in the autumn of 1932 because "her father had impressed upon her that she courted danger for herself if she continued to share her life with a Jewess" (Wolff, 1980, p. 109). She was also arrested by a member of the Gestapo in 1933 accused of being a woman dressed as a man and also a spy. After her release, her apartment was searched and she soon fled Germany travelling to Paris then to London. Her book on gesture was written in French (it was translated into English by Anne Tennant, a friend and love interest). The impact of the Third Reich upon the manuscript, therefore, manifests itself in the chosen language of composition and the country of publication, England.

Additionally, Wolff hints at the psychic distress displacement can cause. She writes of a particular patient: "the exaggeration of her gestures when she spoke about past miseries might be explained by the fact that she was a refugee who had suffered a great deal before she came to this country" (Wolff, 1945, p. 144). Wolff had first-hand experience of the shattering effects of exile. Her reasoning that gesture can register anguish may have been based on her own experiences. Here, Wolff signals gesture's autobiographical potential. The body may be inscribed by specific events, possibly chronicling an individual's past experiences by way of styles of gesture. In this instance, an excess is detected by Wolff in the patient's gesticulations that betrays her previous misfortunes. Paolo Mantegazza takes this line of thinking further, suggesting that gesture can form an intergenerational memory. He attributes the lack of expansive gestures amongst Jews to centuries of persecution (Mantegazza, 1889, p. 204).

The research on gesture conducted by Efron and Wolff demonstrates that the history of gesture studies is bound up with events in Nazi Germany. Gestures also play an important role in a later effort to attest to Nazi genocide, Claude Lanzmann's 1985 film *Shoah* (Dir. Claude Lanzmann, 1985, France) which now forms my focus. This film is analysed in four ways: firstly, I consider the way gesture contributes to Lanzmann's idea of incarnation. This is followed by an analysis of how gestures in the film potentially foster a sense of empathy. The relationships between gesture, memory and trauma are then discussed. Finally, gesture at the level of the camerawork in *Shoah* is examined.

Reiterative gestures

Henrik Gawkowski, a former train driver, leans out of a stationary steam locomotive's cab, looking back the length of the train as if towards its transport. A sign for Treblinka is visible behind him. Nodding slightly as he does so, he makes a throat-slitting gesture by running his right hand's index finger left to right across his neck. Towards the end of this action, there is a slight upturn of the finger towards the ear and raise of the elbow as the curve of the larynx is traced. Shortly afterwards, Gawkowski will rapidly repeat the gesture again twice, yet less emphatically, less theatrically, than this instance. The gesture will be mentioned and performed several more times in the next half hour of Lanzmann's documentary *Shoah*. It is a descriptive visible utterance, portraying the act of having the throat slit by a knife. Gawkowski makes his gesture for Lanzmann's camera, for the documentary's audience. It repeats a past gesture, comprising the same physical action as one Gawkowski witnessed years ago, yet is made in radically different circumstances. This visible utterance nevertheless points back to its prior incarnation.

This signal, or variations of it, was a familiar sight to those being transported to death camps by rail during the Holocaust. It is an action which is described in the Sonderkommando member Zalman Gradowski's account of a transport passing through Treblinka. This account, each character of which comprises a defiant act given the grim circumstances of its composition, was buried in the grounds of the crematoria at Birkenau shortly before Gradowski was murdered in 1944.[3] Gradowski writes:

Each traveller looks outside, scouring the area with his eyes. Perhaps something will be seen, perhaps some hint will be found to reveal the truth; perhaps a voice will be heard to tell them where they are being transported and what lies in store for them. How terrible: two young Christian girls are standing down there; they look up at the train windows and pass their hands across their throats. The onlookers have understood the hint; shuddering, they turn silently aside. (Gradowski, 1985, p. 185)

It is clear from Gradowski's description, and from reports in *Shoah*, that the Jews imprisoned in the transports were subject to a continuous gestural assault as they journeyed to their deaths. In *Shoah*, during his description of arriving at Treblinka as part of a transport, Richard Glazar recounts that when an old man on the train gestured to a young farmhand outside: "Where are we?" The kid made a "funny gesture" in response. Glazar demonstrates it by placing his hand around his throat and shaking his head repeatedly. This causes his neck to rub against the webbing between the thumb and index. He repeats this gesture a second time shortly afterwards yet ends it differently, gliding his hand, which he holds horizontally, palm downwards, across his throat. This gesture makes the throat visible and the deadly significance of the action therefore becomes more legible.

The film cuts from Glazar's testimony to that of some farmers from Treblinka who relate making the gesture to new arrivals in the transports. *Shoah* has moved from the viewpoint of the recipient of the gesture to the perspective of the gesturer. The gesture made by the farmers is rapid comprising of just the index finger held horizontally run quickly across the neck. Lanzmann asks: "But what does that gesture mean?" One farmer repeats the action, explaining as he does so that it signals to the Jews "that death awaited them". He ends this clarification smiling, his palm open, offering his devilish gloss to the interviewer. It is clear that the gesture acts as synecdoche. One instance of fatal injury, having the throat cut, comes to stand for murder in general.

The gesture is futile, an appallingly ineffectual way of signalling the industries of mass death awaiting those on the transports. It has no value as metaphor.

Lanzmann, however, draws on the power of this ghoulish visible utterance to reveal the mind set of those who made use of it. In *Shoah,* he appears to harness the capacity of what Rebecca Schneider describes as "reiterative gesture" as a means to preserve a past time (Schneider, 2011, p. 37). For Schneider, gestures can potentially carry material traces of the past into the present, blurring any simple demarcation between times. In a live performance such as a historical re-enactment, participants "position their bodies to access, consciously and deliberately, a fleshly or pulsing kind of trace [of the past] they deem accessible in a pose, or gesture, or set of acts" (Schneider, 2011, p. 37). This trace is frequently emotional. Gesture permits the past to be felt in the present. The farmers in *Shoah* are not consciously seeking such an experience yet Lanzmann's choreography appears deliberately designed to foster it. His idea of incarnation, of a knowledge made flesh, which he links explicitly to gesture during a discussion about *Shoah,* appears to prefigure Schneider's (Lanzmann, 1990a, p. 414). Elsewhere, Lanzmann states that his aim is to produce situations that "resuscitate the past as though it were the present" (Lanzmann, 1990b, p. 441).[4] The past here is figured as a physical being, a being revived through gesture. In the case of the farmer asked to clarify the meaning of the throat-slitting action, it is his glee as he does so that betrays the original emotional tenor of the sign. Lanzmann revitalises the man's sadism. He brings the unimaginable present of the man's fundamental hatred back to life.

This technique, the generation of emotional insights through reiterative gestures, has been roundly criticised by Dominick LaCapra who argues that incarnation is the equivalent of acting-out as it understood in psychoanalysis. Acting-out, LaCapra explains, is a situation in which "one reincarnates or relives the past in an unmediated transferential process that subjects one to possession by haunting objects and to compulsively repeated incursions of traumatic residues (hallucinations, flashbacks, nightmares)" (LaCapra, 2007, p. 198). Not all Lanzmann's incarnations appear to fall into this category. The Polish farmer is not haunted by his gesture and Franz Suchomel's spirited rendition of a German song from Treblinka, during which his past jubilation is reawakened, also cannot be aligned with trauma. LaCapra, however, believes that in the interviews with survivors, rather than bystanders or perpetrators, Lanzmann "seems to absolutize acting-out" (LaCapra, 2007, p. 210). In this context, he draws attention to an interview in English with Abraham Bomba, who cut the hair of women who were about to be gassed at Treblinka, which is conducted in a barbershop in Israel. Lanzmann films Bomba seemingly trimming the hair of a friend as he recounts his experiences at the death-camp. Bomba had worked as a barber in New York but was retired by the time the interview was conducted in Tel Aviv.

At one point during the director's demanding questioning, Bomba breaks down and initially refuses to continue. Lanzmann, implores, cajoles and presses him to do so. Bomba eventually relents and resumes his account, lapsing briefly into Yiddish as he does so. It is scenarios such as this which lead LaCapra to contend that Lanzmann's "idea of both the best acting and of truth itself amounts to acting-out, including the breakdown of the victim who cannot go on" (LaCapra, 2007, p. 211). The director is not interested in providing a means for those survivors he interviews to work through their trauma. LaCapra, however, in contrast to Lanzmann's disinterest compellingly argues that the role of secondary witness should be to "reactivate and transmit not trauma but an unsettlement – or what Lanzmann terms 'a sort of suffering' – that manifests empathy (but not full identification) with the victim and is at most an index of trauma" (LaCapra, 2007, p. 221).

Empathic gestures

LaCapra describes empathic unsettlement as an attentive secondary witnessing that does not comprise identification with a victim but instead "involves a kind of virtual experience through which one puts oneself in the other's position while recognizing the difference of that position and hence not taking the other's place" (LaCapra, 2001, p. 78). His definition shares some commonality with that of Edith Stein who describes empathy as a situation in which "the same world is not merely presented now in one way and then in another, but in both ways at the same time" (Stein, 1989, p. 64).[5] For Stein, empathy requires a telling distance. Her remarks on how such states of co-experiencing, of detached communion, come into being are noteworthy.

Gesture plays a prominent role in Stein's exploration of what is and is not empathy. She uses "witnessed gesture" as part of her remarks on how the theory of imitation cannot explain the phenomenon that is empathy (Stein, 1989, p. 22). She also refers to gesture to distinguish looking at another's feelings from sharing those feelings. Stein writes:

> When I "see" shame "in" blushing, irritation in the furrowed brow, anger in the clenched fist, this is a still different phenomenon than when I look at the foreign living body's level of sensation or perceive the other individual's sensations and feelings of life with him. In the latter case I comprehend the one with the other. In the former case I see the one through the other. (Stein, 1989, p. 75)

Here a gesture, the clenched fist, can be interpreted as a sign, as an expression of anger, an index of a state of mind. This response to the gesture, however, is interpretative rather than empathic. An empathic comprehension of the gesture's significance is attained through communing with the gesturer's feelings.

The clenched fist could potentially provide the means to foster this familiarity. Elsewhere, as part of a discussion of sensual empathy, Stein recounts how observing a hand can prompt empathic connection:

> The hand resting on the table does not lie there like the book beside it. It "presses" against the table more or less strongly; it lies there limpid or stretched; and I "see" these sensations of pressure and tension in a con-primordial way. If I follow out the tendencies to fulfilment in this "co-comprehension" my hand is moved (not in reality, but "as if") to the place of the foreign one. It is moved into it and occupies its position and attitude, now feeling its sensations, though not primordially and not as being its own. [...] During this projection, the foreign body is continually perceived as belonging to the foreign physical body so that the empathized sensations are continually brought into relief as foreign in contrast with our own sensations. (Stein, 1989, p. 58)

The discussion here is not of gesture. It does, however, point towards how gestures such as making a fist might provide a comparable stimulus to co-comprehension, this time not of sensation but of emotion. If a clenched fist of the kind discussed earlier is *seen* con-primordially, then the possibility of feeling emotions as well as sensations arises. Stein was, in fact, reluctant to distinguish the two (Stein, 1989, p. 98).

In *A Psychology of Gesture*, Wolff conceives of gesture at one point in terms that resonate strongly with Stein's remarks on bodily positioning as a passage to empathy. Wolff reveals that in striving to understand the reactions of the mental patients she was studying she often "imitated their gestures and postures as a means of realizing their states of mind" (Wolff, 1945, p. 81). Wolff believes that this realisation, a realisation that sounds remarkably like empathy although it is not so called, arises through imitation which, as already discussed, Stein rejects as an explanation for how empathy arises. There is, however, a mutual recognition that attentiveness to bodily comportment can facilitate comprehension of a foreign body's experiences.

Stein and Wolff are also linked in other ways. Both women were born Jewish. They were also at the University of Freiburg at the same time. Wolff credits her interest in existentialism to being taught by "the phenomenologists Professor Husserl and the then Dr. Heidegger" (Wolff, 1971, p. 63). Stein studied for her doctorate with Husserl and worked as his teaching assistant at Freiburg from 1916 until 1922. She also collaborated briefly with Heidegger editing some of Husserl's work. Wolff arrived in Freiburg as a student in 1920. It is, therefore, possible she met Stein. In 1933, when all Jews were dismissed from their jobs, Stein lost her position teaching at the Institute for Scientific Pedagogy in Münster and Wolff lost her post as an apprentice of electro-physical therapy at the *Allgemeinen Krankenkassen Berlin* (Berlin's Public Health Insurance) based at Neukölln. Wolff would leave Germany shortly afterwards eventually settling in England where she continued to face anti-semitism but not the threat of persecution (Wolff, 1969, p. 143). Stein would enter a Carmelite nunnery in Cologne in 1933, later be moved to another nunnery in the Netherlands for her safety yet ultimately be deported from there to Auschwitz where she was murdered in August 1942.

Stein's and Wolff's ideas about empathy can be traced back to their foundation in phenomenology. LaCapra's understanding of the concept, despite similarities with Stein's, emerges from psychoanalysis. Empathic unsettlement arises through transference. LaCapra suggests that "empathy is bound up with the transferential relation to the past, and it is arguably an affective aspect of understanding which both limits objectification and exposes the self to involvement or implication in the past, its actors, and victims" (LaCapra, 2001, p. 102). He argues of the experience of the historian in the context of transference that "when confronting live issues, one becomes affectively implicated and tends to repeat in oneself at some level the processes active in what one tries to understand" (LaCapra, 1998, p. 40). This affective implication, manifested by way of psychic tension, presumably operates like transference in the analytic situation in that it can be generated through verbal and non-verbal expressions. Non-verbal expressions, of course, include gesture.

A professional historian, Raul Hilberg, features in *Shoah*. In one scene, he appears to acknowledge experiencing a repetition of the kind described by LaCapra. It is a scene in which Hilberg explains the significance of a document from Nazi Germany, transport order number 587. Lanzmann asks him: "Why such a document is so fascinating as a matter of fact?" Hilberg replies:

> Well you see when I hold a document in my hand, particularly if it's an original document, then I hold something which is actually something that the original bureaucrat had held in his hand. It's an artefact. It's a leftover. It's the only leftover there is. The dead are not around.

As he delivers his explanation, he can be seen fingering the reproduction of the transport order he has to hand, manipulating it, and lightly stroking the paper. There is a lot that can be deduced from Hilberg's rationalisation for his documentary fascination. The second half of the response stresses the importance of the substance of the record. The piece of paper provides the dead with a kind of material afterlife, through it a trace of their existence remains, albeit as nameless groups. The incriminating list of dates, points of departure and of destination, and numbers of passengers is possibly all that is left of those murdered, the only surviving index of their former presence in this world.

The first half of Hilberg's answer is more disconcerting. He appears to be suggesting in his initial discussion of the bureaucrat that the paper somehow forms a bridge between present and past, between historian and perpetrator. It puts him in touch with the deskbound executioner. In the context of Hilberg's preceding discussion with Lanzmann, the historian seems to be saying that through handling an original document, through following the same gestures as the official, he can enter into his mindset. Physical interaction with the document prompts an unsettling empathic connection which enables Hilberg to grasp the Nazi civil servant's decision-making processes. The insights that this documentary link with the perpetrators provides, awareness facilitated by shared gestures, undergirds the historian's understanding of the destruction of the European Jews as an administrative process. Gesture grants vicarious access to the past.

Gesture, memory and trauma

In her subtle study of *Shoah*, Sue Vice draws attention to the importance of gesture for understanding the past, attesting to it. She discusses, for example, Lanzmann's interview with one of the survivors of Chełmno, Mordechai Podchlebnik. When asked about the gas vans used there, Podchlebnik at one point "even acts out with arm movements the opening of the van's double doors" (Vice, 2011, p. 12). This gesture, which depicts a bodily action, is called kinetographic by Efron (1972, p. 96). There are a number of such gestures in *Shoah*. Franz Schalling, a perpetrator, also employs kinetography in his description of the gas vans at Chełmno. He recounts how the gassing began, stating that the driver "climbed into the cabin after the doors were closed and started the motor". As Schalling says these words he shuts the door with his left hand and then turns a key in the ignition with his right.

This last gesture, a minimal twist of the wrist, also holds a symbolic potential. Schalling's slight motion to portray mass murder in operation is emblematic of the Nazi indifference to Jewish lives. The ability to turn the virtual key in the present, the ease with which it is done, is itself revealing, incriminating. Suchomel also exhibits a callous symbolism of this kind in his interview. As he describes the unloading of a transport by Ukrainian guards at Treblinka, he echoes their command "czipse, czipse, czipse" accompanying the words with tiny gestures to signal that the internees were being beaten at the same time as the order was given. These gestures are not properly kinetographic. They portray an action but wholly inadequately. They are more symbolic, although like Schalling's not intentionally so, the ease with which they are made betraying Suchomel's callousness.

In Adam Kendon's *Gesture,* many of the examples used to illustrate particular forms of gesticulation relate to remembrance (Kendon, 2004). Gesturing can form a key means by which to communicate the past, be it former actions, previously known objects or prior emotions, in the present. This communication is sometimes intentional but, as in the case of Schalling and Suchomel, also often involves unconscious elements. It is these elements which can be registered through transference. Lanzmann, in fact, sometimes ends up mirroring Suchomel's gestures as happens in the discussion of the "funnel" to the gas chamber at Treblinka which Vice examines (Vice, 2011, p. 45). This may be part of an effort to build rapport or ironise yet, as occasionally seems the case, it may additionally be a symptom of affective contagion. Lanzmann's arm movements during his discussions with Suchomel intermittently seem unsettlingly similar. The discussion of the funnel which they enter into is a key example.

There are also numerous instances in which survivors employ kinetographic gestures alongside their oral testimony. Filip Müller, for instance, uses actions of this kind to describe his efforts to move slimy corpses in a water-filled pit in a field near Birkenau. The Nazis ordered Müller and others to stack the bodies. They were, however, slippery as they had been submerged overnight. As Müller recounts this event, he reaches his right and then left arm towards Lanzmann who is off camera. The filmmaker in this moment occupies the position of the body of a dead woman as Müller's gestures return him to the field. The survivor clasps his fingers together in a fist as he relates trying to grip the hands of the corpse. They were too slick and he ended up losing his hold and falling backwards into the water. As he describes this, he withdraws his arms so that his right forearm is perpendicular with his upper arm and his left arm is crossed over his chest. In this horrific account, words and gestures combine to capture the experience. Lanzmann's ability to bring about such moments, such instances of acting-out, may foster working-through in a way that is overlooked by LaCapra.

In order to grasp how this manifestation of working-through materialises in *Shoah*, it will be necessary to examine LaCapra's conception of the relationship between acting-out and melancholia and working-through and mourning. LaCapra states that:

> In acting-out one has a mimetic relation to the past which is regenerated or relived as if it were fully present rather than represented in memory and inscription. In psychoanalytic terms, the acted-out past is incorporated rather than introjected, and it returns as the repressed. Mourning involves introjection through a relation to the past that recognizes its difference from the present and enacts a specific performative relation to it that simultaneously remembers and takes at least partial leave of it, thereby allowing for critical judgement and a reinvestment in life, notably social life with its demands, responsibilities, and norms requiring respectful recognition and consideration for others. But with reference to trauma, acting-out may be a necessary condition of working-through, at least for victims and in certain ways, for all those directly involved in events. (LaCapra, 1998, p. 45)

Acting-out is a situation in which the experience of the past is unmediated. Working-through enables the cut of difference, severing past and present, which allows mourning to occur. Mourning is accompanied by the transition of an experience into the memory of an experience. Freud relates that this occurs through the ego accepting the "verdict of reality" that the object being mourned no longer exists and, therefore, severs its attachment to it (Freud, 1917/1991, p. 265). LaCapra's linking of mourning with the emerging capacity for critical judgement connects the process with thinking.

LaCapra acknowledges that acting-out and working-through are "in general intimately linked" processes (LaCapra, 1994, p. 205, 1998, p. 45). This implies that where acting-out is found the activity of working-through is also likely present. LaCapra, in fact, recognises the possibility that *Shoah* might be "closer to mourning and working-through – or at least more effective in relating acting-out and working-through – than [his] argument allows" (LaCapra, 2007, p. 221). One way in which working-through might be seen to occur is through Lanzmann's capacity to encourage accounts of the past that utilise both gesture and speech. The research of David McNeill into gesture, whilst not psychoanalytically informed, is illuminating here. McNeill argues that thinking comprises "a dialectic of gesture imagery and verbal/linguistic structure" (McNeill, 1992, p. 245). The two channels of gesture and speech evolve together, grow together, until the final stage, in which they emerge synthesised as what McNeill calls "surface utterance" (McNeill, 1992, p. 220). In this moment of synthesis, "language and gesture are combined into one unified presentation of meaning" which is "an act of communication, but also an act of thought" (McNeill, 1992, p. 246).

McNeill's description of this co-emergence of gesture and speech as sign and thought can be applied to Freud's report of the fort/da game played by the boy as a means by which to assuage his anxiety at his mother's absence. This game, combined as it is of synthesised gestures and of vocalisations, can, in fact, be read as an early manifestation of the dialectical process identified by McNeill. It consists of throwing a reel tied to string over the edge of a curtained cot and then pulling it back, actions accompanied by vocal utterances. As the reel is thrown, the imperfect utterance of "fort" ("gone") is made and when the spool is pulled back the child exclaims "da" ("there"). Freud states that much greater delight is attained when the reel is successfully retrieved from the cot using the string. This does not always happen. The fort/da game, as an aggressive reliving of loss, exhibits aspects of acting-out. Its pleasurable dimension, however, suggests that there must also be an element of working-through present. The game possesses the capacity to alleviate distress in some way.

The mother's departure is, of course, temporary. It cannot be equated with loss as Freud discusses it in relation to mourning and melancholia. It does nevertheless seem that a transition to symbolisation occurs in the game. The loss of the mother is memorialised through the reel and, more importantly, the gestures and vocalisations that accompany the game. Jacques Lacan recognised that on one level the game was about the attainment of a capacity for representation. He argues that the child's action "destroys the object that it causes to appear and disappear in the anticipating *provocation* of its absence and its presence" (Lacan, 1977, p. 103). Slightly later he reiterates this point suggesting "the symbol manifests itself first of all as the murder of the thing, and this death constitutes in the subject the externalization of his desire" (p. 104). Lacan's focus here is on how the vocal utterance as symbol stands in for the lost object and, by doing so, does away with it. He fails to acknowledge the role played by gesture in the game, the way the hand dismisses the mother and invites her return, and how it contributes to this matricide. I would argue, as Luce Irigaray recognises, that both gesture and vocals are crucial for understanding the game (Irigaray, 1989).

The fort/da game forms the beginnings of representational practice. This practice, as McNeill identifies, comprises both speech and gesture. Working-through as manifested in the game, therefore, involves finding words and gestures to substitute for things. It requires instituting language and taking leave of immediate matters. I have argued elsewhere, however, that in cases of massive psychic trauma language can fail to accomplish its usual distancing and differentiating effects (Chare, 2011, 2013b). In these circumstances, the task becomes to re-engage with language through the gesture of writing or another medium. Prior to encountering McNeill's work, however, I had not recognised the centrality of gesture to all acts of utterance perceiving it as distinct from speech and capable of being pared from it. I had considered gesture as a form of pressure pointing towards aspects of psychic life beyond signification (Chare, 2013c, pp. 190–207). Now I am struck by how trauma might produce situations in which the dialectic identified by McNeill becomes stalled. The survivor of a traumatic event might be able to speak about their experience, or physically act-out parts of it, yet failure to combine these two aspects inhibits their ability to work-through the event, synthesise gesture and speech, and make a full return to language.

In *Shoah*, Lanzmann provides a space through his interviews in which the binding of gesture and speech, their co-emergence, can be fostered. Müller, for instance, in his account of the water-filled pit packed with corpses, makes vivid use of gesture combined with speech to describe his experience. Words alone would not adequately vehicle the horrific sliminess her refers to. McNeill suggests that the unregulated nature of gesture, in contrast with the rules of speech, "allows free play to idiosyncratic imagination" and injects personality into language (McNeill, 1992, p. 251). The synthesis of gesture and speech in Müller's reliving of the event enables him to give the fullest possible expression to the experience. In the instant at which he loses his grip on the dead woman, she also releases her hold on him. He is able to let go of the past, to remember it. In this context, elsewhere in *Shoah*, it is Lanzmann's constant pressing for detail that comprises his therapeutic gift. He draws out gestures through insisting on knowing specifics. In this way, he provides a space through which the dialectic of speech and gesture, if stalled, can be restarted. Through this restarting, survivors can move beyond acting out and towards working through.

Gesture in camera

Given the importance of gesture in communication in general and as an aid to working through in particular, it is troubling how often Lanzmann favours the talking head over the talking hand (as evidenced through frequent close-ups of the faces of his interviewees). This forms a kind of gestural amputation. The face can gesture but many complex signs are produced by other parts of the body. It is remarkable how regularly fingers appear at the edges of frames, hands pop briefly into view, signalling a vital gestural economy suppressed by Lanzmann's preferred choice of shot as performed by his cameraman.

Efron recognised film's value as a means of recording gesture in *Gesture and Environment*. Screening films of specific gestures to observers enabled the researcher to source qualitative analyses. He also draws attention to some of the difficulties he encountered in trying to record spontaneous gestures. He found it hard to film indoors because of poor lighting conditions (Efron, 1972, p. 133). He also did not record audio as he filmed yet recognised that gesture is frequently incomprehensible without knowledge of the speech that accompanied it (Efron, 1972, p. 141). Efron does not, however, consider the act of filming as itself gestural.

It is clear that the camera in most films is directed at something, is indicating incessantly, inherently deictic. It points the viewer in the right direction. Against this ever present gestural ground, however, there are more obvious deictic instances which can be achieved through techniques such as close-up or zoom. In the sequence of *Shoah* that explores the fate of the Jews of Corfu, for example, the camera focuses frequently in the early stages on the concentration camp tattoos of members of the community, zooming in slightly. This subtle, yet repeated, pointing impresses the significance of the tattoos on the viewer. Camerawork is, of course, not the only way that gestures other than those made by people who are being filmed are registered. In the section of *Shoah* that examines the significance of the throat-slitting gesture, the scene in which an anonymous farmer provides an explanation for the visible utterance cuts to another interview, one with smallholder Czeslaw Borowi. The scene of one cutting gesture concludes through a literal cut in the film that leads to another cutting gesture. Cuts, as a part of editing, form indexes of gestures. It is, however, camerawork that has received the most commentary and will form my focus here.

It is through gestures made by the camera under Lanzmann's instruction that an objectionable aspect of *Shoah* emerges. In his incisive analysis of the barbers shop sequence, Aaron Kerner draws attention to how, at the moment Bomba's testimonial narrative breaks down, "the camera zooms in for a close-up of Bomba's face, as we see his facial muscles wince with emotion" (Kerner, 2011, p. 209). This choice of shot is used to signify "an intensified emotional state and directs the audience in how they should respond" (Kerner, 2011, p. 209). The camera points out that the viewer should be feeling something here. It also literally points at Bomba. In the period where the survivor suggests he cannot proceed with the account, he paces repeatedly as if he wants to walk out of shot, to escape the frame. The camera, however, tracks him. It keeps pointing at him. The scene with Bomba is the most obvious instance of this refusal to withdraw, to cease to point. There is, however, also an indication of it in the interview with Müller when he also threatens to break down, shifting in his seat as if he is about to get up and walk away. The camera anticipates his action, moves with him.

The zooming in on Bomba, the close-up of him in deep distress, is abhorrent. It is sticking a finger in his face from distance. The gesture is, of course, one he will probably be unaware of until he views the footage for himself. The zoom in is a physically proximate gesture that registers only belatedly. Lanzmann's pitiless use of this technique in moments of sorrow is in marked contrast to the approach adopted in the documentary *Kitty: Return to Auschwitz* (Dir. Peter Morley, UK, 1979). In the film, Kitty Hart, who is returning to Birkenau for the first time since her incarceration there, breaks down shortly after entering the camp. The film crew are following her and her son and the camera keeps a respectful distance as she composes herself. There is no zooming in. The camera keeps pointing at her yet from afar. Admittedly, there is less temptation to get closer as Hart's back is turned. There is no face to potentially fill the frame. Bomba, however, also briefly turned his back to the camera, a gesture that suggests a wish for privacy, a need for relief. This response shows that although Lanzmann may produce an environment conducive to working through, the way filming is conducted can work against it. Bomba may not register the zoom but he does show an awareness of being filmed, of where the camera is. Lanzmann's handiwork, the camera actions he encourages, sometimes shuts down spontaneous testimonial gestures. In this instance, he also fails to accord Bomba the privacy he requires. By minimising its deictic capacity, the camera in *Kitty*, therefore, displays an ethical gesture that Lanzmann will not countenance.

Wolff believed that the gestures of a person betray their psychological make-up. In the series of plates that accompany the text of *A Psychology of Gesture*, there are photographs of General Ritter von Thoma and Adolf Hitler as well as of the Belgian fascist leader Léon Degrelle and of François Darlan who was, for a time, de facto head of the Vichy government. The hands of Degrelle are "like claws" and his gesture shows "hatred and the will to conquer" (Wolff, 1945, p. 204). Hitler, who has the face of a "maniac" displays a hand gesture that "conveys anxious appeal" and his splayed fingers show "a mixture of anxiety and aggression" (Wolff, 1945, p. 205). All the fascists exhibit gestures which Wolff interprets in negative terms. In *Shoah*, however, with the exception of Suchomel, whose gestural volubility indicates a delight in his conversation with Lanzmann which is at odds with the subject of Treblinka, the gestures of the Nazi officers and officials who are filmed are, on the whole, nondescript. Their minimal gesticulations, of course, hint at suppression. They do not wish to give their emotional state away.

Drawing on Stein's idea that the body can act as a spur to empathy, however, it becomes possible to read the gestures that comprise *Shoah*'s camerawork as prompts to co-comprehension with the state of mind of the director. In the scene with Bomba, Lanzmann's speech coupled with the camera's gesture, communicates a brutal tenacity, a refusal to let go of anything in the search for truth. Kerner has stated that the film-maker "sadistically prods victims" (Kerner, 2011, p. 179). This prodding is verbal. He also, however, mercilessly points at them. It is in these moments that gesture in *Shoah* becomes profoundly troubling. The gesture is dissimilar to the callous indifference to another communicated by Schalling as he virtually murders a vanload of Jews with a twist of his wrist. Lanzmann, of course, does not set out to hurt and, as already demon-strated, actually generates situations that potentially help, if not to heal, then to mitigate psychic pain. The close-up of the face, however, does not adequately record these con-ditions. The lens, instead, captures a trembling individual who wants to be elsewhere yet is held fast. The camera at these moments indexes a disturbing lack of compassion. Through the empathic insights its actions prompt, the camera reveals that Lanzmann, at times, seems to have no capacity for empathy.

At other moments, however, the camerawork reveals an awe-inspiring poetic sensi-bility and level of sensitivity. This occurs, for instance, when Lanzmann exploits the suppression of camera gesture to incarnate the past during an account by Jan Piwonski (a former assistant pointsman at Sobibór railway station) of the day the camp went silent shortly after construction was completed. As he is recounting this event, the cam-era cuts from him to a static shot of railway tracks. A woman walks along one side of them as Lanzmann queries "It was the silence that made them understand?" to which his translator responds "That's right". The woman has disappeared from view when Lanzmann asks, "Can he describe that silence?" The camera remains unmoving as the translator relays the question. Piwonski answers: "It was a silence. Nothing was going on in the camp. You saw nothing. You heard nothing. Nothing moved." During this intense scene, outwardly prosaic, the absence of camera action figures this silence. In *Analysing Sign Language Poetry*, Rachel Sutton-Spence explains that for Deaf people "silence is a visual experience of stillness and a lack of movement" (Sutton-Spence, 2005, p. 112). Lanzmann presents the viewer, the gestural listener, with a comparable silence. The camera has no movement and, therefore, indexes no manual operations. It shows no signs of life. This enables it to revive the sense of deathly quiet described by the man. In a remarkable recognition of the apparatus's gestural power, the stilled camera also comes to embody the dead.

Acknowledgement

I am grateful to Liz Watkins and Dominic Williams, and the anonymous reviewer of an earlier draft of this article for their helpful comments and insights.

Notes

1. This essay uses the 1972 reprint of Efron's book which was retitled *Gesture, Race and Culture*.
2. For a general discussion of National Socialism and race science see Dan Stone's *Histories of the Holocaust* (Stone, 2010, pp. 160–202).
3. This document is explored in more depth in my forthcoming book, co-authored with Dominic Williams, *Matters of Testimony*.
4. My translation. All translations are my own unless otherwise stated.
5. I explore Stein's ideas in more depth in my essay "On the Problem of Empathy: Attending to Gaps in the Scrolls of Auschwitz" (Chare, 2013a).

References

Chare, N. (2011). *Auschwitz and afterimages: Abjection, witnessing and representation*. London: I.B. Tauris.

Chare, N. (2013a). On the problem of empathy: Attending to gaps in the Scrolls of Auschwitz. In N. Chare & D. Williams (Eds.), *Representing Auschwitz: At the margins of testimony* (pp. 33–57). Houndmills: Palgrave Macmillan.

Chare, N. (2013b). Symbol re-formation: Concentrationary memory in Charlotte Delbo's *Auschwitz and after*. In G. Pollock & M. Silvermann (Eds.), *Concentrationary memories: Totalitarian resistance and cultural memories* (pp. 103–113). London: I.B. Tauris.

Chare, N. (2013c). Encountering *Blue Steel*: Changing tempers in cinema. In G. Pollock (Ed.), *Visual politics of psychoanalysis: Art and the image in post-traumatic cultures* (pp. 190–207). London: Tauris.

Efron, D. (1972). *Gesture, race and culture*. The Hague: Mouton.

Freud, S. (1917/1991). Mourning and Melancholia. In A. Richards (Ed.), *The Penguin Freud library: On Metapsychology* (Vol. 11, pp. 251–268). London: Penguin.

Gradowski, Z. (1985). Writings. In B. Mark (Ed.), *The Scrolls of Auschwitz*. (S. Neemani, Trans.). (pp. 173–205). Tel Aviv: Am Oved.

Irigaray, L. (1989). The gesture in psychoanalysis. In T. Brennan (Ed.), *Between feminism and psychoanalysis* (pp. 127–138). London: Routledge.

Kendon, A. (2004). *Gesture: Visible action as utterance*. Cambridge: Cambridge University Press.

Kerner, A. (2011). *Film and the Holocaust: New perspectives on dramas, documentaries, and experimental films*. New York, NY: Continuum.

Lacan, J. (1977). Function and field of speech and language. In A. Sheridan (Ed.), *Écrits: A selection* (pp. 30–113). London: Routledge.

LaCapra, D. (1994). *Representing the Holocaust: History, theory, trauma*. Ithaca, NY: Cornell University Press.

LaCapra, D. (1998). *History and memory after Auschwitz*. Ithaca, NY: Cornell University Press.

LaCapra, D. (2001). *Writing history, writing trauma*. Baltimore, MD: Johns Hopkins University Press.

LaCapra, D. (2007). Lanzmann's *Shoah*: "Here there is no Why". In S. Liebman (Ed.), *Claude Lanzmann's Shoah: Key essays* (pp. 191–229). Oxford: Oxford University Press.

Lanzmann, C. (1990a). Le lieu et la parole [Place and speech]. In M. Deguy (Ed.), *Au sujet de Shoah: Le film de Claude Lanzmann* [About shoah: The film by Claude Lanzmann] (pp. 407–425). Paris: Éditions Belin.

Lanzmann, C. (1990b). De l'Holocauste à *Holocauste* ou comment s'en débarrasser [From Holocaust to *Holocaust* or how to get rid]. In M. Deguy (Ed.), *Au sujet de Shoah: Le film de Claude Lanzmann* (pp. 426–442). Paris: Éditions Belin.

Mantegazza, P. (1889). *La physionomie et l'expression des sentiments* [Physiognomy and the expression of feelings] (2nd ed.). Paris: Alcan.

McNeill, D. (1992). *Hand and mind: What gestures reveal about thought*. Chicago, IL: Chicago University Press.

Schneider, R. (2011). *Performing remains: Art and war in times of theatrical reenactment*. London: Routledge.

Stein, E. (1989). *On the problem of empathy*. Washington, DC: ICS Publications.

Stone, D. (2010). *Histories of the Holocaust*. Oxford: Oxford University Press.

Sutton-Spence, R. (2005). *Analysing sign language poetry*. Houndmills: Palgrave Macmillan.

Vice, S. (2011). *Shoah*. Houndmills: Palgrave Macmillan.

Wolff, C. (1945). *A psychology of gesture*. London: Methuen.

Wolff, C. (1969). *On the way to myself*. London: Methuen.

Wolff, C. (1971). *Love between women*. London: Gerald Duckworth.

Wolff, C. (1980). *Hindsight*. London: Quartet.

That spectacular supplement: martial arts film as reality

Paul Bowman

Cardiff University, Cardiff, UK

This chapter contributes to the long-running debates about the relations between representation and reality. It is informed by Rey Chow's and Meaghan Morris's questioning of the need to position oneself in and write from any simple 'position' or identity. What the chapter advocates for is neither an identity nor even a politics, but rather a way of approaching film that concedes the inevitability of its connections with other realms and registers, via the specific case study of martial arts films and their supplementary relations to wider discourses, ideologies and embodied practices. Beginning from Kyle Barrowman's critique of my earlier work, and then adding insights from both Jacques Derrida and Chow, the chapter approaches the problematic of representation and reality by way of a consideration of film fight choreography. The discussion covers a range of examples of recent Chinese-language martial arts films, from the first *Ip Man* film (Dir. Wilson Yip, Hong Kong, 2008) to Wong Kar-wai's film *The Grandmaster* (Dir. Wong Kar-wai, Hong Kong and China, 2013). These have been chosen because they at one and the same time fetishise the 'faithful' representation of 'real' martial arts styles while also *thereby* showing them in an impossibly perfect light. Given this paradoxical double status of the image – at once faithful to the real and yet *by the same token* utterly impossible and utterly unreal – they exemplify what Brooks Landon once termed the 'aesthetics of ambivalence' that is at the heart not only of martial arts film choreography and martial arts film spectatorship but also martial arts practice.

Introduction: grandmasters and masterclasses

When Ip Man meets Gong Er in unarmed combat near the beginning of *The Grandmaster* (Dir. Wong, Hong Kong, 2013), the narrative of the film has already made it clear that this is not merely about individual versus individual. Rather, it is about style versus style. Indeed, the duel replays the much mythologised folk and cinematic convention of the rivalry between so-called Northern and Southern Chinese martial arts styles (Hunt, 2003). However, the fight between Ip and Gong is also a complication of these broad categories because, as has already been made clear in the film, Ip Man is a representative of one *particular* Southern style (*wing chun*), and as such, his victory would 'prove' the supremacy not merely of Southern styles per se, but actually of one *particular* style – *wing chun*. Of course, *literally*, the duel will primarily establish the supremacy of one or the other combatant, but this only matters because they are the *representatives* of larger institutions.

In other words, this combat is tokenistic – gestural. It is not all-out conflict; rather, it is carried out via tokens and gestural transactions. This extends from the macro-scale, wherein one duel between two people can signify the supremacy of an entire institution (or indeed, region), down to the component ingredients of the fight itself. Most noticeable, perhaps, is the ready stance – the pose adopted by each fighter before the fight itself. The ready stance plays a key visual role in each of the many films that have been made about Ip Man since the first years of the twenty-first century. These films include *Ip Man* (Dir. Wilson Yip, Hong Kong, 2008), *Ip Man 2* (Dir. Wilson Yip, Hong Kong, 2010), *The Legend Is Born: Ip Man* (Dir. Herman Yau, Hong Kong, 2010) and *Ip Man: The Final Fight* (Dir. Herman Yau, Hong Kong, 2013), as well as – most famously – Wong Kar-wai's *The Grandmaster* (Dir. Wong Kar-wai, Hong Kong and China, 2013)[1]. In all of these films, Ip prepares for combat by sliding one foot, moving his arms, and sinking into a characteristic ready stance of *wing chun*. More often than not, at this point, Ip will also declare his identity, his hometown and his style ('Ip Man, Foshan, Wing Chun'). In *The Grandmaster*, the ritualism and decorum of the martial arts duel is emphasised, with combatants typically inviting each other to fight with the polite word *qing* ('please').

The fight between Ip Man and Gong Er is a beautiful affair. It takes the form of exchanges of impeccably executed techniques, all clearly depicted so as to be recognisable to martial artists. The exchanges are filled with attacks, counters, glances and even (thanks to slow motion) lingering gazes. After each short burst of combat, ready stances are regained and the combatants return to the fray. As the quick glances of combatants become the lingering gazes of two people evidently becoming increasingly attracted to each other, the staging, choreographing, filming and editing ultimately show the conflict becoming more *eros* than *polemos*. Indeed, the erotic sensuality of fight scenes such as this led more than one online reviewer to ask whether this could even be classed as a 'martial arts film' at all.

Nonetheless, whether art film, martial arts film or artistic martial arts film, Ip Man's gestures, postures, ready stances and techniques are consistently and impeccably those of *wing chun*. Indeed, DVD extras, 'making-of' clips and publicity films around *The Grandmaster* often showed the actors undergoing rigorous martial arts training in preparation for filming. It is certainly a film steeped in highly specific, refined, even rarefied stylistic knowledge. At one point during the fight with Gong, Ip notices that she has changed her ready stance and has adopted *his wing chun* stance. In response, Ip changes his ready stance. He adopts the stance that Gong Er had hitherto been using, characteristic of her 'sixty-four hands' style. Having each acknowledged the other's gesture, they proceed to fight using the movement-principles and techniques of their opponent's style.

This is a switching of roles and styles that serves to illustrate not the supremacy of one style over another but rather the individual genius of each of the practitioners. For it demonstrates their mutual ability to apprehend, comprehend, appreciate and even perform a style totally different to the one they have spent countless hours mastering. The gesture here is double. Through the performing of the physical gesture of the ready stance of the other's style, Ip and Gong gesture to the fact that they each 'get it', they each 'show' that they understand how the antagonistic style works; and not only that, but that they have, in a sense, already 'learned' it, simply by sparring against it.

Indeed, in this and other ways, *The Grandmaster* offers a kind of masterclass in martial arts pedagogy. But what kind? Or, phrased differently: What is the relationship of this 'martial arts' film to reality, or at least to practices and discourses of martial arts? As already hinted, many martial arts film fans did not enjoy this film – some even disputing its status as a martial arts film. However, I want to develop a reflection on the relationship between film and 'reality' by insisting on the observation that the fight choreography in *The Grandmaster* is, in a sense, *hyper-faithful* to 'real' martial arts. The techniques are always perfect. But this very perfection – combined with the conventions of its cinematic rendering that emphasise its idealistic beauty – causes problems for martial arts aficionados and others who seek to assess martial arts films in terms of their 'realism', or rather, whether or not they are 'realistic'. And it should be noted at the outset that martial artists are not the only ones who assess choreography in these terms: as someone who both studies and researches martial arts, I am frequently asked by non-martial artists whether the martial arts or fight choreography in this or that film is real, authentic, genuine, or realistic, and so on. Accordingly, my discussion will engage with current debates around realism, but it will displace them into the realms of 'culture' – and specifically *pedagogy*. However, unlike many explorations of martial arts and pedagogy, in what follows I will insist on maintaining attention on what we might call a cinematic or *spectacular supplement*, in connecting cinematic and non-cinematic martial arts discourses via what Rey Chow proposes are culturally specific 'affective modes' and 'affective tendencies' (Chow, 2007). The ultimate aim here is to show that the discourses of realism and indeed reality can be developed in ways that at least gesture to the importance of film within culture.

Fighting realism

To begin with 'realism': a recent study of realism by Kyle Barrowman takes issue with a range of approaches to film fight choreography, including my own (Barrowman, 2014; Bowman, 2010). However, Barrowman primarily targets the arguments of such key writers on martial arts action cinema as Hunt (2003), Teo (2008, 2009) and Bordwell (2000). His critique of my own is only a stepping stone on the way to his primary objective, which is to rescue the work of Bazin from the kind of reductive common sense consensus that he believes is based on a (non)reading that reduces Bazin's work to a caricature, and thereby forecloses its potential productiveness for thinking about the relations between cinematic and other realms of reality (Bazin, 2005b, 2005a).

The topic of the relationship between filmic and other realms of reality (or indeed between representation and reality per se) is an enduring and vexed problematic. It is shared not only by classical philosophy and contemporary film studies but also by all studies of media effects, from debates and moral panics about the effects of images to every academic and political field that ever becomes exercised by such matters as 'negative images' of regional, class, national, ethnic, gender, sexual or any other kind of group or identity. The frequency of febrile responses to cinematic images *even in film studies* once caused Meaghan Morris to complain that such responses evince 'a strictly armchair way of seeing or not-seeing films which first views them as evidence of some social or political mess, then treats them as guilty stand-ins for that mess – and wages a war of attitude on other viewers' (Morris, 2001, p. 171). Rey Chow goes even further, and argues that the disciplinary concerns of film studies itself have long been wedded and welded to questions of groups and identities (Chow, 2007).[2]

At the heart of such issues, Barrowman proposes, are questions of realism. According to Barrowman, my work on martial arts has little time for realism. Indeed, he proposes that 'in an effort to "checkmate" the notion of realism for use in discussions of martial arts cinema' my own argument, in *Theorizing Bruce Lee*, is that the sloppy scuffle between Hugh Grant and Colin Firth in *Bridget Jones' Diary* (Dir. Sharon Maguire, UK, 2001) is in a peculiar way more realistic than the fights in films such as *Way of the Dragon* (Dir. Bruce Lee, Hong Kong, 1972), precisely because the fight in *Bridget Jones' Diary* is full of 'mistakes, misses, and clumsiness' (Barrowman, 2014; Bowman, 2010).

However, in assessing the comparison I make between the choreography of many martial arts films and the fight scene in *Bridget Jones' Diary*, Barrowman replaces all of the films I mention with one: *The Matrix* (Dir. The Wachowski Brothers, USA, 1999). He does so in order to make a claim about 'reality' – not cinematic realism, but reality outside the cinema, reality on the ground, so to speak, or reality 'in the real world', real reality, reality per se. And after doing this he goes on to use this claim to attempt to 'checkmate' his representation of my position. As he writes:

> For purely heuristic purposes, this is a useful observation that helps one recognize the departure from reality in a film like *The Matrix* (1999) when Keanu Reeves' untrained computer geek character instantly knows martial arts and can execute techniques at an extraordinarily high level, something neither Grant's character nor Firth's character were able to do once they engaged in combat [in *Bridget Jones' Diary*]. In making this move, however, Bowman misses the hole it leaves in his argument, for comparing a fight between two untrained civilians to a fight between two renowned experts and expecting the combative texture to be identical (either expecting them both to look as skillful as *The Way of the Dragon* or as sloppy as *Bridget Jones' Diary*) is a terribly egregious attempt at elevating a contingency to a universal (and the egregiousness is compounded by the fact that this position also overlooks the similarly contingent nature of the techniques used for filming sequences of martial arts action). (Barrowman, 2014, unpaged)

This is a stimulating rejoinder to my work, but it is not the way that I would either represent my argument or construe the 'terribly egregious hole' in it. For my argument, at least my own reading of it, was not that the fight in *Bridget Jones' Diary* was more real than the fights in other action films, but rather that precisely what is comedic about it is an effect achieved by virtue of its deliberate difference from many – perhaps all – conventional action film fight choreography. In the deliberateness of this difference it thereby passes comment on action fight choreography by basing its primary characteristics on all that is conventionally excluded from action film fight choreography – the misses, the slips, the trips, the fumbling, the scuffling and the general lack of proficiency or mastery either of technical skill or of the environment. It is funny because of the way it goes against the norms and expectations of 'straight' fight choreography, the way it is almost a study of all that is repressed in what we might ironically call – with a respectful bow to queer theory – the 'pugilonormatvity' of most fight choreography. It certainly evinces the messiness of contingency.

In other words, the reason for my juxtaposition of very masterful (and 'serious') fight scenes with a very messy (and comic) scene was to complicate the understanding not of realism or genre in films but rather the complexity and messiness of *non-cinematic* reality. Consequently, my rejoinder to Barrowman is to suggest that in seeking to refine and complicate the theoretical problems of realism *in film*, he does so via a reciprocal set of universalising or simplifying propositions about *non-cinematic reality*. Stated bluntly, there is evidence here that Barrowman's phantasy is that 'in reality' a real Jason Bourne, Colt, Nico or a Tang Lung *really would* beat an untrained Mark Darcy or Daniel Cleaver.

Unfortunately, once we start speculating on what would 'really happen' were the 'real' Jason Bourne to go toe to toe with the real Tang Lung, we enter the realms of a very commonplace fantasy within martial arts discourse. The exemplary questions in this fantasy are either 'who would win, Bruce Lee or Mohammad Ali?', or 'which style is best?' I have written about these debates before, yet I have assiduously avoided joining in with them in their own terms (Bowman, 2010, 2013, 2015). This is because there are so many reasons *not* to enter into 'who would win' speculation. Anecdotally, I have seen fights where the 'objectively' superior fighter tripped and fell and hence lost the fight. I personally have beaten far superior fighters myself – somehow – and, conversely, there have been times where I have been beaten by complete novices. And so on. Add your own examples.

Barrowman's critique of my work culminates in his specific contribution to the debate on realism – the notion of 'combative realism':

> On the one hand, given the lack of training and martial arts experience of the characters fighting in *Bridget Jones' Diary*, one could hardly expect a masterclass in martial arts, thus validating the film's claim to combative realism specifically as a result of the *absence* of technical skill; on the other hand, given the considerable training of the characters fighting in *The Way of the Dragon*, one could hardly expect buffoonery, thus validating the film's claim to combative realism specifically as a result of the *presence* of technical skill. Bowman's mistake was to think that there was any useful way of comparing these cases according to a universal notion of 'Realism' in the first place [13]. Just as there is no universal Bazinian Realism the criteria for which are completely met by *The Crime of Monsieur Lange* (1936), *Citizen Kane* (1941), and *Journey to Italy* (1954), there is no universal Combative Realism the criteria for which are completely met by the fight scenes in *The Adventures of Fong Sai-yuk* (1938), *Enter the Dragon* (1973), and *Here Comes the Boom* (2012). (Barrowman, 2014, unpaged)

Barrowman's exploration of the notion of 'combative realism' is fascinating. However, it seems salient to note that subtending and silently structuring the argument at this point are two equally problematic dimensions: first, an implicit universalising (reductive) proposition about 'reality' – a proposition that Barrowman himself actually distances himself from if and when posed explicitly (as we will see in the following extract); and second, a taxonomic ordering desire that Barrowman has picked up most directly from Leon Hunt who, in *Kung Fu Cult Masters*, tried to enumerate different forms of 'authenticity' or 'authenticity effects' in martial arts film (Hunt, 2003). Barrowman critiques Hunt's regressive move away from 'realism' and into 'authenticity', but he picks up the same taxonomic, ordering and hierarchising impulse. And the desire to map out and organise the world into some kind of order or hierarchy can be regarded as symptomatic of what Jacques Derrida would have called a metaphysical desire, or what Rancière would associate with a desire to police the world into 'proper categories' and put everything into their 'proper places' (Derrida, 1981; Rancière, 1999).

Of course, to his credit, Barrowman's larger aim is merely to insist, along with Miriam Hansen – whom he quotes on this matter –, that the problems of cinematic realism simply will not go away, no matter how much we might want them to. He believes I want them to. As he writes:

> Bowman … writes off realism as essentially useless in discussing martial arts cinema [and] flat-out proclaims that there exist greater demands for scholars studying martial arts cinema

than analyzing 'those easy forms of perfunctory evaluation which proceed in terms of making claims about "real" martial arts practice versus cinematic "tricks"'. (Bowman, 2010, p. 71)

I still agree with my quoted self on this point, and will elaborate on it in the next section. I think it is crucial, and not only for thinking about realism (combative or otherwise), but more importantly for displacing the discussion away from a focus on film *exclusively* and into such realms as those of *documentary* and *pedagogy*. My intention is less to write off realism than to write away from it, or rather, away from the disciplinary contexts of its formulation. This is because my concerns with film have never been internal to the discourse of film studies, but rather with the relations between films and other practices, their place within wider discourses and networks of representation, belief and practice. Consequently, 'realism' remains a concern, inasmuch as it will never stop returning, as a question, a challenge, a threat, a promise, a possibility; but the fact that its unequivocal arrival seems permanently deferred does not stop martial arts films from 'working' – from having effects – within discourses that stretch from the screen to phantasmatic to philosophical to haptic and embodied (or embodying) realms, registers and contexts (Barrowman, 2014; Downey, 2014; Hunt, 2003, 2014; Morris, 2001, 2004; Spencer, 2014). I stand by the contention, made by Brooks Landon, reiterated by Leon Hunt, quoted by me and approved of by Barrowman, that martial arts film spectatorship involves an 'aesthetics of ambivalence' – an investment in two contradictory registers at the same time: on the one hand, the fantasy of escapism via identifying with (for example) often impossibly phallic heroes, and on the other hand, an investment in ideas of documentary 'realism', or the desire to see action sequences within fight scenes that seem 'realistic', or at least possible.

In this context, my aim is not to dismiss realism, but to displace the debate explicitly into one that addresses the relations between any genre of representation and wider practices and discourses. Consequently, I would concur with the general thrust of Brooks Landon's and Leon Hunt's discussions of the aesthetics of ambivalence, at least inasmuch as it provokes us to consider approaching *any* martial arts fight choreography either as a kind of documentary or as an argument about reality, and indeed (therefore) as ineradicably pedagogical. To take things even further, and to invert and displace the debates accordingly, the consideration of filmic representations of martial arts as always making reference (however allusive) to *documentary*, or *documenting*, or *showing*, and as always-possibly having *pedagogical* potentials, suggests that it may also be important to consider 'reality itself' – at least the reality of martial arts teaching and learning – as always making some supplementary reference to the cinematic, perhaps even 'being' in some sense cinematic, although not simply hyperreal in the crude Baudrillardian sense that organised *The Matrix*.

Cinematic reality

Too much of a fixation on cinematic realism can close down consideration of a perhaps more interesting proposition: the idea that reality might be in some way cinematic (Geiger and Littau, 2013). Perhaps reality always has a greater chance of being cinematic than cinema ever had of being either realistic or realist. As curious as it might seem, a proposition like this can in fact reasonably be made, by making reference not to a theory of ontology but to a very widely assumed theory of the subject. (Indeed, theories of ontology often rely on an implicit theory of the subject, suggesting that a theory of the subject is more fundamental to thinking about reality than even supposedly non-subject-centred theories of ontology, such as those that sometimes circulate in contemporary philosophy.)

So common is this tacitly assumed theory of the subject that it operates not only in film studies but also in cultural studies, anthropology, sociology and beyond. The constitutive ingredients of it boil down to two propositions: first, that the subject be regarded first as *constitutively incomplete* and, second, as *performative*. Both of these ideas are dominant today, and derive from many sources, although perhaps none more clearly than Lacanian strands of poststructuralism. In these, the human subject is understood as formed via processes of identification and mimesis in relation to an external object or field.

From here, it becomes clear that there may be no good reason to exclude TV, film and other media from the potential field of and for identification and mimesis (Mulvey, 1975). Yet, the objection may be raised that sociologists and psychologists of many stripes have long searched for ways to establish the 'influence' of external stimuli such as these, but that there has been a general inability to find stable, reliable and programmatically predictable relations and effects between, so to speak, 'cinematic cause and embodied/subjective effect'. However, the failure of empirical approaches to find them does not mean that such relations do not exist. Rather, it might just as easily be taken to illustrate the limits of empirical approaches in the study of connections and possible 'influences'. Such a limit would arise because the hope of finding regular or programmatic predictability in relations and effects must rest on a tacit belief in the regularity and programmatic predictability both of *contexts of experience* and of the *subjects* (who may or may not be) having the 'same' experience. Yet none of these things are certain. Individual histories and hence everything else thereafter can – perhaps must – be regarded as singular. Of course, there are, here and there, processes of stabilisation, regularisation and attempted homogenisation – think of Althusser's classic postulation of ideological state apparatuses, or Adorno and Horkheimer's fears about the standardising effects on viewers of mass-produced 'culture' and so on (Adorno *et al.*, 1979; Althusser, 1977). And, of course, identifications and affective bonds can be group, mass, national, religious ethnic, and so on. (Laclau, 2005). The occurrence of such moments, periods and contexts supports the argument that subjectivity is constitutively incomplete and performed via mimeses based on identifications, at the same time that the contingency and complexity of subjectivity outflanks and outweighs the viability either of any 'hypodermic needle' or 'monkey see, monkey do' hypothesis about effects.

Accordingly, rather than focusing either on the questions of adjudicating whether, when and where films may or may not live up to one or more idea(l) of 'realism', or if and when 'real life' is 'influenced' by film, literature, music or other media, it seems more productive to explore the ways in which these putatively separate realms (real life, on the one hand, and representation, on the other) *supplement* each other. My argument will be that, when it comes to martial arts (both as experienced in film and as experienced in other areas of discourse, including, of course, the discursive experience of practicing and performing martial arts) the main conduit that both articulates and obfuscates the realms of reality and representation – the point of connection, contamination or cross-fertilisation, that can 'communicate' the contents of one realm into the context of the other – is the notion of *gesture*.

Theoretically, analytically and methodologically, the key term calling out for deployment here – in the context of incompletion and the constitutive character of relations to external objects – is *supplement*. My understanding of the term is derived from Derrida's exploration of the peculiar status of the word in a wide range of texts, particularly of European philosophers (Derrida, 1976). Derrida's reading of both the word itself (in the philosophers' arguments) and of the specific things they were discussing when they used the word 'supplement' zones in on the paradoxical *marginal centrality* of supplements. The supplement is deemed to be something secondary, that yet cannot be done away with, excluded, got rid of. The supplement seems to be a secondary add on, but without it, the primary thing could and would not be what it is or becomes, because it is what it is or becomes what it becomes by way of the supplement. Derrida finds many examples of supplements, to which we can add more: the relation of writing to speech is one of his most famous, for instance; or masturbation to sex; technology, tools or prostheses to the human; representations to reality; or indeed imagination, dreams and interpretations to reality and truth.

In my own analyses of martial arts discourse, this understanding of the supplement has enabled me to reconcile the idea of cinematic and other forms of representation or fictional/dramatised performance with that of 'real' martial arts discourse – whether that discourse takes the form of practical exercises in training, such as formal drills or free sparring, or whether it takes the form of spoken or written words about martial arts, as well as online how-to 'documentaries' and instructional videos. My sense is that the putative separation of these realms (the fake/filmic from the real/actual) is an unnecessary metaphysical convention and that to maintain it in academic discourse is to miss the crucial interplay of elements from each side of the screen. Both discursive contexts evoke, allude to, challenge, elaborate on, contest, explore, comment on and *supplement* each other. Film-fantasy supplements fighting philosophy, and vice versa, in ongoing unpredictable dialogic relations (Bowman, 2010). Martial arts and action film representations of fighting are informed by (and formed from) many areas of martial arts discourse, at the same time as they propose models of what real fighting might really be like, which itself provokes or stokes martial arts desires, fantasies and discourses; such that the reality of martial arts practice can be said to be in some sense supplemented by the cinematic.

Examples I have discussed before range from the impact of 1960s and 70s martial arts choreography on the uptake of the practice of Asian martial arts the world over to the impact of the fight choreography of films such as *Batman Begins* (Dir. Christopher Nolan, USA, 2005), *Mission: Impossible* (Dir. Brian De Palma, USA, 1996), *M:I-2* (Dir. John Woo, USA, 2000), *M:I-3* (Dir. J. J. Abrams, USA, 2006), *Mission: Impossible – Ghost Protocol* (Dir. Brad Bird, USA, 2011), *Mission: Impossible – Rogue Nation* (Dir. Christopher McQuarrie, USA, 2015) and *Jack Reacher* (Dir. Christopher McQuarrie, USA, 2012) on the uptake of the new martial arts that were featured therein. This was first called 'Keysi Fighting Method', but it soon fractured and fragmented into 'Keysi', on the one hand, and 'Defence Lab' on the other (Bowman, 2014). Other cases include the once subterranean but recently more visible influence of Filipino martial arts in Hollywood choreography, via the work of Bruce Lee's student Dan Inosanto, and especially Inosanto's student Jeff Imada; the *Fight-Club-ization* of martial arts and other films in the wake of *Fight Club* (Dir. David Fincher, USA, 1999), which itself came in the wake of the Ultimate Fighter Competition (the UFC), and the increasing incorporation of obviously Mixed Martial Arts (MMA) inspired fight choreography into blockbuster productions, such as, for instance, *The Expendables* (Dir. Sylvester Stallone, USA, 2010), which incorporates many techniques recently popularised by MMA competitions, such as the arm-bar and the guillotine (Bowman, 2015). At the other end of this spectrum, 'real' fight clubs have emerged (bars and nightclubs where patrons can engage in hand-to-hand combat), and there have been famous cases of MMA fighters in competitions such as the UFC incorporating cinematic techniques into their competition fighting, from spinning elbow strikes taken from *Ong-Bak: Muay Thai Warrior* (Dir. Prachya Pinkaew, Thailand, 2003) to flying kicks propelled by bouncing off the cage wall, inspired by *The Matrix*, to one famous knockout kick copied directly from the famous 'crane kick' that is used at the end of *The Karate Kid* (Dir. John G. Avildsen, USA, 1984) (Bolelli, 2014; Downey, 2014; Spencer, 2012).

In all cases, the logic is gestural and performance is mimetic. Every move has a semiotic value, in a discourse that is equally and ineradicably shot through by the aesthetics of ambivalence – ambivalence about reality, perhaps, and about the place of action fight choreography within it, certainly. Dramatic techniques like those seen in the movies are *at one and the same time valued and disdained*. A knockout spinning kick in the ring, cage or octagon is rightly deemed 'unbelievable' – in the double sense of being amazing because rare, and hence simply unbelievable in the sense of not credible – not reliable, not predictable – not something you would want to assume would always work 'in reality'. But even outside of the discourse of practicality and reality versus impractical spectacularity and unreality, aesthetic questions arise. Female MMA champion Ronda Rousey's devastatingly fast and unequivocal win by throwing, holding and repeatedly punching her opponent into knockout in the 2014 UFC is regarded as both realistic and yet always somehow inferior to her win by throw and arm-bar in the 2015 UFC. This is because the arm-bar has the discursive status of 'pure', 'clean', 'technical', 'safe', 'reliable' and so on, whereas the rapid pulverisation of her opponent the year before has the status of 'brutal'. Even practical efficiency is aesthetic.

But it is not universal. The aesthetics of practical efficiency themselves change. Today, MMA knockouts by jumping or spinning kicks are regarded with ambivalence because they have the discursive status of being both high skill *and* high risk. They are eyed with both interest and suspicion because the current configuration of martial arts discourse – one that has been consolidating itself since the first UFC competitions in the early 1990s, when the Gracie style of Brazilian Jiujitsu began to prove itself in 'reality martial arts' competitions – is one in which grappling and ground-fighting have become *hegemonic*. Because of the success of grappling and ground-fighting, they have come to define today's dominant common-sense understanding of what fighting is 'really like'. But this will not be permanent. This discourse moves and modifies.

The point to be emphasised here is that every move, no matter how 'real' or 'unreal' it is deemed, has, first and foremost, a semiotic value. That value is always constituted in a discursive network that skips freely from film to formal training and from format to format. Thus, just as the UFC questioned the need for rules in martial arts competition in the early 1990s, so we might question the need for a strict demarcation of 'film studies' from 'cultural studies', especially around the discourse of martial arts, which easily and arguably always traverses the supposedly separate realms of fiction and reality.

Conclusion: sentimental martial fabulations

The disciplinary separation of film studies from cultural studies is an academic gesture whose net result is the shackling of thinking and enquiry into unnecessarily separated orders. To reactivate their interimplication and imbrication, I have been emphasising the supplementary relations between film and other aspects of culture, such as lived daily life and daily practices. But perhaps the matter of realism, or more helpfully perhaps, the matter of what Barrowman reformulates as 'combative realism', deserves further attention. In order to conclude, I will propose a different way to approach such matters, informed by a reading of Rey Chow's argument about sentiments and affects in different filmic and cultural discursive contexts. Of most relevance is *Sentimental Fabulations* (Chow, 2007), in which Chow proposes an approach to understanding the works of certain Fifth-Generation Chinese film makers by exploring the relations between attachment to values that are older and other than those of the cinematic image, in what she calls an 'age of global visibility'. For present purposes, Chow is useful here because her work offers a provocative and stimulating way to reconfigure questions not only of realism but also of reality, at the same time as offering a way to rethink what I am proposing is the essentially gestural character of martial arts culture, at least whenever it meets filmic and other kinds of representation.

Unfortunately, Chow herself rarely mentions martial arts, whether inside or outside films. The closest she ever comes is one or two occasions in which she merely mentions the existence of 'martial arts films'. One such occasion takes the form of a list of 'Chinese things'. In this list, 'martial arts films' are mentioned as an example of a familiar category of commodity or practice among other familiar types or stereotypes of 'Chinese stuff'. However, in Chow's work, such mentions are never *mere* listing, in the sense of the abusive failure to read or take seriously the object or topic being mentioned. Rather, such mentions occur in moments of conceptual reconfiguration, as in the following remarkable passage from the introduction to *Sentimental Fabulations*:

> With respect to the recent Western European and North American fascination with East Asian cinema, the first question to ask, then, is this: should we try to direct such fascination back at some authentic, continuous Asianness lying beyond the alluring cinematic images, or would it not be more pertinent to see Asianness itself as a commodified and reproducible value, made tantalizingly visible and accessible not only by the filmic genres of the action or martial arts comedy, the love story, and the historical saga but also by an entire network of contemporary media discourses – economic rivalry, exotic cuisine, herbal medicine, spiritual and physical exercise, sex trade, female child adoption, model minority politics, illegal immigration, and so on – that are at once sustained by and contributing to the flows of capital? Part of my goal in this study is to argue that Chinese cinema since the 1980s – a cinema that is often characterized by multinational corporate production and distribution, multinational cast and crew collaboration, international award competition activity, and multicultural, multiethnic reception, as well as being accompanied by a steady stream of English-language publications, written (not infrequently by those who do not speak or read Chinese or consult Chinese-language sources) for an English-reading market – is an inherent part of a contemporary global problematic of becoming visible. As much as belonging in the history of Chinese culture, the films involved should also, I contend, be seen as belonging in the history of Western cinema studies, in the same manner that modern Asia, Africa, and Latin America, properly speaking, belong in the history of modern European studies. (Chow, 2007, pp. 12–13)

One important dimension to the work of Chow that I want to draw attention to here relates specifically to the fact that despite foregrounding the complexity and near ubiquity of commodified media/representational images in the contemporary age of visibility, she neither abandons non-media reality nor makes facile or febrile statements about the 'death' of reality. Thus, although there may be no 'authentic, continuous Asianness lying beyond the alluring cinematic images' – indeed, although the very idea of an authentic continuous Asianness may itself be the product of the alluring cinematic images that conjure it up – and although we should 'see Asianness itself as a commodified and reproducible value'; Chow's aim is neither to try to kill nor to ridicule any desire of or for it. It is rather to emphasise that all of this is '*made* tantalizingly visible *and accessible* not only by the filmic genres of the action or martial arts comedy, the love story, and the historical saga *but also by an entire network of contemporary media discourses*' (emphases added). If more and more areas of life are entangled within, captured by, experienced in relation to and constituted through 'an entire network of contemporary media discourses', Chow does not abandon the question of *the rest*, the *remainder*, the *remnants*, *traces*, or *residues* of something at least apparently former and other than contemporary media discourses. This is precisely where the notion of the sentimental comes in:

> If contemporary cultures are caught up in what I have been referring to as global visibil-
> ity – the ongoing, late capitalist phenomenon of mediatized spectacularization in which the
> endeavor to seek social recognition amounts to an incessant production and consumption
> of oneself and one's group as images on display, a phenomenon in which subjectivity has
> become, willy-nilly, object-ivity – how do we come to terms with older – or increasingly
> estranged – forms of interpellations such as self-restraint, frugality, filial piety, compliance
> with collective obligations, inconspicuous consumption, modesty about exhibiting and thrust-
> ing oneself (including one's body parts and sexual interests) forward as a cause in public,
> and so forth, wherein the key is not exactly – perhaps exactly not – becoming visible? How
> might we go about handling the tenacity, in the midst of global visibility – itself a new kind
> of aggressive, oftentimes oppressive, reality – of residual significatory traces of a different
> kind of social behavioral order? Such traces [are] often emergent in the form of a vaguely
> anachronistic affect whose mere survival points to another modality of attachment and iden-
> tification – and whose noncontemporaneity stands in mute contrast to the glamour of global
> visibility… (Chow, 2007, pp. 22–23)

In other words, Chow proposes that the sentimentality of many Fifth-Generation films is precisely the residue or symptom not simply of 'something old', but rather of 'the old, now lingering in the enigmatic form of an intensity (in the form of some emotionally guarded and clung-to inside) that seems neither timely nor fully communicable' (2007, p. 23). Significantly, she adds that the sentimentality she regards as the 'predominant affective mode' (p. 14) of many Chinese films is 'neither timely nor fully communicable – *especially not across cultures*' (2007, p. 23, emphasis added), even though she regards it as 'an inherent link to the nexus of becoming visible' (2007, p. 23). This lack of smooth cross-cultural communicability arises because, to Chow, it bespeaks and speaks back to 'the remains of a collective cultural scaffold'. Indeed, what Chow wants to draw into visibility is what she calls the 'sentimental interstices – the remains of a collective cultural scaffold – that lend the images their support' (2007, p. 23).

The key point to note here is that what is being developed and deployed by Chow is an argument about the complexity of relations between film and culture. The second point to note is that Chow is working through and helping to find a way to make sense of the very familiar theme of cultural difference. As anyone who reads reviews of Hong Kong and Chinese films released for Anglophone audiences in the USA or UK will be aware, reviewers make repeated observations about the films' frequent 'excessive sentimentality'. This is certainly so in relation to Hong Kong and Chinese martial arts films, which are often clearly structured by the kinds of sentimentality that Chow identifies in relation to the non-*martial* but very definitely *art* films that she examines.

To refer back to our opening discussion of *The Grandmaster*: the flurry of Hong Kong and Chinese films released between 2008 and 2013 that each – to coin a phrase – 'sentimentally fabulated' Bruce Lee's *wing chun* kung fu teacher, Ip Man, all make excellent examples to consider. Elsewhere, I have focused on the way these films nostalgically reactivate and 'replay' Bruce Lee, with a peculiar 'afterwardsness' that is entirely appropriate to their object (Bowman, 2013). After all, Ip Man came before Bruce Lee historically (he was Lee's teacher), but he was only reinvented as some kind of Chinese cultural hero long *after* Bruce Lee, in the *wake* of Bruce Lee and *because of* the earlier global fame of Bruce Lee. As mentioned earlier, these films include *Ip Man*, *Ip Man 2*, *The Legend is Born: Ip Man* and *Ip Man: The Final Fight*, as well as Wong's *The Grandmaster*. There are also closely related films that reactivate and replay Bruce Lee via different stand-ins, such as *Legend of the Fist: The Return of Chen Zhen* (Dir. Andrew Lau, Hong Kong and China, 2010), which reincarnates Chen Zhen, the character Bruce Lee played in *Fist of Fury* – or, more precisely, it reincarnates the Chen Zhen played by Jet Li in *Fist of Legend* (Dir. Gordon Chan, Hong Kong, 1994), a remake of the Bruce Lee film, *Fist of Fury* (Dir. Lo Wei, Hong Kong, 1972).

However, as well as in terms of their 'afterwardsness' and the ways they use stand-ins for Bruce Lee – in what seems to amount to a concerted rethinking of the post-1997 relations between Hong Kong and China (Bowman, 2013) – it is equally possible to read these films in terms of their sentimentality. To give another example: during the same period, *Bodyguards and Assassins* (Dir. Teddy Chan, Hong Kong and China, 2009) was released. This is a martial arts film the strongest and perhaps most widely remarked feature of which was its painstaking recreation of Hong Kong *c.* 1905. Reviewers noted this detail, praising it and recommending it to viewers accordingly. At the same time, reviews also warned Western viewers to brace themselves for lashings of sentimentality of the variety that Chow calls the most 'conventional understanding … of the sentimental', namely 'an affective orientation/tendency, one that is often characterized by apparent emotional excess, in the form of exaggerated grief or dejection or a propensity toward shedding tears' (p. 15). Exactly this form of sentimentality is present throughout *Bodyguards and Assassins* and many other Hong Kong and Chinese martial arts films of the same period.

However, Chow continues, 'when examined closely, such emotional excess is only a clue to a much broader range of issues' (p. 15). For instance, she argues that it is eminently possible to 'understand the sentimental not only as an instance of affect but also as a relation of time', and specifically 'as an affective state triggered by a sense of loss' or as 'the symptom of the apprehension of an irreversible temporal differentiation or the passing of time' (p. 15). In light of the fetishistic overvaluation of a nostalgically memorialised Hong Kong (or Shanghai) of times gone by in all of the films mentioned earlier – especially, perhaps, *Bodyguards and Assassins*, which actually gained fame in part *precisely because of* its reconstruction of an older incarnation of Hong Kong, that city 'of disappearance' (Abbas, 1997) – Chow's argument seems not only plausible but actually compelling.

In other words, as well as the question of film's relation to reality with which we began, we are now also faced with a range of other cross-cultural questions. For Chow:

> The pertinent question to be derived from these cross-cultural considerations is not exactly how to apply them to Chinese film or how such 'Western theory' does not fit 'Chinese reality' but rather the question of a particular discursive relation: how can the symptoms of prominent affective tendencies, as detectable in certain films, be theorized in relation to the foundations and practices of social interaction? With this question in the foreground, the sentimental,

instead of being equated with the occurrence of affective excess per se, can more fruitfully be rethought as a discursive constellation – one that traverses affect, time, identity, and social mores, and whose contours tend to shift and morph under different cultural circumstances and likely with different genres, forms, and media… (Chow, 2007, p. 17)

Viewed from here, the supplement to the question of 'realism', combative or otherwise, would be the element of 'the symptoms of prominent affective tendencies, as detectable in certain films, [needing to] be theorized in relation to the foundations and practices of social interaction'. This is not to say that the fight between Ip Man and Gong Er is somehow simply or actually 'realistic', but rather that the mode of its construction and configuration is indicative of, immanently entangled within and gesturing towards a 'discursive constellation', at once 'lost', 'to come', 'permanently deferred' and in processes of deformation and becoming. Our own place or orbit within the discursive constellation may, then, perhaps be intimated by our intellectual and gut responses not only to the idealised gestures and (im)perfect techniques but also the gazes exchanged by Ip and Gong.

Notes

1. Elsewhere, I have connected this flurry of cinematic interest in Ip Man to the post-1997 renegotiation of Hong Kong 'Chinese' cultural identity (Bowman, 2013), and connected them with related films that rework themes associated with Bruce Lee – a real-life student of Ip Man's kung fu. Such films include *Legend of the Fist: The Return of Chen Zhen* or *Fist of Legend*.
2. This present work, too, is involved in the long-running debates about the relations between representation and reality. But it is informed by Chow's and Morris's questioning of the need to position oneself in and write from any simple 'position' or identity. Indeed, what it advocates for is neither an identity nor even a politics, but rather a way of approaching film that concedes the inevitability of its connections with other realms and registers, via the specific case study of martial arts films and their supplementary relations to wider discourses, ideologies and embodied practices. Beginning from Barrowman's critique, and then adding insights from both Derrida and Chow, the chapter approaches the problematic of representation and reality by way of a consideration of film fight choreography. The discussion covers a range of examples of recent Chinese language martial arts films, from the first *Ip Man* film (2008) to Wong Kar-wai's film *The Grandmaster* (2013). These have been chosen because they at one and the same time fetishise the 'faithful' representation of 'real' martial arts styles whilst also *thereby* showing them in an impossibly perfect light. Given this paradoxical double status of the image – at once faithful to the real and yet *by the same token* utterly impossible and utterly unreal – they exemplify what Brooks Landon once termed the 'aesthetics of ambivalence' that is at the heart not only of martial arts film choreography and martial arts film spectatorship (Hunt, 2003; Landon, 1992;) but also martial arts practice (Bowman, 2010, 2013).

References

Abbas, A. (1997). *Hong Kong: Culture and the Politics of Disappearance*. Minneapolis and London: University of Minnesota Press.

Adorno, T. W., M. Horkheimer, and J. Cumming. (1979). *Dialectic of Enlightenment*. London: Verso Editions (Distributed by NLB).

Althusser, L. (1977). *Lenin and Philosophy and Other Essays*. London: New Left Books.

Barrowman, K. (2014). Action aesthetics: Realism and martial arts cinema, Part 1. Theoretical considerations. *Off Screen*, 18 (10). Available online at http://offscreen.com/view/action-aesthetics-pt1

Bazin, A. (2005a). An aesthetic of reality: Neorealism. In H. Gray (Ed.), *What Is Cinema? Volume 2* (pp. 16–40). Berkeley, CA: University of California Press.

———— (2005b). The ontology of the photographic image. In H. Gray (Ed.), *What Is Cinema? Volume 1* (pp. 9–16). Berkeley, CA: University of California Press.

Bolelli, D. (2014). How gladiatorial movies and martial arts cinema influenced the development of the ultimate fighting championship. *JOMEC Journal,* 5, 1–15. Available online at http://cf.ac.uk/Jomec/Jomecjournal/5-june2014/Bolelli_Gladiators.pdf

Bordwell, D. (2000). *Planet Hong Kong: Popular Cinema and the Art of Entertainment.* Cambridge, MA: Harvard University Press.

Bowman, P. (2010). *Theorizing Bruce Lee: Film-Fantasy-Fighting-Philosophy.* Amsterdam and New York: Rodopi.

———— (2013). *Beyond Bruce Lee: Chasing the Dragon through Film, Philosophy and Popular Culture.* London and New York: Wallflower Press.

———— (2014). Instituting reality in martial arts practice. *JOMEC Journal,* 5, 1–24. Available online at www.cardiff.ac.uk/jomec/jomecjournal/5-june2014/Bowman_Reality.pdf

———— (2015). *Martial Arts Studies: Disrupting Disciplinary Boundaries.* London: Rowman and Littlefield International.

Chow, R. (2007). *Sentimental Fabulations, Contemporary Chinese Films: Attachment in the Age of Global Visibility, Film and Culture Series.* New York: Columbia University Press.

Derrida, J. (1976). *Of Grammatology.* Baltimore and London: Johns Hopkins University Press.

———— (1981). *Dissemination.* London: Athlone.

Downey, G. (2014). 'As Real as It Gets!' Producing hyperviolence in mixed martial arts. *JOMEC Journal,* 5, 1–28. Available online at http://cf.ac.uk/Jomec/Jomecjournal/5-june2014/Downey_MMA.pdf

Geiger, J., and K. Littau. (2013). *Cinematicity in Media History.* Edinburgh: Edinburgh University Press.

Hunt, L. (2003). *Kung Fu Cult Masters: From Bruce Lee to Crouching Tiger.* London: Wallflower.

———— (2014). Enter the 2-disc platinum edition: Bruce Lee and post-DVD textuality. *JOMEC Journal,* 5, 1–12. Available online at http://cf.ac.uk/Jomec/Jomecjournal/5-june2014/Hunt_BruceLee.pdf

Laclau, E. (2005). *On Populist Reason.* London and New York: Verso.

Landon, B. (1992). *The Aesthetics of Ambivalence: Rethinking Science Fiction Film in the Age of Electronic (Re)Production.* Westport, CT and London: Greenwood Press.

Morris, M. (2001). Learning from Bruce Lee. In M. Tinkcom and A. Villarejo (Eds.), *Keyframes: Popular Cinema and Cultural Studies* (pp. 171–184). London: Routledge.

———— (2004). Transnational imagination in action cinema: Hong Kong and the making of a global popular culture. *Inter-Asia Cultural Studies,* 5 (2), 181–199.

Mulvey, L. (1975). Visual pleasure and narrative cinema. *Screen,* 16 (3), 6–18.

Rancière, J. (1999). *Disagreement: Politics and Philosophy.* Minneapolis: University of Minnesota Press.

Spencer, D. (2014). From many masters to many students: Youtube, Brazilian jiu jitsu, and communities of practice. *JOMEC Journal,* 5, 1–12. Available online at cf.ac.uk/Jomec/Jomecjournal/5-june2014/Spencer_BJJPractice.pdf

Spencer, D. C. (2012). *Ultimate Fighting and Embodiment: Violence, Gender, and Mixed Martial Arts.* New York: Routledge.

Teo, S. (2008). *Hong Kong Cinema: The Extra Dimension.* London: British Film Institute.

———— (2009). *Chinese Martial Arts Cinema: The Wuxia Tradition.* Edinburgh: Edinburgh University Press.

The disquiet of the everyday: gesture and *Bad Timing*

Liz Watkins

School of Fine Art, History of Art and Cultural Studies, The University of Leeds, Leeds, UK

An analysis of *Bad Timing* discerns gesture as a vital, but often overlooked aspect of the representation of gendered bodies and the female voice. While gesture can be read of performance or a specifically cinematic inflection of narrative form, a study of gesture and parapraxis in the stasis of the body and silence in language discerns a subject position that disquiets, inscribing as it does the everyday violence in the image of woman and is evocative of a crisis in the historical representation of women in cinema.

Cinematic discourse produces socially inscribed representations of sexed bodies. For Mary Ann Doane, cinematic bodies become the site of regulation as the technologies that modulate and animate the human form disclose prosodic and contingent gestures for analysis (Doane, 2002, p. 1; Väliaho, 2010, p. 25, p. 31).[1] From Muybridge's chronophotographic studies of gesture to Stephen Heath's reading of Charcot's Salpêtrière Iconographie of hysteria, the body is both produced and inscribed by the effects of the symbolic.[2] Heath tells us that Charcot's photographic records submit gestures "to the clarity of meaning in narrative [...] the spectacle of the lessons which contemporary pictures and prints pick up: the excited audience, the master, the young woman in a series of pathetic scenes according to a script" (Heath, 1978, p. 58). Whilst symbolic inscriptions form "socially appropriate bodies" (Grosz, 1989, p. xv) gestures trace the intersections of the body with language and memory in solitude and social interaction where the possibilities and limits of communication are at play. Gestures can underscore or unsettle meaning in conversation, betray a default in an exchange of information or operate as an affective trace of what remains unspoken in silence. An analysis of gesture as a facet of performance and as a specifically cinematic inflection of narrative form in *Bad Timing* (Nicolas Roeg, 1980) finds that the repetition or reflection of a bodily movement and the nuance that a sleight of hand betrays as reciprocity or disconnection in dialogue, traces instances where subjective memories intersect with a history articulated by others. From "gestures that are frighteningly carefree" and which involve the heroine, Milena's "whole body" to the film's seemingly "excessive and superficial" (Maslin, 1980, p. 70) attention to the flicker of a hand and the mirrored orientation of a gaze interweave a gendered system of representation and the history of cinema as a discourse founded on the body and technology (Doane, 1991, p. 79).

The complexity of narrative form in *Bad Timing* elicits a series of unstable subject positions in an economy of scopophilia and the desire to know, which situates the disillusion of classic narrative cinema historically (de Lauretis, 1984, pp. 84–87; Wilson, 1999, p. 278). Although not a feminist film or simply eliciting the distanciating effect of art house cinema (Miller 1994/2004, p. 327), *Bad Timing* draws from the style and content of film noir with a theme of surveillance that is familiar to political thrillers of the 1970s and the inflection of a love story in its intimacy and disavowal (Ross, 1995, p. 195) to call an economy of knowledge that is gendered into question through a process of rewriting that situates images and shots in new contexts. The investments and counterpoints of the network of power in *Bad Timing* align masculinity with narration and scopophilia (Wilson, 1999, p. 178), whilst Milena has been read as enacting "a bodily, affective register that is opposed to knowledge and understanding" (Ross, 1995, p. 199): the detective's determination to re-establish the chronology and order of an ellipsis in the account that Milena's lover offers of her suicide attempt is intercut with an assembly of her impulsive gestures, such as the shudder and flex of her hand, which betrays inconsistencies in their verbal exchange. Associative editing and the cross-cutting of shots from different locations and the chronological disordering of events in to a film that unfolds in flashback contribute to the destabilisation of processes of "visual and narrative identification" (de Lauretis, 1984, p. 88; Pym, 1980, pp. 11–112). The fragmentary effect of editing opens a space in which to read gesture as a register that is both operative in and indicative of the alignment of sexuality, violence and the female body in cinema as a historicised and gendered discursive form. *Bad Timing* enacts the disillusion of a textual system in which the subject is positioned ideologically. Close proximity and control of the film's heroine, Milena Flaherty, are insinuated as the locus of desire in relation to a masculinised subject position that is temporarily aligned with Stefan Vognic as her husband and dissuaded lover, Alex Linden as a psychoanalyst and Inspector Netusil as detective (Mulvey, 1981/1989, pp. 30–31). Each of them temporarily offers a point of orientation for the spectator in a scenario which plays on sadism through visual analysis as the desire to know and of inciting a change in another (Mulvey, 1975/1989, p. 22). Speech is aligned with the narration of events throughout which gestures, as an effect suggestive of the repressed, solicit attention. Such modulations of meaning in language appear to be ephemeral, but also retrace memories which seem to haunt the body in movements that signal discontent, a mark of reticence in a mirage of complicity. Between body and language, gestures trace an economy of exchange and resistance in the gendered discourse of cinema.

In *Bad Timing*, this complex process of associative editing elicits connections between minute details such as the imagery of hands to be found in a brooch on Milena's jacket or the repetition of a gesture.[3] In his study of the power structures in *Bad Timing*, Ian Penman notes that the narrative is articulated "through a compulsive – and useful- catalogue of individual habits, characteristics and possessions" (Penman, 1980, p. 107). For example, as Alex reflects the movement of a desk clerk who lifts her curled hand to her lower jaw, his response incorporates a disruption in the repetitive tapping of his fingers (Figure 1).

The sequence cuts between them, each time closer to their hands and marking the temporality of their exchange as Alex's determined movement draws attention to the clerk's bodily tic and his own hesitation to accept the words spoken. The critical play of this gesture disturbs the reciprocity of conversation with a sleight of hand. The

Figure 1.   Alex's critical play in the reflection of a gesture in conversation.

deictic function of a gesture is also marked in the direction of a character's look as it is taken up by that of another (Kendon, 2004, p. 2). The connections are swift and yet compelling in a film otherwise described as a "labyrinthine" configuration of frag- mented scenes and images intercut into narrative form (Brooke, 2007, pp. 86–87; Lapsley, 2009, p. 20; Maslin, 1980, p. 70). The illegibility of *Bad Timing* lies in the discontinuity of Alex Linden's account of Milena Flaherty's suicide attempt.[4] In a con- versation about Milena in her absence, the mirroring of a gesture as Alex and then Inspector Netusil look off-screen is followed by a shot of her in the stupor of an over- dose; an image that disturbs the chronology of their exchange and is revelatory of Alex's miswriting of the event. This gesture marks an instance like Kendon's concept of a parenthesis in the verbal articulation of a tale (2004, p. 137). For filmic discourse, a parenthesis which denotes a pause in speech introjects meaning on to the words spo- ken. Gesture performs a similar function earlier in the film as Milena's invitation to a conversation away from the physicality of sexual intercourse is countered by Alex's petulant remarking of language as his territory.[5] Alex's protests at Milena's desire to talk attributes to her a reticence to consider the issues he would choose to discuss. This plays on the economy of power for which the body and language are intermedial of knowledge and exchange in their relationship and in doing so, positions her as focus of the conversation rather than a participant. A subsequent sequence intercuts shots of a conversation mediated by a telephone; the gestures of each reflect those of the other, despite their different locations, whilst Alex's speech marks an intermittent response to the slurred words uttered by Milena. Alex records and replays the distressed phone calls Milena makes throughout the duration of her attempted suicide, before travelling a circuitous route to her apartment where he pulls the phone cable from her reach, an action which thwarts the possibility of her summoning assistance. Thus, Alex marks his territory in language, whilst gestures as ephemeral movements that inflect meaning in speech to reveal an economy of exchange and resistance operative between the body, language and memory. The privileging of vision and language in relation to knowledge in film and its analysis remains open to a reading of the significance of gesture as a form of expression which lies between language and the sublimation of the body (Butler, 1989, p. 90).

The articulation of meaning in this sequence is both through anomalies in Alex's spoken account and the counterpoint of gestures. In *The Psychopathology of Everyday Life* writing-mistakes, misreading and chance actions can reveal "an unintended display of candour" (Freud, 1901/1991, p. 169). In their immediacy of gesture trace the effects of latent desire called into play by context and conversation. Nervous saccadic movements such as Alex's tapping of a pen knife in his hand mark the "idle play" which "regularly conceals a sense and meaning which are denied any other form of expression" (Freud, 1901/1991, p. 250). Milena's repetitious flicker of a hair pin signals the subtle reciprocity of bodily movement as integral to the formation and exchange of meaning in conversation.[6] Conversely, "bungled actions", such as Alex Linden's inadvertent glance toward Milena's bed where crumpled sheets trace the absence of her body, deviate from the intended expression of the speaker (Freud, 1901/1991, p. 178 and pp. 220–221). Such "chance symptomatic actions" seem inappropriate (Freud, 1901/1991, p. 215) to the intentions of the subject, a residual effect of the transgression he seeks to conceal from Inspector Netusil, that is, his ravishment of Milena as she lays unconscious on her bed. The surreptitious gesture of his glance traces the reactivation of what has made an impression as a memory trace, which even if forgotten from consciousness, can be reawakened. Similarly in conversation, Netusil's comment that the toxic effects of the overdose left Milena unable to even "move a finger" is juxtaposed with the jolt of Alex's hand first pressed into the bed sheets and then withdrawn from view (Figures 2–4).

The subsequent image, displaced from the spatial logic of the sequence is of Milena, hospitalised, with a cannula inserted into the skin of her hand. The detective's words elicit a physical reaction in Alex which indirectly betrays his violation and the failure of his compassionate response. These gestures, as parentheses, sketch threads of connection across the temporal and spatial disorder of the images, in which these ellipses manifest the affectivity of material that is otherwise illegible to the system in which it occurs. In this sense, gesture signals something beyond material that is directly represented or comprehensible according to the textual system of the film. For Heath, such instances call to the concept of excess as a paradigm for ideological positions that are considered to deviate from the system of representation. In classic cinema, this

Figure 2.   Alex's inadvertent glance betrays his ravishment of Milena.

Figure 3.   Alex touches the bed where Milena had lain.

Figure 4.   Inspector Netusil's look follows Alex's glance toward the bed.

system is reliant on the repression of feminine desire on which signification depends (Mulvey, 1981/1989, p. 31). The organisation and disruption of the filmic system echoes "the function historically allocated to woman: sexuality, its prohibition" (Heath, 1975a and 1975b, p. 107).[7] Toward the end of the film, Alex's response to Milena's distressed phone calls and then the ravishment are played out in detail. The grasp of her hand as she sits in a disconsolate haze in the corner of the room and later, in close-up, the flicker of her eyelids opening as Alex cuts the remnants of lingerie from her body, mark the retroactive rewriting of this sequence from opening sections of the film. This process of cross-cutting between the time of the investigation and the events that form the focus of Netusil's inquiry signals both the work of memory and the forgetting of the specificity of feminine desire in the filmic system through the demarcation of the female body as the site of difference. The rewriting of this sequence signals suppression of the feminine as the violence implicit in the cinematic articulation of the image of Woman. The complexity of her desires and the violation of the act of efface-ment in Alex's articulation of her history are written on the body: the shudder of her hand and the minute movement of her eyelids signal her vulnerability in the muted response of an overdose. In this last instance, the images rather than performance are gestural as they trace the latent unease in elision of sexual difference in a system that is irresponsive to the specificity of feminine desire.

Jones' note on Freud's concept of parapraxis as an everyday action incorrectly per-formed, indicates it as a temporary disturbance for which no motive can be immedi-ately perceived (1911, p. 478). What is "incorrect" is the inflection of a gesture in a particular context and moment, the forgetting of a word from speech or writing, or the misplacing of an object. Each refers to a sensory perception or motor process. Jones categorises these as: (1) symptomatic acts such as forgetting or a "failure" of seeing or hearing and erroneous perceptions such as false recollection; (2) instances of unin-tended performance or the misplacing of objects that are revelatory of "non-conscious motives of conduct" (Jones, 1911, pp. 256–257). Doane notes that in the *Psychopathol-ogy of Everyday Life*, Freud suggests gestures are determined and that within this framework contingency could be read as a "failure of interpretation" (2002, p. 167). This "failure" is a question of legibility, a hesitation to invest meaning in every contin-gent occurrence, but which as a "failure" of sensory perception (of seeing, touching or hearing as modes of reading) (Jones, 1911, p. 256) marks a disturbance that is symp-tomatic of a system of representation that is proscriptive of gender in the production of knowledge and reliant on an imbalance of power in the subjugation of the feminine.[8]

In *Bad Timing*, the ellipsis in the temporality of Alex's account of Milena's suicide attempt is revealed, through the complexity of cross-cutting and associative editing, as an effacement of the ravishment Netusil investigates. The *bad timing* of the film's title lies in the constant rewriting, the deletions and revisions of a process that produces a text with a history. This history is of cinematic representation and of Milena as femi-nine subject caught between the social and cultural organisation of the body as pre-scriptive of the expression of desires that transgress a heterosexual and monogamous contract that is a point of contention in the film. In a narrative that relies on numerous genres and invokes classic cinema in its disillusion, gestures question and betray the memory of the historical allocation of a disarticulated image of woman. The repetition of images, such as the double take of her apartment sourced from different moments in the plot infers Netusil as voyeur to series of intimate and volatile exchanges. From the darkened space of the corridor, Netusil's perspective of a room in disarray ceases as the camera pans right at a speed which blurs the image. The subsequent shot reveals Alex entering Milena's ornate but orderly apartment as she walks toward him smiling. The spatial continuity of the juxtaposed shots emphasises an ellipsis in the chronology of the narrative. Alterations in the arrangement of her room trace the imprint of inhabi-tation, from a drift of papers fallen from the shelf and the detritus of clothes, cigarettes and ash cast from everyday incidents of movement, to the upturned bottles, bed sheets twisted under the grasp of her hand and the drag of her unconscious body. Whilst de Lauretis notes that "excess, the sexual, physical, and domestic 'disorder' that […] in the movies marks women who choose to be outside the family" (de Lauretis, 1984, p. 91), such images trace the sediment cast-off of diurnal movements, of paths worn through habit and instances of deviation to offer an archaeological trace of Milena's life. The tension of memory and narrative echoes the "history behind things being kept in place in 'order' on a writing table" (Freud, 1901/1991, p. 190) and the fascination of parapraxis, of miswriting, or a misplaced object. Memory is operative in the emplacement of objects and the history that can be read of their disarray, not simply as disorder, but as a site that demands to be deciphered. This "disorder", the fragmentation that is associated with a feminine subject position, is echoed in the narrative structure of *Bad Timing*. The historical image of woman in classic cinema is invoked by the complexity of associative editing and critiqued by the work demanded of the spectator by the differences marked in repeating a gesture, such as the flicker of Milena's hand, which disquiets, inscribing as it does the everyday of violence in the image of Woman.

The recurrence of certain images throughout the film and the series of images, which belie the cinematic illusion of movement and modulate, the body return us to the sequence of photographic studies which constituted Charcot's iconographie of hysteria and reveal the complex interrelations of language, body and the symbolic. The succession of static images infers bodily movement through the segmentation of the hysteric's gestures as they unfold over time.[9] As a translation, this photographic process diminishes the hysteric's voice in to notes in the accompanying text leaving her gestures to mark the "absence of speech across the body" (Heath, 1978, p. 82). This "silence" then can be interpreted as the forgetting in and of the orders of discourse that is replicated as an effect of the technology in presenting an incomplete account. The abstraction of the hysteric's gestures into a series of still images is the staging of a scene from fragments dislocated from their context on to the image of woman and of which a new narrative is written. The duration of study is intercut with elisions in a temporality of movement, that is formulated by the selection and effacement of information. The process of miswriting in narrative, as the repetition of an image situates it in a new context, can be discerned as a filmic process which itself takes on a gestural function, where two threads of association converge to elicit a failure in a cohesive filmic system. Such repetitions, when they register as an inconsistency, trace fractures and mistiming in the story told and which, in *Bad Timing*, are symptomatic of discontent. As Alex walks into Milena's apartment, she lies uneasily against the corner of her bed. A reverse shot of Inspector Netusil retracing Alex's footsteps notes her absence. The film repeatedly returns to this corner of her room: from a gesture which beckons Alex to her bed, to the unconscious shudder of her hand and later the fall of his and then Netusil's gaze. Here, technology inflects the viewer's perception as the differences between the two shots of Milena's apartment are marked by a comparison. The juxtaposition of two gestures through the process of associative editing can mark a concept like parapraxis, like a slip of the tongue, in the filmic system as the "convergence of two causal series" in narrative form (Laplanche, 1999, p. 105) neither of which is determinate of meaning, but is symptomatic of an "excess of message" (Fletcher, 1999, p. 45) that is disquieting in its timing.[10]

In *Bad Timing*, the abstraction of the image of woman is entangled in the cross-cutting of shots as a symptom of cinema as a discourse to which the body, temporality and technology are integral. Both Doane and Väliaho refer to the series of static images that constitute the chronophotographic studies of body and movement made by Muybridge and Marey. Whilst for Doane (1991, p. 79, 2002), the cinematographic offered a seemingly permanent record of transient details, of the minutiae of facial expressions or the ephemeral movement of gestures that could be discerned amidst the apprehension of bodily movement in a series of still frames that belie the temporality of the moving image, Väliaho (2010, p. 29) suggests the technologies that animate representations of body and gesture signal a crisis in a subject position which he links to modernity as a shift in consciousness and thinking of time and memory. Such studies echo Charcot's photographic documentation of hysteria where gestures are the manifestation of the affectivity of the repressed. Freud's note that "hysterics suffer mainly from reminiscences" (Freud & Breuer, 1895/1991, p. 58) is read by Heath to suggest that "fiction film suffers from its reminiscence of the woman, its problem of memory, the memory it seeks to control, again and again" (Heath, 1978, p. 102) of irreducible sexual difference. Milena is not depicted as a hysteric, but among the variously disordered threads of *Bad Timing*, the practice of associative editing, marked by repetition, calls for a network of connections to be traced and in doing so formulates a subject position that is evocative of a crisis in the historical representation of women in cinema. Although the subject position constructed around Milena through a flashback indicates the pathologisation of a female protagonist similar to that noted by Doane of the women's pictures of the 1930–1940s (1991, p. 76), the rewriting implicit in the film form of *Bad Timing,* which was initially circulated in the early 1980s when the complexities of female sexuality and questions of cinema and representation affected the reception of the film, if not its production, address the spectator as "historical woman" (de Lauretis, 1984, p. 102).

Gestures, although transient, are caught in a discourse that plays on both memory and the immediacy of perception as the rewriting of each instance through associative editing formulates a text with a history. The contested reception of *Bad Timing* is contiguous with "investments and counter-investments" that are operative in the power structure of the film as it sits uneasily in a cinema which is otherwise ideologically complicit as a system of representation by which a society chooses to represent itself (de Lauretis, 1984, pp. 85–87). In the opening section of the film, the subject position attributed to Milena is constructed through ambiguous point-of-view shots, dialogue and gestures that are reciprocated in conversation, thus indicating her participation in an exchange of knowledge and an economy of power. This sequence marks the dissolution of her marriage to Stefan Vognic, which is depicted by the scene in which they drive across the Austrian–Czechoslovakian border. As they stand opposite each other on the bridge at dusk with rain falling, Stefan's distressed inhalation of breath stutters a lament that remains unspoken. This pause, as a gesture in itself, is expressive of the questions which remain unanswered in the distraction of lighting a cigarette, a ritual that is shared as Milena strikes the match and his hand covers the flame. This sequence cross-cuts between them, to offer a series of point-of-view shots that marks their interaction. The editing of the film, as each shot cuts closer to the cigarette, the match and then the familiar practice that Stefan and Milena share in its lighting, else the correlation of a repetitive movement of Milena's hair pin and Alex's penknife, each tapping the object on their hand, directs the viewer's attention to the subtleties of meaning that are communicable in their interaction. However, Milena's gestures become less legible to the context of the conversations in which they occur as each instance is displaced through the repetitive process of editing and cross-cutting which invests them with new meaning. Milena's gestures connect to those of other characters less frequently as the film progresses and gradually begin to mark asymmetry in communication as an uncertainty in the text. However, this illegibility is embedded in conversation as a discontinuity in the exchange of information and as a "failure" of sensory perception inferred by the text and that can be discerned by the spectator. For Freud, such opacity to cognition invests the peripheral details of chance or happenstance as sites close to meaning that are perceptible through their connection to material that is deemed more significant in the system of representation in which they occur. The fractures in *Bad Timing*, which de Lauretis reads as addressing the spectator as "historical woman" (1984, p. 102), infer the temporality of a parapraxis that Laplanche notes is not:

reducible to its materiality. A slip of the tongue is no more *nor* less real materially than a correctly pronounced word. But a slip does not boil down to each of the interlocutor's conceptions of it, which are often incomplete and reductive. It conveys a detachable, observable message, which is partly interpretable by psychoanalysis. (Laplanche, 1999, p. 170)

The materiality of a gesture as parapraxis, of miswriting in a film text, is not explicative of its meaning for either conversant. For Freud an instance of parapraxis must be temporary, not particularly unusual "within the limits of the normal" and, so if perceived, then considered an instance of chance (Freud, 1953/1891, pp. 300–301). Every gesture, forgotten detail or word eludes meaninglessness as for Freud it can in part be retraced to the impression of a memory but forms only an unwitting reaction to it that intersects with present context. The fragmented text through which Milena's gestures emerge, if not the intentional work of conscious perception occur in the repetition of the image, which like a tremor on a web of connections solicits the spectator's attention to affectivity of discontent in the convergence of threads of association that can be traced throughout the film's narrative form.

For de Lauretis, it is the achronology of *Bad Timing* that draws the spectator into a process of recognition and its effacement. This practice of rewriting addresses the spectator as historical subject as it foregrounds the ineluctably cinematic and elusive immediacy of *now* and the indeterminacy of *nowhere* to position the feminine at the borders:

> It is such a figure, constructed by the montage as a memory of borders, contradiction, here and there, now and nowhere, that addresses me, spectator, as historical woman. And it is just in the split, in that non-coherence between registers of time and desire, that figural and narrative identification are possible for me, that I can pose the question of my time and place in the terms of the film's imagining. (de Lauretis, 1984, p. 102)

In *Bad Timing*, gestures signal the disquiet of the everyday, of the familiar of cinema and its scenarios to question the "imagining" of the film (de Lauretis, 1984, pp. 99–102). The recurrence of a scenario in which Milena leaves a lover details the gesture of returning a ring or a door key as a symbol of a bond that is invoked in its negation. In the shots that follow the lighting of cigarette on the bridge, the hesitant resignation of her wedding band to Stefan is countered by her reassurance that "it's not really like going away". Her remark is diminished by his painfully minimal response that it is not so "for you". In this sequence, the film continues to cut between Milena and Stefan, the shots alternating between the perspectives attributed to each of them in turn. Each image is initially framed at an ambiguous angle, before the camera closes in on a series of gestures. These movements detail an exchange that enacts empathy in the different meanings that can be discerned as such gestures are interwoven with dialogue.[11] The second instance is intercut with shots of a bridge, which marks the border as a site of exchange, of mediation and refusal. Milena places a key on the bedside table as she turns toward the door and away from Stefan's tired and reproachful glance. Smiling, she walks and looks directly toward the camera in acknowledgement of its presence. The emphasis on the fetishistic display of Milena, who is so frequently the focus of others, from the fall of a furtive glance to the words exchanged between investigators and lovers, is countered by the return of a key which signals a decision to leave and disturbs the economy of power, knowledge and desire familiar to classic narrative form.

An emphasis on interactions and conversations in *Bad Timing* as film which reconfigures aspects of the love story and film noir discerns gesture as a vital, but often overlooked aspect of the representation of gendered bodies and the female voice.

Milena's speech is nuanced and provocative; full of questions rarely met by a response. There is a sequence that recurs throughout the film in which her voice is recorded on an answer machine. The film cuts between shots of Alex as he replays and interrupts the sound of her distress with the touch of button and the visual record of her gradual intoxication.[12] The mediation of the tape machine and Alex's manipulation of her speech, marks the disembodiment of her voice as his actions, rather than the words spoken orientate the spectator's interpretation of the image. In her analysis of the power structures of gender and the female voice in cinema, Kaja Silverman notes a similar scenario, in which the female voice is recorded and replayed in *Klute* (Alan J. Pakula, 1971).[13] In each of these films, the heroine's voice is disembodied as it registered on tape (Silverman, 1988, p. 81).[14] The female voice is "often shown to coexist with the female body only at the price of its own impoverishment and entrapment. Not surprisingly, therefore, it generally pulls away from any fixed locus within the image track, away from the constraints of synchronization" (1988, p. 141). Composed and inscribed by the symbolic, the human form becomes a signifying complex of gestures which operate between a body that is discursive and anatomical. Gestures which signal stasis or change mark an introjection that disturbs expression in language or narrative and projects meaning on to the voice of another (Silverman, 1988, p. 81, p. 221, p. 224). The projection of masculine desire on to the female voice can be discerned in Alex's registration of the guttural rasp of Milena's breathing through the meandering sentences of her plaintive phone call. This imbalance of power disembodies her voice as a precursor to the ravishment scene in which she remains silent, but for the flex of her hand and the shudder of her eyelids opening, each of which is figured in her absence by the direction that Alex and then Netusil look. The intromission of a gesture which may signify psychical activity, the mimicry of bodily movement may conceal asymmetry in the reciprocity that is otherwise imagined of "communication" (Laplanche, 1999, p. 126).[15] In such instances, the gestures of the other, despite their observable form, can breach the boundaries of subjectivity to be experienced as unpleasure. The effraction of the borderlines that inscribe the subject of marks the violence of the internalisation of the gestures of the other as both performance and text intersect to destabilise the subject positions that are constructed as potential points of identification for the spectator and that recur throughout Roeg's film. Repetition solicits attention through the familiarity and difference marked by its recurrence in various contexts and participates in rewriting the scenography of desire to mark the "now" of Milena's sexed body:

> which the montage succeeds in making present at once conscious and unconscious, alive and dead, there and not there: never totally unconscious, for it moves and gasps, shivers and groans – registering sensations, unknown perceptions, feelings perhaps – even in the deep coma of the emergency room and the ravishment scene (especially then). (de Lauretis, 1984, p. 101)

Her gestures disrupt the double temporality of the investigation and the elusive historical event that the rewriting the ravishment through the film narrative evokes. Gestures play on the question of (il)legibility in narrative, that is of recognition of the "irreducible difference" (de Lauretis, 1984, p. 101) of the excess of feminine desire marked on the body and in language, where performance and text intersect. Of the ravishment, the sadism in the semblance of intimacy can be found in Alex's utterance of his love for Milena as the meaning of his words is eroded, displaced into a symptomatic repetition against the saccadic movements of his hand, once curled in the cyclical caress of his hair, now, uninvited yet touching her neck. Her call for compassion unrequited, the sexual act is played in detail. High-angle shots of Alex leaning across her torso are intercut with those captured from the locality of her shoulder as he cuts the remnants of lingerie from her body. Milena shudders, her eyes wide open yet drifting from consciousness as the progression of the sequence is severed by the sound of a woman screaming. This vocal expression is not synchronised with the image of Milena, but Netusil's dramatic gesture of dragging sheets from the bed up close to his face, an action that intimates evidence as it infers the residue and odor of a stain: he beseeches Alex to confess.

Between the body, language and technology, gestures trace the complex relation of history, memory and the image of Woman in narrative cinema. In *Bad Timing*, the forgetting of feminine desire is sketched as the miswriting or false recollection of a scenography that reveals the operations of a gendered economy of knowledge and power. In the final section of the film, on a sidewalk in New York, Alex catches sight of Milena in quiet conversation with her friends. As she looks back in silence, a scar, the index of a body that lives and suffers, traces the fall of her neck. Her refusal of a verbal response is marked by a moment of stasis – she pauses as she turns toward him – a gesture and image in which the causal threads of body, language and memory converge in the disquiet of the everyday, of the latent unease of the cinematic articulation of feminine desire at the borderlines of what is (il)legible to the "language" and subject positions of narrative cinema as a socially invested space.

Notes

1. The tutoring of the body into a social and cultural form is made visible through the materiality and system of cinematographic representation as a series of still images that belie the illusion of movement and the increasingly complex temporalities of the emergent narrative form of cinema.

2. The symbolic refers to the effects of a social order and language on the formation of subjectivity according to the demands of a paternal authority, which is dependent on the suppression the feminine.

3. The misdirection constituted by this sleight of hand reveals a level of interpretation. The mediation of reading the gesture through the translation of a bodily register into language, dispels the immediacy of response and betrays the work of conscious recognition which is already in the dimension of meaning (Merleau-Ponty, 1964, pp. 7–8; Said, 1967, p. 62).

4. Ross notes that in the women's films of the 1940s, romantic relationships were based on "intimate confessions and a sharing of emotions and life stories" (1995, p. 198). A similar practice is sketched out in conversations between Milena and Alex, but diminished or refuted by the distraction marked by a gesture. This can be found in Milena's momentary captivation in the flight of an insect as Alex speaks evocatively of the changing architecture of a city in which he feels at home.

5. Their exchange escalates as she riles him and is met with the ill-judged response of a violent and sexual encounter.

6. Although the bodily tics and expressions of Alex and Milena rarely connect in conversation, those of Alex and Netusil are so entwined, so insidious that they seem to "establish a parallel, a duet, a duel" (Maslin, 1980, p. 70). Following Netusil's comment that "we are not unalike", the sequence divulges a close-up of his arms interwoven with those of Alex, clasping the sleeve of his jacket and imploring a confession, whilst the camera turns to focus of the repetitive movement of Alex's hands as a mark of his hesitation to respond.

7. My development of an analysis of gesture in *Bad Timing* draws from my short essay on cinematic excess: Watkins, Excess, Cinematic. 2013. *Encyclopaedia of Film Theory*. eds. E. Branigan and W. Buckland. New York: Routledge, pp. 178–181.

8. Wallesch, 2004, pp. 389–399 addresses Freud's early neurological studies of aphasia as the forgetting of words.

9. Heath notes that Charcot's photographic studies are attentive to the duration of the hysteric's symptoms. The images as a sequence emphasise repetition rather than "disorder" and so call for interpretation (Heath, 1978, pp. 57–58).

10. In his 'Introduction' to Laplanche's *Essays on Otherness*, Fletcher refers to the "excess of message", which eludes each interlocutor's understanding of a slip of the tongue in conversation, where neither "causal series" is determinate of meaning (1999, p. 45).

11. In the shots that precede this exchange as they cross the border, Milena's discontent belies their interaction. As Stefan hands his passport to Milena, he does not turn to see, as the spectator does toward the periphery of image, the curiosity in her expression at the familiarity of this action. The tilt of her head and the turning of the passport in her hands constitute a gesture that denotes her comprehension and unease at the familiarity of his actions.

12. A close-up of Alex's wrist watch set at almost 20 minutes past 10 o'clock betrays the delay that he manipulates in responding to Milena's plea. The image of the watch precedes a shot of Milena in her apartment where the rhythmic ticking of a clock can be heard, measuring each second closer to irrecoverable damage from her overdose.

13. Also see Gledhill's seminal 1978 analysis of the female voice in Klute.

14. Silverman's analysis is specific to *Klute* and does not extend to *Bad Timing* (1988, pp. 81–84). The heroine of *Klute*, Bree differs from Milena as she speaks in a voice-over to offer a perspective that undermines the content of the image.

15. Laplanche revisits Freud's notes on gesture, parapraxis and verbal communication in a critical reading of Lacan's conceptualisation of language as univocal (1999, pp. 91–93).

References

Brooke, M. (2007). DVD review: Nicolas Roeg. *Sight and Sound, 17*, 86–87.

Butler, J. (1989). Sexual ideology and phenomenological description: A feminist critique of Merleau-Ponty's *Phenomenology of Perception*. In J. Allen & I. M. Young (Eds.), *The thinking Muse, feminism and modern French philosophy* (pp. 85–100). Bloomington, IN: Indiana University Press.

de Lauretis, T. 1984. *Now and nowhere: Roeg's Bad Timing. Alice doesn't: Feminism, semiotics, cinema* (pp.84–102). Bloomington, IN: Indiana University Press.

Doane, M. A. (1991). *Femme fatales, feminism, film theory, psychoanalysis*. London: Routledge.

Doane, M. A. (2002). *The emergence of cinematic, modernity, contingency, the archive*. Cambridge, MA: Harvard University Press.

Fletcher, J. (1999). Introduction: Psychoanalysis and the question of the other. In J. Laplanche (Ed.), *Essays on otherness*. Oxon: Routledge.

Freud, S. (1953/1891). *On Aphasia*. London: Imago Publishing.

Freud, S., & Breuer, J. (1895/1991). *Studies on hysteria*. (J. Strachey [1953], Trans.). London: Penguin.

Freud, S. (1901/1991). *The psychopathology of everyday life*. (J. Strachey, ed., A. Tyson [1966], Trans.). London: Penguin.

Gledhill, C. 1978. *Klute* part I: A contemporary film noir and feminist criticism. In E. Ann Kaplan (Ed.), *Women and film noir* (pp. 26–35). London: BFI.

Grosz, E. (1989). *Sexual subversions, three french feminists*. New South Wales: Allen & Unwin.

Heath, S. (1975a). Film and system: Terms of analysis part I. *Screen, 16*, 7–77.

Heath, S. (1975b). Film and system: Terms of analysis part II. *Screen, 16*, 91–113.

Heath, S. (1978). Difference. *Screen, 19*, 51–112.

Jones, E. (1911). The psychopathology of everyday life. *The American Journal of Psychology, 22*, 477–527.

Kendon, A. (2004). *Gesture: Visible action as utterance*. Cambridge: Cambridge University Press.

Laplanche, J. (1999). *Essays on otherness*. Oxon: Routledge.

Lapsley, R. (2009). Cinema, the impossible, and a psychoanalysis to come. *Screen, 50*, 14–24.

Merleau-Ponty, M. (1964). The Primacy of Perception. In M. E. James (Ed.), Evanston, IL: Northwestern University Press.

Miller, T. (1994/2004). *Psycho's Bad Timing*: The sensual obsessions of film theory. In T. Miller & R. Stam (Eds.), *A companion to film theory* (pp. 323–332). Oxford: Blackwell.

Mulvey, L. (1975/1989). *Visual pleasure and narrative cinema. Visual and other pleasures* (pp. 14–26). London: Palgrave Macmillan.

Mulvey, L. (1981/1989). *Afterthoughts on "Visual pleasure and narrative cinema" [visual and other pleasures* (pp. 29–38). Palgrave Macmillan: London.

Maslin, J. 1980, September 21. Film: Roeg *Bad Timing* starring art Garfunkel. *New York Times*, p. 70.

Penman, I. (1980). *Bad Timing*: A codifying love story [review]. *Screen, 21*, 107–110.

Pym, J. (1980). Ungratified desire: Nicolas Roeg's *Bad Timing*. *Sight and Sound, 49*, 111–112.

Roeg, N. (Director). (1980). *Bad timing*. Great Britain.

Ross, T. (1995). Nicolas Roeg's *Bad Timing*, fabulising the author among the ruins of romance. In L. Jayamanne (Ed.), *Kiss me deadly: Feminism and cinema for the moment* (pp. 180–220). Sydney: Power Publications.

Said, E. (1967). Labyrinth of incarnations: The essays of Maurice Merleau-Ponty. *The Kenyon Review, 29*, 54–68.

Silverman, K. (1988). *The acoustic mirror: The female voice in psychoanalysis and cinema*. Bloomington, IN: Indiana University Press.

Väliaho, P. (2010). *Mapping the moving image: Gesture, thought and cinema 1900*. Amsterdam: Amsterdam University Press.

Wallesch, C. W. (2004). History of Aphasia: Freud as Aphasiologist. *Aphasiology, 18*, 389–399.

Wilson, K. (1999). Time, space and vision: Nicolas Roeg's don't look now. *Screen, 40*, 277–294.

Image as gesture: notes on Aernout Mik's *Communitas* and the modern political film

Patricia Pisters

Faculteit der Geesteswetenschappen, Capaciteitsgroep Media & Cultuur, Amsterdam, The Netherlands

Walking through Aernout Mik's exhibition *Communitas,* dwelling in the encounter with the people and situations in front of and on the screens, one is struck by the cinematic and political qualities of the gestures in these powerful video installations. In this article I will develop some film-philosophical reflections on the silent performative force of the image as gesture and as politics. Drawing on Giorgio Agamben's "Notes on Gesture", Robert Bresson's "Notes on the Cinematographer" and Gilles Deleuze's reflections on the modern political film, I will contextualize Mik's work in the tradition of the modern political film. Being in between language and image, a go-between that connects people, things and the world, the gesture belongs to ethics and politics more than to aesthetics. Characters in Mik's work perform gestures that express the possibility of resistance and of the possibility of a shared community, a gesture which is shared by the artist, his actors and the visitors of the exhibition alike. Just like the modern political film the video works manage to change our perception of familiar situations via a simple tic, a spasm or a shared bodily posture.

Walking through Aernout Mik's exhibition *Communitas,* dwelling in the encounter with the people and situations in front of and on the screens, one is struck by the cinematic and political qualities of the gestures in these powerful video installations.[1] In this article some film-philosophical reflections on the silent performative force of the image as gesture and as politics will be explored.

White suits, black hats

A good place to start Aernout Mik's exhibition *Communitas* is the three-channel video installation *White Suits, Black Hats*, composed of archival images of the EYE Film Institute Netherlands. Mik (2012) selected silent images from the 1920s and 1930s from the colonial Dutch Indies presented on parallel screens: recordings of parades, funerals, dances and physical exercise but also images of tea and rubber factories, work in the rise fields, traders, all kinds of Dutch companies ranging from Heineken's beer brewery to the "Oranje Hotel" and other scenes of daily routines in the Dutch Indies such as missionaries in action.

While Mik usually presents original material in his installations, as a found footage piece *White Suits, Black Hats* nevertheless offers significant entrance points into his work, firstly because the images are silent. Most of Mik's video installations are without sound and therefore have a silent cinema quality.[2] The silence of the images emphasizes quite literally the bodily movements and gestures of the people on screen. On a more abstract level this also allows us to see the image itself as gesture, rather than as spectacle. In the first part of this article I will elaborate on this notion of the image as gesture as discussed by Giorgio Agamben. Besides silent cinema, the cinematographic style of Robert Bresson will be another important reference to develop this idea in respect to Aernout Mik's work.

Secondly, implicated actually in the idea of the image as gesture, but explicitly evident in the historical political situation of the colonial times in which the images from *White Suits, Black Hats* were made, is a reflection on the political and ethical dimensions of images. The images of *White Suits, Black Hats* are from a period of emerging political transition. While the colonial power relations between the colonizers and the colonized were still in place in the Dutch Indies, elsewhere in the world communist revolutions had already inspired emancipatory movements for "the people". Eisenstein's revolution films, for instance, are exemplary for the classic political film, where the ruling classes are resisted with an enormous sense of community and intensive hope for revolutionary change for "the people". But what happened with this notion of "the people?" In the second part of this article I will look at the development of the modern political film as put forward by Gilles Deleuze and discuss the ways in which Aernout Mik's work is a form of political cinema with other means.

Notes on gesture

Let me first return to the silent cinema qualities of Mik's work. In film history and theory, the visuality (or muteness) of the moving image has often been related to the realm of the spectacle, to the dominance of the eye, the frenzy of the visible and the ideology of the power of the gaze, often controlled by patriarchal or imperial masters. Giorgio Agamben's short text, "Notes on Gesture" claims an alternative genealogy for grasping the powers of the moving image (Agamben, 2000, pp. 48–60). Agamben starts his reflections on cinema by arguing that the scientific experiments of Gilles de la Tourette on the human gait allowed for a new take on gesture, walking being one of the most basic gestures. De la Tourette is of course mostly known for the syndrome named after him, and I will return to that condition later on. But first it is important to note the connection that Agamben makes between Tourette's studies on motion, such as his footprint reproductions and the invention of the cinematograph by Muybridge and Marey. Agamben claims that humanity had lost the gesture in the early nineteenth century because they had become frozen in symbolic representation, for instance, the gesture as an expression of moral character in Balzac's work, and given way to the interiority of psychic life (2000, pp. 50–53). Science and cinema, according to Agamben "leads images back to the homeland of gesture" (2000, p. 56).

For Agamben "cinema has its center in the gesture" and therefore it goes beyond aesthetics and "belongs essentially to the realm of ethics and politics" (2000, p. 56). So by focusing on the gesture, a certain ethics and politics of the image is foregrounded. Agamben explains that gesture differs from *action* and from *making*. Gesture stems from the word "gerere", "*to carry or to carry on*". And thus what characterizes gesture is that something is carried or carried on: something is being endured and supported (2000, p. 57). The gesture as *endurance* breaks with the idea that action (or producing something) needs to have a goal, an end:

Nothing is more misleading for an understanding of gesture, therefore, than representing, on the one hand, a sphere of means as addressing a goal (for example, marching seen as a means of moving the body from point A to point B) and, on the other hand, a separate and superior sphere of gesture as a movement that has its end in itself (for example, dance seen as an aesthetic dimension). [...] If dance is gesture, it is so, rather, because it is nothing more than the endurance and the exhibition of the media character of corporeal movements. *The gesture is the exhibition of medialtiy: it is the process of making a means visible as such.* It allows the emergence of the being-in-a-medium of human beings and thus it opens the ethical dimension for them. (Agamben, 2000, p. 58)

Human beings in "pure and endless mediality", that is what gesture relays. Agamben argues that "cinema's essential 'silence' (which is not necessarily related to the presence or absence of a sound track)" shows us the sphere of pure means, the gesturality of human beings (2000, pp. 59–60). "The gesture is essentially always a gesture of not being able to figure out something in language" (2000, p. 59). So the gesture is neither image nor language, but mediation between the two. In this mediation, the gesture also implies a shared endurance in time, a participation in the world in its making, in an endless go-between of things and people. In gesture, we weave the fabric of the world between life and art. Mik's *Touch, Rise and Fall* can perhaps elucidate what the gesture as endurance and mediality means in concrete art practice.

Touch, rise and fall

The situation that *Touch, Rise and Fall* makes us encounter is very familiar – at least to post 9/11 humanity in the grip of fear and control. The screens of the two-channel installation are placed on the floor and as visitor we can physically connect to the situations on the screens. We see people at airports, a typical shared "non-place" of contemporary modernity (Augé, 1995). They are waiting, enduring time together (Figure 1). While I

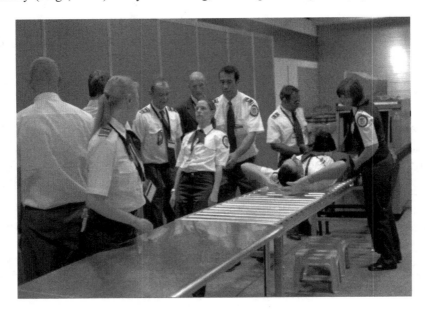

Figure 1. *Touch, Rise and Fall*, two-channel video installation (Mik, 2008).
Note: Courtesy carlier l gebauer, Berlin.

was sitting on a bench opposite of the work, other visitors sat on the floor for a while, just like the tired passengers at the airport or walked along the line of people in the image. The gestures of walking and of waiting, very literally started to make connections between art and life. We not only recognize the situation but also connect to it due to the way the video installations allow a human scale in the events. The words, "touch, rise and fall", also indicate this dimension of the gesture that is expressed in this work where there is no total divide between us, the visitors and the actors.

Nor is there an enormous difference between the security officers and the passengers. We see moments where the security officers are "killing time", fighting playfully with one another; their office space looks like a joyless bedroom in an asylum centre rather than an office. At other moments they pull themselves through the security scanner or they sink on the floor in bored waiting – just like the passengers. But as they put on their blue gloves, this seems to be the cue for stepping into their assigned role and starting to search all luggage. Dolls and stuffed animals bought at the gift shop are considered as suspicious and cut open, an action which seems all the more violent in light of the common humanity that was exposed just moments before. And then, all of a sudden, after all the checking and cutting, everybody is simply allowed to pass through the checkpoints. The alarm lights are all red, but no bag nor body is searched any longer. The security guards stand inoperative, almost mesmerized and no longer able to perform their controlling gestures, perhaps realizing the endlessness of it all.

In these moments we can sense the difference with television programmes such as *Border Security* (Seven Network, Australia, 2004) that has hundreds of episodes in which security personnel are followed at the Australian airport borders, looking for criminals, drug dealers and illegal immigrants. They are actually experts on reading gestures and body language. And they are all doing their jobs in full sincerity. But these television images are no gestures in Agamben's definition, they remain on the side of representation and more specifically on the side of representing the law. The common gesture of mediated and shared humanity is not given to us. The possibility for resistance is not part of these series. This does not mean that this is not possible on television, but it is not given *in Border Security* where a voice-over explains the rules and regulations and the "blue gloves" never leave the hands of the officers to humanly touch, rise and fall.

Middlemen

Let me move back to the exhibition. From where I was sitting and observing *Touch, Rise and Fall,* I could also see another installation, *Middlemen* from 2001. This work was made before 9/11 and is maybe one of the most well-known works of the exhibition. Here again, the scene is familiar, certainly after 9/11 and the subsequent financial crisis that we are still in. And yet it is eerily strange as well. Here, we see stockbrokers in a crisis situation, not being able to act or make a deal; the only movements left are gestures of the people in the scene: some characters write aimlessly something on their note block; others sit down moving in a stiff way, one man is running back and forth, others have bodily tics or make sudden spasmodic jerking movements (Figure 2).

Again, from my bench I noticed that visitors immediately connected to these movements, some even embodying the intensities of the gestures by imitating the spasms and tics. In the installation itself I was also affected by the sometimes

Figure 2. *Middlemen*, single-channel video installation (Mik, 2001).
Note: Courtesy carlier 1 gebauer, Berlin.

spasmodic movements of the camera itself, making sudden zoom movements, literally shaking the image. And at one point one of the machines in the middle turns around, uncontrolled by anyone. We have here an ecological crisis landscape where people, objects and technology move on the same level and to which we can connect on an embodied level. In "Notes on Gesture" Agamben addresses this loss of control of motor and speech coordination in Tourette's syndrome and remarks that after Tourette's description of the disorder it seemed to have disappeared for decades, only to reappear in the 1970s when Oliver Sacks reports three cases of Tourettism in a few minutes while walking along the streets of New York. He then puts forward the hypotheses that:

> in order to explain this disappearance is that in the meantime ataxia (lack of voluntary coordination of muscular movement), tics, and dystonia (abnormal muscle contractions and twisting) had become the norm ant that at some point everybody had lost control of their gestures and was walking and gesticulating frantically. (Agamben, 2000, p. 52)

This is where we are in *Middlemen*: a visionary point of view on our current situation where we all seem to have lost control, in any case collectively in the financial world and to which we can only connect by uncontrolled gestures. Upon closer inspection we see that one of the persons is actually a mannequin, a doll figure that imitates the movements of his human double or is it the other way around. Most of the time Mik does not use professional actors and so his characters do not perform in any conventional way. They all seem more like living dolls, puppets that are in the grips of something intolerable.

Notes on the cinematograph

This style of performing brings Mik's work in relation to a precursor in cinema, the films of Robert Bresson. In his "Notes on the Cinematographer" Bresson reflects in short and powerfully poetic statements about his filmmaking: "your film is not made for a walk of the eyes but to be penetrated by it, to be completely absorbed by it" (Bresson, 1977, p. 97, my translation). We recognize here the connecting, inserting and interfacing power of the sensibility of the gesture. It is impossible to do justice to Bresson's thoughts and observations, but one element is of particular interest in reference to the video installations of Mik. Instead of actors Bresson prefers to talk about "models". Like Mik, he mostly worked with amateurs, actors without acting habits who are able to perform in such a sober and blank way that they lay something bare to the camera that does not seem to belong to themselves, through gesture, excavating inward movements that endure at a deeper level: "If, on screen, the mechanisms disappears and the phrases you have made them say, the gestures you have made them make, have become one with your models, with your film, with you – then a miracle" (Bresson, 1977, pp. 41–42, my translation).

So what Bresson wants to bring out of his models, is an intensity that lies beneath the overload of images that we know, to reveal "the connections that wait beings and things to live" (1977, p. 81, my translation). Bresson's film style is very restraint and his "models" will never express any psychological or dramatic emotions. And yet the "cinematographer" explores a new way of sensing, his style is one of affection-images, as Gilles Deleuze characterized Bresson's films (Deleuze, 1986, pp. 108–111). It is a tactile style, full of hands in close-up and other techniques to make the felt and the gesture primary. For instance, Bresson's last film, *L'Argent* (1983), presents interesting parallels to Mik's style. In *L'Argent,* forged money is around and at the beginning of the film we see how a simple worker, Yvon Targe, is duped by a shopkeeper who has decided to pass on the forged money that he himself accepted earlier that day. Because of the restrained way of filming, every shot in medium close-up fragments filmed spaces and brought out the gestures of the actors more than anything else. Even with sound this is a "silent film" in the sense that Agamben meant in his "Notes on Gesture". The blank performance of the models, in both physical and vocal performance brings out intensity in jerks. Because of the lack of orientation – we never get a full establishing shot that allows spatial orientation – aesthetically these images have a vertiginous effect. Space is composed fragment by fragment. And in this way, precisely because we cannot orientate ourselves, the image becomes affectively expressive, tactile and full of potentiality. As indicated, Deleuze has defined these as affection-images that work directly on our senses first, before they mean anything. This type of constructed space Deleuze calls "any-space-whatever":

> Any-space-whatever is not an abstract universal, in all times, in all places. It is a perfectly singular space, which has merely lost its homogeneity, that is, the principle of its metric relations or the connection of its own parts, so that the linkages can be made in an infinite number of ways. It is a space of virtual conjunction, grasped as pure locus of the possible. (Deleuze, 1986, p. 109)

Back in the exhibition space, watching the puppet-like performances in *Middlemen*, interchanged with looking at *Touch, Rise and Fall*, Bresson's style comes to mind. The dominant use of medium close-ups, often we see only feet or middle parts of the body, as well as the breaking of the image over several screens from different vantage points.

This breaks up and fragments the space, creating a similar affective style that transcends any psychology: characters are not motivated by a cause-and-effect chain but express and impersonal event, a gesture of the world. The "non-place" of the airport then turns into an "any-space-whatevers" full of potentialities. And this gives us the feeling that, in spite of all the control and loss of control, something is still possible, and that a connection can be made. Just like in *L'Argent* some police officers step into a bakery not to arrest somebody but just to buy some baguettes, such kind of a connecting gesture can be made in Mik's world.

Several scenes of *L'Argent* take place in court. Yvon Targe is innocently accused of forging money. He gets away the first time, but because of the scandal loses his job and gets involved in a hold-up. He appears in court a second time, again based on false accusations and ends up in prison. After three years he is released, during which time his little daughter has died, his wife left him. He then makes a conscious choice to become the criminal he was judged to be, kills several people and turns himself in: this time guilty "by choice".

Shifting sitting

Thinking of these moments in *L'Argent* the next installation *Shifting Sitting* (2011) presents another court scene.[3] Here, a Berlusconi lookalike figure appears in the benches. The personal and collective dramas of money as presented in *L'Argent* and *Middlemen* have become completely political. In *Shifting Sitting,* we don't have an innocent man who is wrongly convicted and who in turn takes his fate upon him, but we have a guilty man who knows how to shift and bend the media, politics and the law to make him appear innocent. What is more, judges, accused and public take at certain moments each other's places. Many people even chose literally the "mask" of Berlusconi. We could say that perhaps here we have entered in the nightmare of the gesture – where everything connects indeed, and in such an uncontrollable way that money, politics and justice have become unpredictably interchangeable (Figure 3).

In gestural terms we can say that the whole system has become spasmodic, the trias politica, the separate legislative, executive and judicial bodies gone awry. The whole situation seems so surreal that it seems laughable though crying would be more appropriate. Is there a way to wake up from this nightmare? Let us move to the last installation that I would like to discuss, *Communitas* (2010) the centre piece of this exhibition where the questions of politics presents itself again, under the burning question of its possibility, under all these conditions of crisis. In our contemporary age and day, it is still possible to have something "in common?"

Notes on the political film

In cinema this notion of the common (that binds "the people") has found its expression in political cinema. Here I am referring again to the cinema books of Gilles Deleuze where he remarks that the political film, such as the Russian revolution films of Eisenstein, has changed. The biggest modern political filmmakers – Deleuze situates modern cinema after Second World War, starting with Italian neo-realism ranging from Alain Resnais to the Egyptian films of Yousef Chahine and Palestinian films of Michel Khleifi – have this in common: they know how to show "the people", who are always present in classic political cinema and also "what is missing" (Deleuze, 1989, p. 215). This is the first big difference with classical and modern political cinema. In Soviet

Figure 3.   Shifting Sitting, three-channel video installation (Mik, 2011).
Note: Courtesy carlier 1 gebauer, Berlin.

cinema, but also in American cinema (Ford, Vidor) there are people. In all the colonized parts of the world, too, at the beginning of the decolonization struggles after Second World War there is "a people" that can be addressed in order to raise emancipatory consciousness. But this does not last for long: the euphoria of independence changes soon into disappointments about dictatorships, crisis and migration. And so the acknowledgement of a people who are missing becomes the new basis on which political cinema is founded: "Art, and especially cinematographic art, must take part in this task: not that of addressing a people, which is presupposed already there, but of contributing to the invention of a people" (Deleuze, 1989, p. 217).

The second big difference with classical political cinema is that the political and the private are no longer separate. "[I]n modern political cinema, where no boundary survives to provide a minimum distance: the private affair merges with the social or political immediate" (Deleuze, 1989, p. 218). And so, raising awareness and revolution is no longer the basis of political cinema. No longer is it a "becoming conscious" that makes a film political. Rather political cinema consists of

> putting everything into a trance, the people and its masters, and the camera itself, pushing everything into a state of aberration, in order to communicate violence as well as to make private business pass into the political, and political affairs into the private. (Deleuze, 1989, p. 219)

Showing these conditions of the impossible is what constitutes the modern political film.

The third difference that Deleuze distinguishes is related to the fact that the people only exist in the condition of minority, which is why they are missing. The modern political film has been created on this fragmentation, this break-up of the people. We get shattered states of emotions or drives, a plurality of stories and intertwined lives. One of the consequences is that individuals get a different, more gestural in Agamben's words, relation to the world: no longer one of representation but of resonance, of contact between inside and out, between the private and political. In Deleuze's words:

> Communication of the world and the I in a fragmented world and in a fragmented I which are constantly being exchanged. It is as if the whole memory of the world is set down on the oppressed people, and the whole memory of the I comes into play […] The arteries of the people to which I belong, or people of my arteries. (Deleuze 1989, p. 221)

The last words are a reference to director Yousef Chahine's embodied relation to Alexandria ('Alexandria-I, I-Alexandria' in the Alexandria Trilogy: *Alexandria … Why?* (1979); *An Egyptian Story* (1982) and *Alexandria Again and Forever* (1989)).

The final difference between classic and modern political film is that the author/filmmaker/artist needs to decolonize all kinds of myth, and becomes a sort of intercessor, becoming part of his film:

> The author takes a step towards his characters, but the characters take a step towards the author: double becoming. Story-telling is not an impersonal myth, but neither is it a personal fiction: it is a word in act, a speech-act (or a performance) through which the character continually crosses the boundaries which would separate his private business from politics, and which itself produces collective utterances. (Deleuze 1989, p. 222)

So what we see here is that the modern political film does not produce "the myth of a past people" even though everything is permeated with memories, but it produces "the story-telling" or performance of "a people to come" (Deleuze, 1989, p. 223). The work of art creates itself as a foreign language in a dominant language, precisely in order to express an impossibility of living under domination. So let me make all this more concrete with an example of a modern political film, to point out the connections to both the work and style of Bresson and the video installations of Aernout Mik.

Elia Suleiman's trilogy on 'the Palestinian situation', *Chronical of a Disappearance* (1996), *Divine Intervention* (2002) and *The Time that Remains* (2009), very powerfully shows what the modern political film entails. Far from making cinema a matter of representing the people, a raising of consciousness, he shows that the modern political film is made under conditions of the impossible. Elsewhere I discuss these films more elaborately (Pisters, 2012), but for now it is important to see how as director Suleiman, as a silent witness, walking, observing, waiting, in his films, becomes part of their performance: a mutual becoming of the filmmaker, his characters and the world. The film and the filmmaker, insert themselves quite literally in the fabric of fiction and reality, which is not an impersonal myth and nor purely his personal story. Rather he performs a silent embodied, endured, engaged gesture as a sort of Bressonian model. In a striking scene, some Israeli soldiers shout through their megaphone to some dancing youngsters, who simply ignore the commands. But while commanding, the soldier's body cannot help moving to the rhythm of the music. What we sense is a mutual sharing of rhythms and intensities of life, a mutual becoming, even of "oppressor" and "oppressed". It is this affective level of a common humanity that Bresson searches in his style as well. The film in itself – as film – is political because it becomes part of the invention of a people. It exists, not just as a fantasy but operates as a material/immaterial gesture between the possible and the impossible.

Communitas

I think we have already seen, for instance in *Touch, Rise and Fall* and in the way that visitors of the exhibition embody the affects and gestures of the people on the screens, how Mik's work follows a poetics of the modern political film. While all of Mik's installations are political in this sense of the gestures, the fabrics of the world that we share, *Communitas* refers even more explicitly to the idea of "the people". Set in the Palace of Culture and Science in Warsaw, this building that was a gift of Stalin to the Polish people in the 1950s, was used for party meetings. However, while the location is very specific, the space is fragmented over several screens and the causes or aims of the meetings are undefined (Figure 4). What we see is not a political meeting with an aim or a programme but a people in the making through gesture, as a pure means, as a "Means without End" (Agamben, 2000). Quite literally, *Communitas* presents as a gesture as/of a shared feeling of resistance. Or, again quite literally, as a gesture as endurance in Agamben's sense: the video installation has a duration that invites visitors to participate in the endurance of the political gesture. The people on screen in the rally also eat there, and fall asleep.

Or, perhaps they have not fallen asleep – but have died. The image stays persistently open to all these possibilities, including the violence that is implied. The motionless bodies in red velvet chairs recall the virtuality of our collective memory that is implied in all of Mik's images: we all remember the horrific images of Chechen rebels and hostages that died in their red theatre chairs of a Moscow theatre in 2002 through the violence and the poisonous gas that was used to break the resistance. We cannot help seeing that violent dimension of the images as well, that violent dimension of the political gesture.

Figure 4.   *Communitas*, three-channel video installation (Mik, 2010).
Note: Courtesy carlier l gebauer, Berlin.

And yet, under the conditions of the people that are missing, it is the "performative energy", as Aernout Mik refers to his work in the exhibition catalogue, and of the possibility of any kind or form of resistance that we share here in the work (Mik in Milewski, 2011, p. 211). Or to quote him more fully:

> There are all these streams of action that suddenly crystallize into a certain moment, like the possibility of resistance by the people. These appear almost like after-images that viewers carry with them and which can develop into their own cells of possibility. They offer something, and that's how I want to work. That's why it's political, even if few people in the political world would have any idea how to relate to my work. (Mik, 2013, p. 4)

Insurgence

In 2012, in Montreal, in the wake of the global occupation movements, students in Montreal protested for seven months, everyday and every night against the raise of tuition fees for higher education. In the end they did win, although maybe not for long. However, what was more important, what made this movement and this film political is the collective gesture of resistance, the shared affective energy that, in the words of Aernout Mik could be even called an erotics of the group:

> an erotic sameness in which members of the group are all equally part of that group and physically engaged with each other or determined by each other. There is something that connects and spreads through the group and sometimes spreads from people into objects, creating a kind of animism. (Mik, 2013, p. 3)

This is what we can feel and endure in the collective film *Insurgence* which was made by the Collective Cinema Epopee, 2012. But this is what also can be sensed as the political gestures of the people at the squares in the Arab world, in the park in Turkey, in the streets of Brazil.[4]

And this is what we can feel in the work of Aernout Mik. In the exhibition space as a collective space, we start to connect to the people on the screens – each one of us on his or her own way, taking out new images or new perceptions on known images, and perhaps some energy for our own gesture of resistance whenever possible or necessary. Aernout Mik as a "political filmmaker" in his own singular way shows us that art and life are made of the same gestures where the common can be found. In a way we are all Bressonian models, knowing or at least sensing that "life cannot be rendered by photographic recopying of life, but by the secret laws in the midst of which [we] can feel models [ourselves as models] moving" (Bresson, 1977, p. 77). Here, we have the landscape of a political ecology where everything connects.

What struck me upon leaving the exhibition space was that the silence of the works, also made the visitors silent – the exhibition space felt like a church, all I heard was sometimes somebody coughing, some whispers, footsteps every now and then. But in this collective space, there is no priest, no leader pointing the way – all there is, are images as gestures, and gestures as images to connect to in a thousand different ways. Leaving the museum, the images of the installations still returning in my mind, I felt like having been a "model" in a political film.

Notes

1. The exhibition *Communitas* took place between 4 May and 25 August 2013 at the Stedelijk Museum Amsterdam. This article was initially conceived for the Public Programme alongside the exhibition. See http://www.stedelijk.nl/agenda/tentoonstelling-aernout-mik-communitas. Commissioned by Teatr Dramatyczny, Warsaw and the Biennial de Sao Paulo with additional support from the Mondriaanfonds.
2. *Raw Footage* (2006) and *Convergencies* (2007) that are made from found documentary material from among others Reuters and ITN are with sound.
3. Commission by Jeu de Paume, Paris; Museum Folkwang, Essen; Stedelijk Museum, Amsterdam; additional support by the Mondriaanfonds, the Netherlands Filmfund and the European Cultural Foundation.
4. I am referring here to the Arab Spring revolution on the Tahrir Square in Cairo on 2011, the Gezi park demonstrations on the Taksim Square in Istanbul in 2013 and the social protests in Sao Paulo, Rio and other Brazilian cities in 2013.

References

Agamben, G. (2000). *Means without end: Notes on politics*. (V. Benetti & C. Cesarino, Trans.). Minneapolis and London: University of Minnesota Press.

Augé, M. (1995). *Non-places: An introduction to supermodernity*. (J. Howe, Trans.). New York and London: Verso.

Bresson, R. (1977). *Notes sur le Cinématographe* [Notes on the cinematograph]. Paris: Gallimard.

Bresson, R. (Director). (1983). *L'Argent*. France: Eos Film and France 3 Cinema.

Chahine, Y. (Director). (1979). *Alexandria, Why?* Egypt: MISR International Films.

Chahine, Y. (Director). (1982). *An Egyptian Story*. Egypt: MISR International Films.

Chahine, Y. (Director). (1989). *Alexandria Again and Forever*. France: La Sept/MISR International Films.

Collective Cinema Epopee. (Directors). (2012). *Insurgence*. Canada: Cinema Politica.

Deleuze, G. (1986). *Cinema 1: The movement-image*. (H. Tomlinson and B. Habberjam, Trans.). London: The Athlone Press.

Deleuze, G. (1989). *Cinema 2: The time-image*. (H. Tomlinson & R. Galeta, Trans.). London: The Athlone Press.

Mik, A. (Video Artist). (2001). *Middlemen*. Berlin: Carlier l Gebauer.

Mik, A. (Video Artist). (2008). *Touch, rise and fall*. Berlin: Carlier l Gebauer.

Mik, A. (Video Artist). (2010). *Communitas*. Berlin: Carlier l Gebauer.

Mik, A. (Video Artist). (2011). *Shifting sitting*. Paris: Jeu de Paume and Stedelijk Museum.

Mik, A. (Video Artist). (2012). *White suits, black hats*. Amsterdam: EYE Film Institute Netherlands.

Mik, A. (2013). *'Group erotics' interview with Aernout Mik, part II*. Art It. Retrieved July, 2013, from http://www.art-it.asia/u/admin_ed_feature_e/g3eGAEolFRrVKTW9HDat/?lang=en

Milewski, T. (ed.). (2011). *Aernout Mik Communitas*. Amsterdam: Aernout Mik Stedelijk Museum Amsterdam & Edition Folkwang/Steidl.

Pisters, P. (2012). *The neuro-image: A Deleuzian film-philosophy of digital screen culture*. Stanford: Stanford University Press.

Suleiman, E. (Director). (1996). *Chronicle of a disapearance*. Palestine: Centre National de la Cinématographie (CNC), Independent Television Service (ITVS), Media Programme of the European Community.

Suleiman, E. (Director). (2002). *Divine Intervention*. France: Film Stiftung Nordrhein-Westfalen, Gimages, Arte France Cinema, Ognon Pictures.

Suleiman, E. (Director). (2009). *The Time that Remains*. UK: The Film, Nazira Film, France 3 Cinema.

Monroe's gestures between trauma and ecstasy, *Nympha and Venus*: reading the cinematic gesture "Marilyn Monroe" through Aby Warburg

Griselda Pollock

Centre CATH, University of Leeds, Leeds, UK

This analysis of Marilyn Monroe's image and performance falls between theories of gesture and the work of Aby Warburg on the *pathosformel*: a formulation that encodes and transmits affects through configurations of the imaged body. Warburg suggested that we read images as condensations and mnemonic forms of passion capable of holding and transmitting such formulations. It is this function that accounts for persistence, survival and recurrence of formulations in contradistinction to explanations that elevate one culture's aesthetic forms and naturalise their capacity to recur and be used by later cultures, as for instance, Greek iconographies and mythologies serving as standards which later cultures return to and use because of inherent aesthetic superiority. Refusing these aestheticizing and Eurocentric alibis, Warburg proposed an implicitly transcultural understanding of iconization that lies between the unbound affective condition and symbolic distanciation and representation. The image is a mediating space charged with energies that can lead to regressive acting out or to transformation akin to Freudian sublimation. By deploying Warburg's understanding of the bodily configuration and the activity of its attributes in a study of the image of Marilyn Monroe, it is possible to identify the gestures of a filmed body in a series of films that produced a representation of both sexuality and sexual subjectivity that exceeds both. The figuration of "Marilyn Monroe" counters the ascription to her person and performance of a spontaneous sexiness in order to re-read its effects in terms of the conflicts of post-war American culture oscillating between a traumatic depressive state and the ecstatic: the binaries identified by Warburg.

The gesture is the exhibition of a mediality; it is the process making a means visible as such. (Agamben, 2000, p. 58)

I propose a reading of the cinematic and photographic image of "Marilyn Monroe" as a figuration of the classical prototypes *Nympha* and *Venus*. To do so, I shall construct a picture atlas (Figure 1(a–d) and 2(a–f)) inspired obliquely and transgressively by the art historical enigma of the wordless *Mnemosyne Bilder-Atlas* created by Hamburg art historian Aby Warburg between 1926 and 1929 (Figure 2(a)), that is to say, well into the era of cinema itself (Warburg, 2003). Refusing to treat Warburg's *Bilder-Atlas* as merely a study of images of objects that yielded iconographic lineages, philosopher Giorgio Agamben insists that Warburg's project should be understood instead as a "representation in *virtual movement* of Western humanity's gestures from classical Greece to Fascism" (Agamben, 2000, p. 54, my emphasis).

Figure 1(a). Sam Shaw, Location Shoot New York 1954, silver gelatine photograph. (Courtesy of Sam Shaw Family Archives)

Figure 1(b). Sam Shaw, Location Shoot New York 1954, silver gelatine photograph. (Courtesy of Sam Shaw Family Archives)

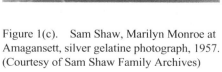

Figure 1(c). Sam Shaw, Marilyn Monroe at Amagansett, silver gelatine photograph, 1957. (Courtesy of Sam Shaw Family Archives)

Figure 1(d). Sam Shaw, Marilyn Monroe at Amagansett, silver gelatine photograph, 1957. (Courtesy of Sam Shaw Family Archives)

By means of four images on one page of my scrapbook, (Figure 1) I want to suggest that we might (re-)discover, in the middle of the twentieth century, and in the context of the American culture machine that was Hollywood cinema, the persistence, revivification and re-articulation of certain affective gestural "formulae" for "life", and furthermore, "the feminine figuration of life". Warburg traced these formulae from classical Greece via the migration of images through Indian translations and then back into the art of the European, Christian Renaissance and finally into his proto-fascist present in the 1920s by assembling a montage of images that exceeded his ability to translate them into any form of academic narrative or historical representation. He visualised and medialized an effect of transmission, persistence and revivification via images by considering images as *formulae*. A pre- or proto-cinematic use of photomechanical reproductive technology enabled him to display an assemblage of images that produced knowledge by means of the illogic of the montage whose formation defied all current art historical systems because Warburg identified images as formulae for affects that became encoded and transmitted as gestures.

Transgressing the borders between cinema and the visual arts, visual arts and the photographic image, this chapter is also an exploration of the specificity of the affect and the effect named "Marilyn Monroe" between trauma (the unspeakable affect) and ecstasy (the body possessed by affect) that occurs in the subjectivized space of the image-as-gesture where we might, borrowing psychoanalytical vocabulary, speak also of *jouissance* – intensity undecidable between pain and pleasure. The argument does not rely on any biographical or extra-cinematic interpretation of the actor. Rather, I seek to read inscriptions in the image field of still images and in "stilled" film sequences. My first "plate" (Figure 1(a–d)) juxtaposes four photographs by one professional photographer, Sam Shaw (1912–1999), of the Hollywood actor formally named Marilyn Monroe (1926–1962). The two pairs date from 1954 and 1957, respectively. Two are still images associated with a shoot for a movie, while the others were taken on a planned photo shoot.

Now known to us only in a photographic record, Aby Warburg's *Mnemosyne Bilder-Atlas* (1926–1929) (Figure 2a) comprised 40 wooden panels covered with black cloth on which Warburg mounted over 1,000 reproductions in combinations that both attempted to disclose the persistence of pictorial formulae and to trace a radically new way of understanding the history of art as a history of images as forms of gestural memory, of stored passion – *pathos* – and transmitted energy derived from what actual bodies had once done in ritual activities. Conversant with the Ritualist Circle of classical studies, Warburg worked from the premise that art emerged from ritual, and ritual from the anxieties and passions experienced and exorcised by vulnerable human beings before forces they could not control (Harrison, [1913] 1959). The nineteenth-century invention of photography enabled Warburg to create exploratory surfaces on which he could combine images as distinct from their material, often fixed-in-place and objective forms elsewhere as paintings, coins, sculptures, prints and newspaper cuttings. This montage revealed no identity, similarity, descent or influence. The Atlas format made visible, however, if not yet speakable, what could only be intimated in creating such constellations of the psychologically invested "image", namely the *persistence of affective formulation across images* that were at once paradigms of certain *pathosformulae* and the diverse instantiations that created the paradigm of a gesturality, which, however, never preceded them: a structuralist insight *avant la lettre*.

Figure 2(a).   Aby Warburg, *Mnemosyne Bilder-Atlas*, Plate 46: *Ninfa.* (Courtesy of the Warburg Institute, London)

What Warburg assembled were the *pathosformulae* – the formulations of intense affect and its potential connotations on many registers – from pagan antiquity through to their recurring re-appearance up to his own modern age of photojournalism. Although his project intriguingly co-emerged with musically accompanied "mute" and sometimes hand-tinted black-and-white cinema – his dissertation on *Primavera* (1482) and *The Birth of Venus* (1483–1485) by Sandro Botticelli was published in 1893 (Warburg, [1893] 1999) – Warburg did not engage with the cinematic image or its supplements, the film still and the publicity photograph. My pictorial atlas, as mode of research, seeks to do just that.

Can we extend Warburg's project or use his method to inquire into the potency and persistent currency of images of Marilyn Monroe as an instance of a cinematic *pathosformula* at once originating its paradigm in a new medium while being an instantiation of a deeper, longer and even mythic register in image culture that resurfaced in or returned to American cinema? Do these images (Figure 1(a–d)) offer us merely static poses before a camera or can they be read in relation to a gestural theory of cinema even though none of them is a cinematic image? Explaining Giorgio Agamben's thesis on gestural cinema, Benjamin Noys writes of the paradoxical relation between still image and cinema that delivers back to us through their medialization, as image to the second power as it were, the social gestures Agamben identifies as being lost through the fragmentation effects of chronophotographic forensic analysis of the body's actions:

> The power of cinema, and the power of cinematic montage, is to free the image from its frozen state and transform it back into gesture. It can reveal the potential of the image, and release what has been frozen in the image. Montage is not simply a repetition of the identical, because in repetition this dynamic potential of the image is returned to us. On the other hand "stoppage" in montage interrupts the stream of images. It brings the image to a stop and exhibits it as such, again as gesture. In this way these two opposing conditions, repetition and stoppage, both work to free the potential of the image and to return it to the movement of the gesture. (Noys, 2004, n.p.)

There are differences of effect and affect in this quartet which take us beyond their usual function as "photographs of Marilyn Monroe", posing in the first two instances before the camera as part of a publicity stunt during the location shooting of the film *The Seven Year Itch* (Dir. Billy Wilder, USA, 1955) and being informally photographed on the beach near her home on Long Island in the latter two. In each case, I suggest that the second of each two pairs achieves an effect distinct from their partners that is not connected to the quality of the photograph as such. To establish this argument, I shall need initially both to acknowledge and to clear a path beside the dominant discourse on Monroe and sexuality in terms specific to ideological and psychocultural readings of cinema. This enables me then to mobilize Agamben's discussion in his essay on "Gesture" in an analysis of Aby Warburg's concept of a *pathosformula*. From this digression into the history of art and one painting by Botticelli (1445–1510) in particular, I return to readings of sequences from several of Marilyn Monroe's films of the mid-1950s in which I aim to use unexpected concepts and methodologies to discern the affectivity of the work of the actor between pose, expression and gesture. Two of these opening images by Sam Shaw, I shall suggest, deliver their gesturality in the space between the classical formulae of the figurations of the feminine as "life" in the figures known as *Nympha* and *Venus*, the latter understood as goddess of Spring, rather than of sexuality in a modern sense.

Marilyn Monroe in the discourse of cinema and sexuality

"Marilyn Monroe" is a phenomenon of cinema in terms of the body she offered to cinema and how it used her body, as well as in terms of the face she created for and used in cinematic performances. Although it is agreed that the medium at which Marilyn Monroe excelled was, in fact, that of still photography (Benzel, 1991; McCann, 1988), it was as a phenomenon of Hollywood cinema during the 1950s that "Marilyn Monroe" was made the figure of sexuality and vice versa. The cinematic performances created by the actor Marilyn Monroe pushed at the limits for the representation of the sexuality in a Hollywood cinema still policed by the Hays Code (Mulvey, 1996). At the same time, scholars such as Richard Dyer argue that Monroe's screen image articulated contradictory discourses on female sexuality refashioned in and by American culture during the 1950s.

An emergent discourse on sexuality was advanced by the photomagazine for men, *Playboy*, launched in December 1953 with a photograph of Marilyn Monroe on its first cover and with the *Golden Dreams* calendar nude photograph by Tom Kelley as its first centrefold. Another, the research-based sexological discourse on female sexuality was intensified in August 1953 by the scandal attending the publication of Alfred Kinsey's revealing report on *The Sexual Behavior in Human Female* propelling ideas about female sexual anatomy and pleasure into public debate (Kinsey, [1953] 1998). Significantly, this was the same year in which cinematically, Norma Jeane Mortensen known as Norma Jeane Baker became the star body and persona "Marilyn Monroe" as a result of the back-to-back release of three films: *Niagara* (Dir. Henry Hathaway, USA, January 1953), *Gentlemen Prefer Blondes* (Dir. Howard Hawks, USA, July 1953) and *How to Marry a Millionaire* (Dir. Jean Negulesco, USA, December 1953). The year 1953 is thus the key moment of the creation and consolidation of "Marilyn Monroe" as an American icon of sexuality that traversed and figured both the *Playboy* and the Kinsey sexological discourses.

The *Playboy* pinup discourse visually shaped a female erotic body through its coy nudity, focusing intensely on a profile of breasts and buttocks, and through specific poses that proclaim this body's willing availability for masculine pleasure and the projection of masculine fantasies. What Richard Dyer names in addition as a "psycho" discourse – drawing on Freudian theory of the trajectory of "proper" feminine sexuality from infantile, phallic clitoral autoeroticism to its adult vaginal reproductive and passive orientation – can also be interpreted as a masculine fantasy. Although this discourse at least acknowledged a specific female sexuality, it did so by imagining and imaging it as oceanic and formless, engulfing its ecstatic feminine subject.

If Kinsey's report had been clear enough through the widespread empirical research about the fact that women reported the clitoral as the site of their sexual pleasure, a persistent American Freudianism ignored the clitoral in favour of a different image of the locus and effects of female sexuality: the vaginal, which has specific imagistic signifiers. Dyer reviews a range of texts from the 1950s, concluding:

> Characteristic of all these descriptions is that although notionally located in a specific place (the vagina), they evoke the experience that suffuses the whole body in a buffeting, dissolving, waterfalling ecstasy. Where the visible/visual analogue for male experience derives from the penis, for the female it is everywhere. The visual analogue of the vaginal orgasm is the female body itself. (Dyer, 2004, p. 52)

Despite the counter tendency in *Playboy* and related iconographies to bind the female body in tight costume and fetishistic accessories (Mulvey, 1989, pp. 6–13), the female body was thus also envisioned as formlessness, blur, and slackness so that Dyer insists "the presentation of her [Monroe's] body ... is the analogue of the conception of female sexual experience that is expressed in the psycho discourse as vaginal orgasm" (Dyer, 2004, p. 53).

Dyer identifies three critical moments in the Monroe oeuvre that define "Monroeness" in this field of the formless, vaginal, sexual, female body: the filmed back view of her long walk in *Niagara*, a long take of her rear when playing with bat and ball in *The Misfits* (Dir. John Huston, USA, 1961) and the scene of her standing over the subway grate in *The*

Seven Year Itch. Dyer also links facial expression to the formlessness of female sexuality: "Nowhere is this truer than in [Monroe's] most characteristic facial expression, repeated in every film, endlessly reproduced, an expression that even in a still photograph suggests movement, and was well enough described by *Time* as 'moist, half-closed eyes and moist half-opened mouth'" (Dyer, 2004, p. 54).

Although not denying the relevance of Dyer's analysis of this cinematic archive and its cultural history of sexuality and the image, I want to revisit it from a different angle mediated by Giorgio Agamben's approach to gesture that passes through the work of Aby Warburg for whom image is a remembered gesture, stored up energy, a latent promise of the return of both. Referring to Gilles Deleuze and his thesis on the movement image which abolishes the distinction between *poses éternelles* and *coupes immobiles* to produce the paradox of *coupes mobiles* (Noys, 2004), Agamben extends this analysis to the image in general in modernity in which every image carries both the potential stasis of a death mask and the reification of the gesture, while sustaining the *dynamis*: the state of that which is not yet fully realized. The death mask element, considered by André Bazin as the unconscious of all art making (1960), is taken in another direction by Agamben. The death mask effect arises from the voluntary memory while the dynamic is the flash of involuntary memory thus always linking to the whole beyond it of which it is a part. Thus, crucially for my argument, between still and moving image, every image functions now as:

> … fragments of a gesture or as *stills of a lost film* wherein only they would regain their true meaning. And that is so because of a certain kind of *litigatio*, a paralyzing power at work in every image; it is as if a silent invocation calling for the liberation of the image into gesture arose from the entire history of art. (Agamben, 2000, pp. 54–55, my emphasis)

Yet what characterizes the gesture is that nothing is being produced or acted in it, but rather "*something* is being endured and supported which otherwise disposes the meaning of the body as *signifying space*" (Agamben, 2000, p. 57, my emphasis).

Without denying the sexuality of Marilyn Monroe, I am seeking to show another dimension in the image archive that gestures towards *pathos*: affect, an intensity of a different order that contributes to our understanding of what in the images of Monroe ensures persistence and exceeds the justifiable but incomplete sociocultural and semio-ideological reading of "Monroe" (McCann, 1988; Mulvey 1996). I want to reformulate the entwinement of a distinctive mode of desirability and *pathos* through the Warburgian thesis on *Nachleben* (persistence, survival, afterlife) by which the art historian was recording a process that falls between survival, return, and recreation by means of involuntary memory flashing up to re-inject intensity into image forms that risk becoming formulaic: cheesy, tacky, Playboy sexy. "Marilyn Monroe's" difference from the pinup, cheesecake and Hollywood eroticism through which she emerged belongs then in a history of the image rather than just cinema, in the field of affective gesture and the body as *signifying space*.

Pose, gesture, expression: Warburg's *Mnemosyne Bilder-Atlas*

Confronting this archive of image traces of performances before moving and still photography, the former being its own composite of stillness and sequencing that generates the becoming in each still and the memory of its arrest in each sequence without Bazinian mortification, I suggest we can consider "Marilyn Monroe" in relation to three scenes of the body and the face: pose, expression and gesture.

Figure 2(b).   Sam Shaw, View of the Location Shoot for *The Seven Year Itch* (Dir. Billy Wilder, USA, 1955), New York, September 1954 (Courtesy of Sam Shaw Family Archives)

Figure 2(a).   Aby Warburg, *Mnemosyne Bilder-Atlas*, Plate 46: *Ninfa.* (Courtesy of the Warburg Institute, London)

Figure 2(d).   *Dancing Maenad*, Roman relief, second century CE., Rome, Museo Capitolino. Photograph: Scala Archives

Figure 2(c).   The scene of the shoot of a scene from *The Seven Year Itch* on Lexington Avenue, New York 1954.

Figure 2(e).   Sam Shaw, Location shoot, *The Seven Year Itch* (Courtesy of Sam Shaw Family Archives)

Figure 2(f).   Sandro Botticelli (1445–1510), *The Birth of Venus*, 1484–86 tempera on canvas, 72.5 cm×278.9 cm. Florence: Galeria degli Uffizi. Photograph: Scala Archives

Agamben makes much of the concurrent emergence of cinema with cultural-art historian Aby Warburg's concept of the image as *pathosformel* – an affect formula – first articulated in his writings in 1905, a conjunction that reflects back on the relation of still and moving images in the expanded *Bilder-Atlas* of cinema studies. *Formel* derives from the Latin *forma* for shape, likeness and figure but also from *formalis*: serving as a model. Both derive from the Greek φόρμουλα. Formula sounds too mathematical or chemical. Formulation suggests something cerebral or linguistic. There is also a sense in formula of a recipe or a set of ingredients. In motor racing, formula refers to specifications of the engine and so forth. Formula can, however, also be a repeated form of words associated with a ceremony or ritual. It is this sense that is being invoked here.

In his battle with what he dismissed as "aestheticizing art history" that focused on style, form or content, Warburg sought to bridge the issue of figuration and formulation by binding affect – pathos – with its forming. The effect of the *pathosformel* was, furthermore, transmission of affect by means of a *form*ulation that carried the memory of bodily movements as emotionally expressive gestures associated with the freighted and symbolic actions of rituals while also storing up, like a charged battery, the lively energy that represents the disturbance of affect as gesture (Pollock, 2013). Warburg is thus offering us a means of rethinking the dominance of the linguistic, structuralist or semiotic models for the production of meaning which rely on this formula: signifier/signified = sign. *Pathosformel* suggests at once that the body, affected by pathos, passion or suffering, intensity at any rate, is a figuration *for* rather than *of* passionate, subjectivized but not rationalized, corporality.

In his book that also explores the potential correspondence between Warburg's ideas and emerging cinema, Philippe-Alain Michaud explains Warburg's other key concept: an "iconology of the interval" in relation to the idea of a constellation:

> To grasp what Warburg meant by the "iconology of the interval" one must try to understand, in terms of introspection and montage, what binds, or inversely, what separates, the motifs on the irregular black fields that isolate images on the surface of the panels and bear witness to an enigmatic prediscursive purpose. Each panel of the *Mnemosyne* is the cartographic relief of an area of art history imagined simultaneously as an objective sequence and as a chain of thought in which the network of intervals indicates the fault lines that distribute or organize the representations into archipelagos, or … "constellations". (Michaud, 2004, p. 253)

At once "chains of thought" (symbolic linkages) and fault lines (gaps) of disparately relating visual instances, Warburg's novel, and psychological, concept of the image was developed at the historical conjunction where chronophotography arrested the movement of gesture and rendered it alien to the bourgeois subject now dispossessed of her gestures. At the same time, chronophotography offered the means of animating the arrested, stilled movement snapped by the camera to produce a reproduction and an illusion of human action – cinema. Precisely here, Warburg used photographs of painted, drawn, carved and etched *representations* of mobile bodies in unknowing anticipation of the curious form that would come to be invented, *on the other side*, as it were, of the invention by cinema of the illusion of continuous movement: the film still. The still is a photograph that carries its own memory of its actual or virtual part in an illusory, moving whole. It is distinct from the normal photograph since it is made by making an image of what had been a performance across several frames of a film. It is conceptually a momentary holding in view of a mobility composed of the illusion of movement created by passing celluloid through a gate at the rate of twenty-four frames per second. It will be this paradox that enables me to reconfigure a relationship between gestures in stills extracted from a film and photographs made during a film shoot not as arrests of animated images, but as formulae linked conceptually, as I shall soon suggest, to a painting created 500 years earlier.

Above the grate

Marilyn Monroe is perhaps held most of all in cultural memory and cinematic imagination by a photographic still that captures a film shoot on 586 Lexington Avenue at Fifty-Second Street in New York in the early hours of 15 September 1954 during the making of *The Seven Year Itch*, which was directed by Billy Wilder (1906–2002) from a successful stage play by George Axelrod (1922–2003) for Twentieth Century Fox. Dressed by the designer Travilla in a tightly fitting ivory halter-top cocktail dress with full pleated skirt, Monroe was asked to stand above a New York subway grate from which, according to the film's narrative, air regularly rushed up as the subway train passed by, causing her skirt to billow, often uncovering a specially chosen double set of proper, white underpants. Monroe rarely wore underwear. Photographs of this "shoot" (Figure 2(b)), stage managed by Sam Shaw as the appointed stills photographer for the production, reveal the crowds Wilder's calculated publicity had attracted to the scene. Men (Figure 2(b)) gathered in increasing numbers to watch and to photograph in turn the many takes of Monroe's repeated posing and reacting to the rush of air as Billy Wilder figured out what effect he wanted as well as what he would be allowed to show in the final film. Thus we have photographs of Wilder's direction, including his own awkward demonstration of what he wanted Monroe to do, which specifically called for the gesture of a slight forward stoop, bringing the shoulders forward, bending the knees and holding down the flying skirt by placing both her hands in front of her groin (Figure 2(c)). One experimental photograph shows a curious effect that disappears her body into a shape created by the floating material of the uplifted but restrained dress (Figure 2(e)).

In the much-quoted image (Figure 1(a)), which is not seen in the film version, this gesture of covering her sex in modesty becomes its opposite when accompanied by the turn of her head, and the expression we see on the face of the actor. It is perhaps better described as ecstatic rather than oceanic. Formally this image (Figure 1(b)) achieves its intensity through the combination of the curving body line created by bending knees, extending her buttocks, exposing bare legs which then come forward, with the downward thrust of her straightened arms meeting at the groin, the raised and then inward curving shoulders, the turned head, the opened mouth and the closed eyes. The gestures redefine the body's space as pleasure. Yet, as we shall see, far from being a pudic Venus Figure covering her sex in shame or vulnerability, Monroe here enacts, in effect, the figure of the *Nympha*, a different legacy from antiquity that figures the feminine as animating life.

One of the most significant elements of the image's effect as a gesticulation of affect arises, however, from the movement of the dress, created, of course, by an external force of blown air. Yet, in the image, the dress performs as the outward sign of an otherwise unrepresentable moment of *jouissance* on the part of its wearer. In Warburg's sense, it is the gesture of the animated costume – *bewegtes Beiwerk* – that conveys the affect suggested by the body's pose, reminding us that the power lies in the formula itself, not the pose.

Let me read this combination of the body's actions and the performed gestures of the animated inanimate accessories – the movement of the cloth in response to the unseen air – in relation to Warburg's work on image memory, placed by Agamben at the critical and historical point in which forensic chronophotography alienated the bourgeoisie from their gestures only to lead to film which returned the gesture while simultaneously re-affirming its loss. "Cinema leads images back to the homeland of gesture" (Agamben, 2000, p. 55). The homeland of gesture has become the *image-phantasm* of the accessorized body, distanced from the viewing body suspended in cinematic fascination. Thus the image itself develops as a fantasy space, perhaps even a medium, for the body no longer identified with its gesture, but now absorbed phantasmatically back into the potency of the image that moves on screen as a new composite of human gestures with the conflation of human-accessory-mise-en-scène.

It is by this means that it becomes possible to introduce Aby Warburg's research into the curious re-emergence in European-Christian culture during the fifteenth century of the image-tropes, the *pathosformulae*, of pagan antiquity one of whose most charged formulae he named the *Nympha* (νύμφη). This figuration/figuration of the feminine is characterized by the body in movement as in running (you might recall Freud's essay on the exemplum of this form in the bas relief of *Gradiva* [light-footed]), but also by the movement of her garments and hair, not so much agitated as enlivened: "*bewegtes*" is the German adjective (Figure 2(e)). The forms of the accessories, streaming hair and flowing garments, creating the illusion of motion caused by invisible wind, produce an image whose external agitations are the analogue for the invisible interior affective condition of the subject: possessed by jouissant affect. This is different, therefore, from Dyer's notion that with Monroe the entire female body becomes the analogue for one of her sexual organs – *Nympha* being in fact an archaic term for the labia. Instead the body quivers with its "traumatic", that is unspeakable, but subjectively experienced intensity, which may be associated with sexual pleasure but on a register of that pleasure's, momentarily dispossessed, subject.

In her study of "Wind: On a Pictorial Quintessence", Barbara Baert draws on the work of Georges Didi-Huberman to explain that the return from antiquity of the dancing figure in fifteenth-century Italian painting and literature is not merely the sign of a new taste for the antique; it is connected with wind itself:

> But the definition of *ninfa* goes further than that: she is not only an iconography *alla Antica* but a motif of "intensity," which makes life itself in all its mobility/changeability visible in the work of art. *Ninfa* is a dialectic form that, in a single movement – the danced immobility of a princess – modulates the essence of the body with its inner and outer life: desire, which wells up from the corruptible beauty of floating pleats and descending air. Desirability appears on the surface of the mirror by means of the wind. *Ninfa* is the last gust of wind and final responsible party for a much deeper, perhaps the deepest "neurosis" in painting: *desire as pictorial affect*. (Baert, 2014; my emphasis)

I am particularly keen to emphasize the notion of both desirability and Baert's "desire as a pictorial effect" (2014) as what becomes visible through medialization. It is much more than the attribute of the body as object being pictured, or the attribute of the person who expresses it.

In his short book *Nymphs* (2013), Giorgio Agamben introduces a mid-fifteenth-century treatise on dance by the choreographer Domenico da Piacenza, who identifies a crucial, hanging moment within the flow of dance that is named "*phantasmata*". Agamben glosses this term as follows: "a sudden arrest between two movements that virtually contracts within its internal tension the measure and the memory of the entire choreographic series" (Agamben, 2013, p. 8). From this insight he formulates a proposition that binds time, memory and imagination.

Indeed memory is impossible without an image (phantasm), which is an affect, a *pathos* of sensation or of thought. In this sense the mnemic image is always charged with an energy capable of moving and disturbing the body. (Agamben, 2013, p. 8)

Tipping us towards the concept of the gesture, Agamben suggests that Warburg may have known of Domenico's "phantasmata" when in turn he formulated his key concept for the manner in which images of gestures become mnemonic transmitters of affect: *pathosformel*. The image is thus a temporary arrest of that which is imagined and remembered as part of a continuous choreography, itself the *transformed* survival of what had originally been rituals *performed*, storing up the memory of the trauma of affect against which the gestures were first prophylactically drafted. The image within this movement of dance – to which I might compare cinema itself – is thus a stored up energy associated with affect that inhabits this formula.

In the age, therefore, of so-called silent cinema with its affecting audio accompaniment, Agamben explains that the main focus of Warburg's investigations was instead "the gesture intended as a crystal of historical memory, the process by which it stiffened and turned into destiny, as well as the strenuous efforts of artists and philosophers (an attempt that, according to Warburg, was on the verge of insanity) to redeem the gesture from its destiny through dynamic polarization" (2000, p. 54). Agamben continues, however, "Inside each section [of the *Mnemosyne Bilder-Atlas*], the single images should be considered *more as film stills* than as autonomous realities (at least in the same way in which Benjamin once compared the dialectical image to those little books, forerunners of cinematography, that gave the impression of movement when the pages were turned rapidly" (Agamben, 2000, p.54, my emphasis).

To my own initial Atlas page, with images from *The Seven Year Itch*, stills made on the occasion of an attempted shoot for a scene in that work of cinema in which wind blows up from a subway grating to cause "The Girl's" white dress to move autonomously around her still body (Figure 1(a) and (b)), and to the images of the woman, out of role, bathing in the ocean, I now add a painting created by Italian artist Sandro Botticelli between 1483 and 1485 in Florence *The Birth of Venus* (Florence, Galleria degli Uffizi) (Figure 2(f)) which contains both Venus, known as *Venus Anadyomene – Venus Rising from the Sea* – because she was conceived from the sprinkling of divine semen on the ocean and is now being born fully grown from the foamy water, and the *Nympha*, as the scallop shell on which she is carried is read as a symbol of the female vulva.

What are we seeing in Botticelli's *The Birth of Venus*? (Figure 2(f)). We are presented frontally with a tableau that comprises four figures, all mythological, but of different orders of meaning. The central figure, citing a lost Greek sculpture, appears to be standing still in a pose known since, and thus knowingly quoted from, classical antiquity: it is survival and a revival of the *Venus Pudica* first created in the fourth century BCE as the *Aphrodite of Cnidus*. The figure is that of a woman represented in a mode known in art historical parlance as a "nude" (Clark, 1956). As distinct from nakedness, artistic nudity is, according to John Berger, an imposed form of cultural clothing that is inescapable as a permanent condition of exhibition imposed distinctively on the female nude. (Berger, 1972)

Here we are caught between the two. Implicitly naked like a newborn child, rather than unclothed, this Venus figure performs two gestures that imply a form of body consciousness at odds with the innocence we might associate with emerging into the world from the ocean as a pre-cultural body. With one hand, Venus attempts to cover her breasts, exposing one, nonetheless, to clear view. With the other hand she holds a swathe of her long, golden hair over her sex, adding to the smooth and hairless body of classical female nudity a surrogate for her invisible sexual hair. Both gestures articulate vulnerability, convey a sense of unwanted exposure and even betray shame, while implying the presence of a viewing other that has incited such protective gestures of a body rendered nude for its display while remaining exposed in unprotected nakedness. It is important to remember that these gestures have also been interpreted on another register as a kind of affirmation of the divine power of female generativity from the view of whose sacred locus the viewer is being protected (Koloski-Ostrow and Lyons, 1997), reminding us that in classical mythology the multifaceted figure of Venus is the Goddess of Spring, of Life and of Death. This kind of monstrance of potential power and effect associated with an invisibly generative rather than a penetrable female body has to be set against the formal effects of the sinuously fashioned curving of the body and the tilt and turn of the head, which makes its uprightness yield to a kind of proffered passivity before the potentially masculinized gaze of the world here negotiating not the Hays but the Christian code: Venus versus the Christian Eve.

On the left-hand side of the painting, as if floating over the water, winged figures represent the winds blowing the Venusian shell towards the land. On the right-hand side of the painting another female figure in a flowing florally patterned dress with agitated drapery and wildly flowing hair moves towards Venus, offering a cloak with which to clothe the "newborn" woman, thus marking into the visual scene her state of exposed undress. It functions as a reverse striptease. We recognize in the handmaiden on the right the *pathosformel* of the *Nympha*:

> the nymph is neither passional matter to which the artist must give new form, nor a mold into which he must press his emotional materials. The nymph is an indiscernible blend of originariness and repetition, of form and matter. (Agamben, 2007, p. 55)

Agamben continues:

> The nymph is the image of the image, the cipher of the *pathosformeln* which is passed down from generation to generation and to which generations entrust the possibility of finding or losing themselves, or thinking or not thinking. Therefore, images are certainly a historical element. (2007, p. 57)

There is a vast and complicated, and indeed esoteric, field of interpretation of Botticelli's iconographic programme studied brilliantly for his doctoral thesis by Warburg ([1893], 1999). Our iconographic programme for Monroe's images appears less esoteric – *Playboy* and Kinsey via Hays – although I have to acknowledge that I have found on the Internet two images that replace Botticelli's Venus with Monroe posing in the shell of Venus, one in the bathing costume she models in *How to Marry a Millionaire* and the other in the billowing dress from the subway grate scene from *The Seven Year Itch*. But while these iconographical studies may account for the existence of the images, they do not address their affect and the substratum that enables affectivity in the image to exceed their conditions of emergence in time and place. Such is the ground that Warburg sought to expose. So I need now to return with the intuition that *Venus* and the *Nympha*, wind and water, cloth in movement, sustain the charge that makes certain images from the 1950s so memorable to us beyond the claims anyone can make for the aesthetics of the films or the photographic model. Rather than being read as signs of the figuration of sexuality associated with an agent of representation, Marilyn Monroe, two photographs (Figure 1(b) and (d)) surprise us with their reanimation in the modern cinematic/photographic age of the duality posed in Botticelli's painting.

Back to the grate

The scenes we see in the final cut of the film *The Seven Year Itch* of "The Girl" (Monroe's character never has a name) responding twice to passing trains and the delight they caused had, however, to be reshot on the Twentieth Century Fox lot (Figure 2(c)). Most of the original New York shoot was rendered useless as a result of the noise of the almost all-male crowd whistling and hooting and calling to see more in this virtual striptease on the streets. Required repeatedly to take up the pose of standing on the grate allowing the air to expose her body as a man with a wind machine below the grate blew air upwards, Monroe commented wryly to director Billy Wilder during the location shooting that she hoped he was not going to use the extra footage "privately" for his stag nights.

The next plate (Figure 3(a–f)) of my cinema album contains two sets of screen grabs from the final film. These shots are more circumspect than the location shoot (Figure 2(b)). The camera is kept low. The editing fragments the actor's body. The uprush of forced air reveals only Monroe's legs as the dress billows up almost out of sight. There are, however, two sequences, two trains. The first sequence plants Tow Ewell's character at a 90-degree angle to Monroe's right. Masculine trousered legs and brown shoes serve as visual foil to the woman's bared legs in white slingback high heels. The cloth of the classically pleated dress swirls around her legs, dancing in response to the air. Its movement stands in for the pleasure of the absented face of the woman. Is this coded nymphic (Warburg) or vaginal (Dyer)? A second train approaches, viewed with delighted anticipation by "The Girl" seeking again a sensation that pleased her. The camera now functions as an invisible and mobile eye. It begins its own movement, however, several grates to her right, tracking the invisible wind arising from the noisy train, thus entraining the spectator's gaze to this combination of the driven machine below and the natural pressure its movement creates in the unseen tunnel that then lifts "The Girl's" skirts out of view, leaving the sight of the man's trousered legs planted alongside the woman's now completely naked legs and delicately shod feet planted apart. This tamed, yet ultimately shocking, cinematic move creates a narrative that ultimately offers an image of nakedness to an expectant, thus hetero-masculinized, spectator who is, however, denied the ultimate sight repeatedly almost revealed but veiled in the location photo shoot. The cinematic version defers the sight of sex to fantasy while providing the necessary defensive fetishization in the fragment of the exposed legs standing apart in the tight white shoes.

Writing of the effects of the Hays Code on Hollywood cinema in the context of her reflections on Marilyn Monroe, Laura Mulvey argues that censorship did not so much remove sexuality from cinema as displace it from the "realm of a tentative modernity into a new apotheosis of the visual concentrated on woman as signifier of sexuality" (Mulvey, 1996, p. 45). Sexuality became the "unspoken" with the coded body of woman the symptomatic return of the repressed (Mulvey, 1996, p. 45). This insight poses a secondary

Figure 3(a–f).   Sequences of the Subway Grate scene from *The Seven Year Itch* (Dir. Billy Wilder, USA, 1955)

question: Is this scene in *The Seven Year Itch* a risky approximation to another site of the gestural and theatrical performance of sexuality already mentioned in its reverse: striptease?

Barthes' striptease

In his essay on striptease in his foundational collection, *Mythologies*, first published in 1957, Roland Barthes makes a surprising claim:

> Striptease – at least Parisian striptease – is based on a contradiction. Woman is desexualized at the very moment when she is stripped naked. We may therefore say that we are dealing in a sense with a spectacle based on fear, or rather on the pretence of fear, as if eroticism here went no further than a sort of delicious terror, whose ritual signs have only to be announced to evoke at once the idea of sex and its conjuration. (1973, p. 84)

Barthes inverts the notion that striptease is a delayed revelation of a hidden depth. Its process is instead "to signify, through shedding of an incongruous and artificial clothing, nakedness as the natural vesture of woman, which amounts in the end to regaining a perfectly chaste state of the flesh" (Barthes, 1973, pp. 84–85). This takes us back to one dimension of Botticelli's *Venus* at her "birth". Furthermore, Barthes reads the role of the props used in striptease as elements of the rite that serves to keep the unveiled body remote, attached to myth and affect. Then he addresses the movements of the dance. Far from being erotic, the undulations of the dancer "exorcize the fear of immobility" (Barthes, 1973, p. 85). The dance, he adds, "consisting of ritual gestures which have been seen a thousand times, acts on movements as a cosmetic, it hides nudity, and smothers the spectacle under a glaze of superfluous yet essential gestures, for the act of becoming bare is here relegated to the rank of parasitical operations carried out in an improbable background" (Barthes, 1973, p. 86).

"Ritual gestures" cosmetically making the body remote are superfluous yet essential gestures that carry more potential meaning than the narrative action of moving from clothed to unclothed: stripping – exactly what was being called for and repeated in the endless shoot on Lexington Avenue: "let's see more, let's see it again." If we were to see the 1954 event on Lexington Avenue and Fifty-Second Street performed for both the moving and the still camera under a Barthesian lens, the very fact of Monroe remaining ultimately covered, however modestly in plain white underwear, deflects the chastity of ultimate female nakedness in favour of the "dance of pretended fear-inducing disclosure". Her gestures then incite a "delicious terror" for whose repetition the hooting crowd repeatedly called out, directed by Billy Wilder in search of the perfect take and the inference of its privately re-useable excess.

But what do *her* gestures articulate on my other register? What did the actor perform at the level of the image by her cooperation, knowingly or unknowingly, with this paradoxical logic of the striptease when on set in Los Angeles? Here is an actor performing for various kinds of camera. But the production process – that the photographs and the stilled frames I have extracted document – is part of a complex procedure of medialization in which a repressed, inarticulable and contested signified of female sexuality/and sexual pleasure is being produced by a performance of a body's posturing and its clothing's gestures. The archive of the Lexington Avenue shoot and its surrounding photographs allow us to address a different question that requires me to distinguish between the pose, the gesture and expression.

Pose, gesture, expression

What are the subtleties that we might need to detect between the pose and the gesture within the context of this argument?

We say that we *strike* a pose, thus creating a momentary arrest of living movement. A pose can turn us into a picture, as Madonna reminds us in her song "Vogue" which opens with the repeated injunction "Strike a pose" before arriving at a list of Hollywood icons – "ladies with attitude" – to be found on the covers of magazines. We also say that we assume a pose which is thus already a freezing of our being with some anterior notion of a potential meaning already there to be repeated, imitated, re-enacted.

Yet before a camera, the pose becomes more than either "striking" or impersonating. According to Roland Barthes, being photographed is an act by which I assume a way of being that is becoming an image for the gaze. This is an act a double sense. I am the agent of an act – posing – in which I put on an act – the pose – a congealed signifying attitude that has repercussions, momentarily, on what I become: *qua* image. Barthes suggests the following:

> I constitute myself in the process of "posing", I instantaneously make another body for myself, I transform myself in advance into an image. This transformation is an active one: I feel the photograph creates my body or mortifies it. (Barthes, 1982, pp. 10–11)

I want to draw attention to the mortifying effect, a deadliness inflicted as the body is recast by the pose but at the same time the pose entraps us in a "social game" that also empties the posed image of a liveliness associated with affective individuality. "I lend myself to the social game, I know I am posing, I want you to know I am posing but (to square the circle) this additional message must in no way alter the precious essence of my individuality, what I am apart from my effigy" (Barthes, 1982, pp. 11–12).

If, according to Agamben, we no longer are our gestures, we are forced anxiously to watch and monitor the way our bodies emit signs, afraid to give ourselves away. The resulting formal restraint in public interface – what has been named the adoption of masked public presence or *blasé* – may have driven the gestural onto the screen in early cinema. Yet these gestures were thinned from their melodramatic exaggeration on the nineteenth-century stage, from their hysterical excess. Bodies had been powerful instruments of Romantic theatricality on stage in ways that influenced the infamous hysterics of Salpetrière who performed for Charcot's camera as if they were a Lady Macbeth played by Sarah Bernhardt (Didi-Huberman, 2003). Yet, we know that once the cinema arrived, such histrionics appeared unconvincing, too posed perhaps. Without words in what the French beautifully name mute cinema, accompanied by music so not silent, acting was increasingly required to mimic the expressively restrained gestures of new social and intimate exchanges, while also representing a lost world of formerly shared gestural meaning that could convey *pathos*. It would seem that, with the evolution of cinema, the cameras watched and then slowly discovered and exploited specific faces that could produce a new form of expressive, *pathetic*, gesture based on the micro movements of lips, brows and the cosmetically highlighted eyes for which perhaps the almost impassive final close-up of Greta Garbo as the film's eponymous heroine in *Queen Christina* (Dir. Rouben Mamoulian, USA, 1933) might be the paradigm (Barthes, 1973; Doane, 2003). We thus would arrive at the close-up in which action is suspended but affect is not. The close-up is not a pose; it is the covenant between gesture and expression.

If the pose is redefined by Barthes as an "act", what do we mean when we say that we *make* a gesture? Does gesture thus endow the movements of the body or even of the facial muscles with the potential for an intention to produce meaning, but without a reifying or mortifying symbolic signifying system. Let me quote Czech theorist Vilém Flusser of the gesture:

> Gestures express and articulate that which they symbolically represent. I will proceed as if I wished to defend the thesis that "affect" is the symbolic representation of states of mind through gestures. In short I shall try to show that states of mind (whatever that phrase may mean) can make themselves manifest through a plethora of body movements but that they express and articulate themselves through a play of gesticulations called "affect" because it is the way they are represented. (Flusser, 2014, pp. 4–5)

In his phenomenology of gestures, significantly expressed as plural, Vilém Flusser addresses what we do that constitutes a set of actions that at once have no causal explanation and yet also move into the symbolic realm without, however, signifying linguistically. Flusser posits a relation between representation and affect which forms a particular passage between the subject and the world, a subject and others in which the latter, the others, themselves gesturing subjects, must make sense of movements of the other's face/body at the level of discerning affect as an affected condition of another's being: an instance of mobilized inter- and trans-subjectivity. This formulation places the gesture in the space "*in-between*" the symbolic and the non-symbolic, what cannot be spoken. Gesture is suspended between trauma and affectivity whose excess is ecstasy, ex-static, moved and moving. Affect is potentially identifiable with trauma in the psychoanalytical sense, not of a dreadful event so much as that which has not yet been or even cannot be symbolically represented. Flusser's formulation thus poses a dilemma because he is defining gesture as a form of symbolic representation (a stands for b) by means of *expression* and *articulation* through bodily movements that have meaning, namely their agent is being affected by internal or external pressures in ways that can be shared and incite response.

Finally, we, as observers, say that we *read* an expression. This deflects the action from the subject whose expression another seeks to decipher, another who interprets what the subject may not consciously intend: the gesture. A notion of an interiority means that we may be betrayed by our expressions. I am arguing that unprompted expressions can, however, become gestures, the articulation of affect, and that the gesture finally suggests an intending or subjective agent. Gesture thereby endows the visible body with subjectivity. This allows us to consider the image archive that makes "Marilyn Monroe", a cultural image, as also the trace of a specific creative agency, animating the older formulae involuntarily reproduced with a vivifying intensity drawn from a singular feminine subjectivity that projects these images beyond their service to their culture as ideological signs of discourses on sexuality.

In the context of this reflection on the archive of Marilyn Monroe as gesture in cinema, I want thus to distinguish those images in which Monroe is posing, thus actively presenting herself to/for the camera, and allowing herself to be made into, and mortified by, an image by means of the manner in which the image turns the pose into a kind of self-willed objectification, a sacrificial offering to its culture as it were. No doubt it required considerable skill acquired from long practice in work as a model and posing to collaborate so effectively in that process and to yield so completely to it. Against Monroe's brilliant ability to produce fine images through posing for outstanding photographers, I want to set the affects we find in other still and cinematic moments. These moments resist these mortifying effects of the pose and generate a movement, even in still images or stills, which is at once enlivening and affecting. The join is what Flussser is defining as the gesture that is mobilized as an intention to convey affect without any form of its symbolization beyond itself. While it is tempting and even illuminating to locate the pose in the sociocultural order of image construction and posit approvingly certain instances in which Monroe transcended cheesecake, pinup or vamp to produce a supplementary effect closer to Barthes' notion of myth, I am seeking here to make sense, through the Monroe archive, of Warburg's paradoxical notion of an image moment that both stores up energy in a memory form and transmits that liveliness in its precariousness and excess as affect between trauma and ecstasy. In what sense can Monroe be thus read through gesture as a matter of moves not poses?

Movies: "Marilyn Monroe's" moves

As I have already stated, in 1953, three "Monroe" movies were released: *Niagara*, *Gentlemen Prefer Blondes* and *How to Marry a Millionaire*. The first cast her as a murderous wife in a thriller set against the dramatic flows of Niagara Falls, whose natural force served as indirect analogy for the threat posed by her dangerously adulterous desires. In the second, a musical comedy, Monroe played an updated version of Anita Loos' creation of a 1920s flapper and gold digger Lorelei Lee. Finally, in her third film, she plays a delightfully shortsighted model who participates in a scheme to catch a millionaire. The thematics of these films are thus female treachery, superficiality and gold digging.

Can we talk about "her" as gesture in these films? Certainly, Monroe performs certain movements that will come to define her star body as "the body" with various parts of her anatomy cinematically sexualized by isolation, focus, camera angle, and prolonged exposure, as in her walk filmed from behind in *Niagara* already highlighted by Richard Dyer. It is in *Niagara*, however, that Monroe performed a notorious gesture. Her character Rose Loomis is filmed, lying awake at an early hour in her Hays Code regulation single bed, her body clearly naked beneath a single white sheet (Figure 4(a–e)). This is not, however, an implicit moment of striptease; the cloth plays its own autonomous part.

"Rose" is smoking, a gesture freighted cinematically with pre- and post-coital connotations that slipped through the scrupulous censorship applied by the still active Hays Code to all film scripts. "Rose" is lying on her back with her left knee raised, her right leg lounging on the bed (Figure 4(a)). Monroe/Rose moves her raised knee millimetres to its right and then again to the left beyond the point it was originally (Figure 4(b)), thus parting and then clenching and re-opening her legs (Figure 4(c)) and inciting in the viewer a notion of her sex, a touching, and its remembered or desired pleasure, and asserting her own sexuality in this self-owning gesture of memory. Rather than action or scripted exchange, Monroe's draped body thus refutes the comforting anticipation of mere nakedness to reinsert, but not through ritualized movement, the evocation of a woman's body as a site rather than a sight of sexuality. The film closes down this extraordinarily daring gestural moment by ending the scene with the inert body of an apparently sleeping Rose on her side, offering to the viewer its curvaceous silhouette become ritualized image form (Figure 4(e)). I note that the movement of the camera from her left to her right alters the function and agency of the body in the cinematic frame compared to the previous image (Figure 4(d)).

We can contrast what occurs in *Niagara* at the level of transgressive or affective body gesture with the use of the *Playboy* body in the musical performances in *Gentlemen Prefer Blondes* (Figure 5). In the pre-credit sequence, Monroe doubles up with Jane Russell in a "performance" of a song and dance number – *Someone Broke My Heart in Little Rock* – that anecdotally introduces the story of the transition of two sexually used working class girls from "the wrong side of the tracks" to their hunting grounds in Wall Street as a signifier of finance capital and its surplus millions. The synchronized movements of two identically dressed women, outfitted in close-fitting ruby-coloured long dresses with plunging necklines and slits up one leg are on the side of "pure ritual", borrowing, in politened form, burlesque gestures. The two actors mimic, but do not quite replicate, the burlesque moves that simulate sexual activity known familiarly as bump and grind. The choreography alternates between moments of statuesque stillness and energetic striding movements, between gestures using closely held or outstretched arms that close or open the body (Figure 5(a–c)). Punctuating this routine are close-ups of Lorelei/Monroe, seemingly offering the moist vaginal face of which Dyer speaks (Figure 5(d–f)).

Figure 4(a–e).   Rose Loomis in bed from *Niagara*. (Dir. Henry Hathaway, USA, 1953)

In this volume, Laura Mulvey has also focused on a 30-second sequence from the opening of *Gentlemen Prefer Blondes* in her own analysis of the gestures of Monroe, made visible through the current ability of digital translation of films onto DVD to allow analysts to slow down, re-edit and mix the moves the actor makes. What this work reveals for Mulvey is Monroe's "photogenic sensibility" which is composed of artifice (mask and masquerade), pose (animate/ inanimate) and the "intimations of mortality [that] tinge this image of sexual excess" (Mulvey, 2006, p. 172; 2015, p. 12). Both of us thus agree that these gestures correspond to what becomes the paradigmatic screen image of Monroe in terms of figurations of sexuality. I want to make

Figure 5(a–f). Pre-credit sequence *Gentlemen Prefer Blondes*. (Dir. Howard Hawks, USA, 1953)

clear, however, the contrast with the joyous intensity and ecstatic animation conveyed in the second of each pair of Sam Shaw's photographs (Figure 1(b) and (d)) exceed the coded sexuality of 1950s Hollywood cinema that is both epitomized and reworked by Monroe in these roles in contrast to the recurrence of such standardized modes of representing woman as a sexual body. The difference to which I am pointing occurs precisely in the space between pose, including the close-up, which we can see at work here and what I am defining as gesture through a Warburgian notion of the *Nachleben* – the persistence, survival or return – of the archaic *pathos formulae* of "life" and intensity that are figured *in the feminine* but are not confined to the phallocentric, bourgeois and ultimately capitalist concept of female sexuality fashioned for and on offer to masculinity or even female sexuality for itself in the Kinsey discourse.

Bus Stop (1954)

My final plates in the picture album are from the film that follows on from the 1953 trio and *The Seven Year Itch* in 1955. By January 1955, Monroe had left Hollywood, moved to New York where she observed at the Actors Studio, and privately studied, an acting method taught by Lee Strasberg that involved the use of deep body memory to engender a personalized, gestural and psychologically freighted foundation for, rather than a classically trained performance of, a character (Spoto, 1993, pp. 338–342). In seeking to counter her typecasting as the dumb blonde or the treacherous woman, Monroe accepted the leading role in *Bus Stop* (Dir. Joshua Logan, USA, 1956), based on the Broadway play by William Inge (1913–1973), rewritten as a screenplay by George Axelrod (1922–2003). She played an abused but ambitious hillbilly singer – "chantoose" – in a two-bit saloon, The Blue Dragon Café, in a western rodeo town, Phoenix, but only on condition that she had some control over the characterization. For the part of "Chérie", Milton Green, the film's producer and co-founder of Marilyn Monroe Productions, worked with the actor to create a special look – a pasty complexion for a woman who worked all night and slept all day. Monroe also refused the over-glamorous costuming that had been proposed by the Hollywood studio (such as she had worn in her role as a saloon singer in a gold rush town in *River of No Return* (Dir. Otto Preminger, USA, 1954). Instead she searched the studio wardrobe, finally choosing a used and worse-for-wear midnight-blue-and-green sequined corset coupled with laddered fishnet stockings and a ridiculous "tail" attached pathetically to the actor's behind (Vogel, 2014, p. 124; Spoto, 1993, p. 390). Long gloves that were too loose and slid down her arms, requiring regular and awkward adjustments, completed a calculated anti-glamour "look" that shifted the viewer's attention to the character which was performed by Monroe with a carefully crafted Oklahoma-Texas accent and a mixture of a survivor's defiance and precarious vulnerability to any kind of warmth or tenderness.

Against this background, I want to study two scenes in relation to the work of this film as gestural cinema. The first is the anti-performance, as it were, delivered by Chérie in the Phoenix saloon. In her tattered and tawdry costume, with lighting operated by kicking large washing pegs, Chérie sings an off-key, painfully slow rendering of "That Old Black Magic" (1942), a song written by Harold Arlen and Johnny Mercer made famous by the Glenn Miller Orchestra (1942) and by Margaret Whiting (1943) recordings long before Sinatra and Ella Fitzgerald gave very different, more jazz-inflected renditions. Using their 1940s phrasings and "big band" sound, but dressed in only a tired corset, Monroe delivers the song with such evident lack of skill that within a minute the all-male audience turns back to noisy chatter. The camera drops to the level of the audience showing only the legs of the performer in the background as if to underscore the loss of visual pleasure along with the limited audio appeal of the singer (Figure 6(a) and (b)). It is in this context that the movements and gestures Chérie (Monroe) performs become agonizing to watch once the camera, its lowered eye line having broken the usual suture of the scopophilia of the diegetic audience – the guys in the Blue Dragon Café – and displaced it from to the visual pleasure of the cinema audience. The moves the singer then makes are disconnected from the unity of sound and gesture that musical theatre and musical film typically effects in order jointly to secure for the various genres and styles – the unnatural choreography of tap, ballroom, or strutting and bumping – an alibi for their insertion of the spectacular interruption of song and dance into narrative. What do we then see cinema having to do in order to compensate for a purposely de-eroticizing spectacle of a performing woman? (Figure 6(c–g))

The impersonal gaze of setting the scene divides the long shot in which Chérie is kept in view by lighting (Figure 6(h) and (i)). Once the bumptious cowboy erupts into the saloon, the cinematic gaze is identified with him (Figure 6(j)). He is smitten. After a noisy interaction which quiets the indifferent saloon audience, his adoring and mesmerized face is inserted repeatedly into the continuing sequence of Chérie singing. This establishes an alibi for continuing the excruciating scene and sound. Monroe makes Chérie respond to the changed conditions, now singing for someone, animating the tired and borrowed gestures with a different quality that can sustain the impoverished and pathetic quality of Chérie's poor copy of a Hollywood or cabaret performance while infusing it with its own genuine pathos (Figure 6(k–p)). The filming identifies this shift from stilted performance into an intimate exchange by giving us close-ups of Chérie. The film focuses on the intensified delivery of the song in which the embarrassing lack of convincing sexual effect of the body's actions gives way to a more cinematically affective use of micro-facial expression. With this we move into Monroe territory and the capacity for which directors otherwise exasperated with their star forgave her: namely, this actor's ability to deliver herself to the cinematic gaze and thus to *produce* a unique *medial* effect of intensity and interiority that is offered up to the viewer who is at once given the sight and excluded from either possession or self-loss as in Barthes' account of the classic close-up (1973). This is redeemed by the return from the awkward literalness with which Monroe makes Chérie circle her head to the words "round and round I go, down and down I go" to an intense and directed look in which the closed self-absorption of mere seconds before become energized and joyous intensity (Figure 6(r–x)). A close-up of the enthralled Beau before the singer flees the stage indecorously closes the sequence (Figure 6(y) and (z)).

Figure 6(a–z).   Blue Dragon Café Sequence from *Bus Stop*: Chérie's Performance of Old Black Magic (Dir. Joshua Logan, USA, 1956)

It would be easy to argue that the effects of working in the Actors Studio are responsible for the transformation of a brilliant comedienne and musical performer who had become identified with an iconization of sexuality in 1953 into an actor capable of both delivering before the camera and offering to the editor, William Reynolds, the means to create, post-production, this subtle set of subjective transformations. By doing exactly what Giorgio Agamben argued would destroy gesture, and worse, by recutting up the already divisive cutting and sequencing that is cinema itself through this montage of screen shots, I can, I hope in Warburgian fashion, disclose an effect that is the "Monroe-ness" of this film.

A discussion of the final sequence is now necessary (Figure 7). The ending of the film is problematic since the narrative has to accomplish the convincing submission of a woman who has demonstrated her own ambitions and has resisted the awkward and domineering attempt by an immature cowboy to claim and to abduct her by force. The ending of the film rhymes, however, with its opening scene that presents the young cowboy roping a steer in record time and setting off for the rodeo accompanied by the song whose chorus includes the words "If you will marry me". It is clear that this an Odyssey, the immature prince leaving his home to win glory and a bride through a test with animals and Woman. The crossing paths of cowboy Beau and saloon "chantoose" Chérie dramatize the "taming of the wild boy" who treats her as his "angel" and yet in much the same way as the steer in the opening shot, even actually roping her and carrying her off over his shoulder. The denouement in the snowed-in bus stop on the journey back to Montana into which Beau has forced Chérie involves the necessary subjection of the "phallic" boy-child Beau, still thinking he can simply have by taking what he wants, to a paternal "castration" through a thorough and humiliating beating at the hands of the bus driver, not his Mentor-Virgil. Bruised and humbled, Beau returns to say farewell to a now liberated but confused Chérie. (Figure 7(a–l))

In tight close-up, Chérie's head lies on the counter facing the camera while Beau enters the frame and speaks to her averted head, her pallor and his tanned skin contrasting dramatically. As he moves in to speak more gently, excusing her previous sexual experience, his head overlays hers with its troubled but also moved expression. Breaking this intensity, Chérie moves to the other side of the room to rest herself against the bowl of the jukebox onto which she then lays her head. Arms raised to hold her head, face pressed against the machine, we then see her sit up and rest her head in hand, the fingers standing in for a "furrowed brow". Toying with her hair in messy anxiety and emotional confusion, we can see the elaborating gestural language Monroe has created for Chérie to intimate her bafflement before a world that has only been abusive to this child-woman, and which now appears to be offering her what ideology, articulated through cinematic narrative, thinks she should want, despite the fact that, earlier in the film, it has been clear she had her own "line", a goal or an arrow of her own making: to be a star. The film has thus to accomplish a rapid transformation of a resentful, used but independent young woman of the world into a "woman" prepared to give it all up to live amongst the cattle in snowy Montana as wife and home-maker to an uncouth cowboy.

Beau repeats his offer of marriage in the formula of "speaking from his heart". As this scene unfolds Virgil strums his guitar and the first notes of the marriage song reappear to accompany the exchange and assist the narrative shift: Chérie: "Guts is the last thing that you need". Beau: "I don't have any now".

This changes the tone and level of his voice as well as his demeanour. Chérie turns, hesitantly whispering "Yes?" and in response to his declaration that he wants to be with her, the film delivers to us a close-up of Monroe's face (Figure 7(g)). The trembling that could have become a habit for Monroe now endows the character of Chérie with the real pathos of her infinite susceptibility to kindness. With tear-filled eyes in a second close-up: "Why, I'd go anywhere in the world with you *now*, anywhere at all". (Figure 7(i)). In his study of Monroe first published in 1960, Maurice Zolotov reminds us of the difficulty of creating a tight close-up while using the ratios of Cinemascope and documents how Logan pushed his cinematographer Milton Krasner to find a lens that would enable him to show "the fuzz on the cheeks and veins in the eyeballs" (Zolotov, [1960] 1990, p. 292).

This innovative intensity snaps as Cherie breaks out of the frame. In trembling anticipation she launches herself into the arms of Beau with completely unanticipated energy as if she had exploded (Figure 7(h) and (i)). The guitar, now visible, plies the marriage melody once again underscoring what has just been accomplished.

From the slow pace and close shooting that enables every movement of face and body to register, the scene itself explodes into action with other characters and a rush to get everyone onto the bus. This movement is halted by Beau's observation that in the snowy outdoors Cherie is dressed in a ridiculously light coat. Logically, he must be manly and yield his sheepskin jacket to her. The cut is swift. From being in the doorway of the bus, Cherie is now set flat against the backdrop of the bus, holding her coat tightly

Figure 7(a–l).   Bus Stop Reconciliation Sequence from *Bus Stop* (Dir. Joshua Logan, USA, 1956)

about her (Figure 8(a) and (b)). A gesture of hand with finger bent in front of her mouth speaks a naively innocent moment of her own awareness that another person might care for her well-being. The film holds us there to be in this moment, before Beau slowly brings her his opened coat, revealing its fleecy interior. Carl Rollyson, in the only other detailed exploration of this sequence of which I am aware, concludes that "Monroe's gestures, like the whole film are organic" (1966, p. 130) The gestures (Figure 8(c–h)) which it is said director Joshua Logan re-shot, suggesting to Monroe that they should be slower and more luxuriating as she allows herself to be wrapped up, arm by arm, tip towards the ecstatic: her eyes closed, mouth slightly opened, head tilted back, relaxing, yielding, being enveloped. This intensity is excessive and affecting. Clothing once again generates semantic momentum that affectively distracts us from realising the narrative function of this ending. The film in effect positions the newly clothed woman in her sheepskin covering as the substitute for and as the analogy of the steer chased and bound in the opening sequence. The film's rhyming of ending and opening thus "animalizes" Woman. The prince has made his conquest, fought the beasts but also wrestled and won Woman-beast through his coming of age saga.

Watched closely, however, the performance in the enacted scene allows bodily and facial gestures momentarily to counter this dire ideological drive. Narratively, as it must, the film problematically ends with the character Chérie succumbing to the marriage plot that was always the film's purpose. But in performing that submission by means

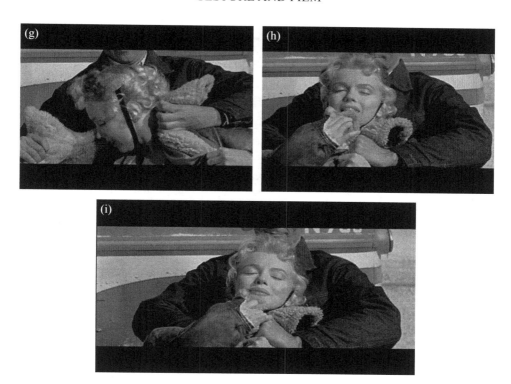

Figure 8(a–i).   Wrapping Sequence 3 from *Bus Stop*. (Dir. Joshua Logan, USA, 1956)

of gestures that are both the medium of affect and the medialization of affect, Monroe endows this otherwise troubling film with a degree of pathos "in the feminine" that lifts it from the mythic project of making a wild boy into a socialized man by means of an ordeal and the winning of his trophy. Monroe's movements trouble the ending of the film with another dimension. At the intersection of cinema and gestural performance, the film makes momentarily visible the violence and abuse inflicted on women, a systemic violence that renders them acutely vulnerable to the longing and yearning for tenderness and care that ultimately moves us. By this "event" before the camera in Monroe's gestures, the gravity of the film is relocated, for this moment, in the feminine.

The challenge in studying the image and cinematic archive that made "Marilyn Monroe" and that Marilyn Monroe made for cinema lies in the balancing of the ideological, industrial and cultural determinants which classical film theory has identified against what was signified through "Monroe" as the excess of the phallocentric psycho-semiotics of sexuality. By means of a gestural analysis, the screen performances that constitute "Monroe" become both a continuation of the history of Western culture's gestures and their formulation as *pathosformulae* and their cinematic *Nachleben*: persistence and transformation. Working with Warburg and the crisis of gesture that cinema both precipitated and to a certain extent redeemed, I am proposing the possibility of discerning a *poiesis* in "Marilyn Monroe" as mediality and performance. That creativity in and as image enables these images associated with the shooting of *The Seven Year Itch*

(Figure 1(a) and (b)) to function in this Warburgian space of Nymphs and Spring or watery pagan goddesses in exile (Agamben, 2007; Figure 1(d)), while also enlivening and renovating the cine-commercial trade in sexuality with an affecting intensity that gestures towards the trauma and ecstasy of feminine subjectivity.

Returning finally to the opening composite plate of my cinematic *Bilder-Atlas*, I have aimed to make visible the plane on which we can discern gesturally affective differences between the photographic performances in certain images (Figure 1(a) and (b)) and that which occurs between others (Figure 1(c) and (d)) that have acquired through this reading a theoretically informed shape, as the difference between the formulaic performance of sexuality in the image and the *pathosformulae* of affectivity and joy in life that rest on the unseen memory of a much longer history of gesture and the image at the intersection of unspeakable and excessive intensity.

References

Agamben, G. ([1996] 2000). Notes on gesture. In *Means without End: Notes on Politics* (pp. 49–62) (V. Binnetti & C. Cazarino, Trans.). Minneapolis, MN: University of Minnesota Press.

Agamben, G. ([2007] 2013). In *Nymphs* (A. Minervini, Trans.). London and New York: Seagull Books.

Baert, B. (2014). Wind—on a pictorial quintessence. *Images: Journal for Visual Studies*, 1. Available online at www.visual-studies.com/images/no1/baert.html [Accessed 20 April 2015].

Barthes, R. ([1957] 1973). *Mythologies* (A. Lavers, Trans.). London: Paladin.

Barthes, R. ([1980] 1982). *Camera Lucida* (R. Howard, Trans.). London: Fontana.

Bazin, A. (1960). The ontology of the photographic image. In H. Gray (Trans.). *Film Quarterly*, *13*(4), 4–9.

Benzel, K. (1991). The body as art: Still photographs of Marilyn Monroe. *Journal of Popular Culture*, *25*(2), 1–29.

Berger, J. (1972). *Ways of Seeing*. London: Penguin Books.

Clark. K. (1956). *The Nude: A Study in Ideal Form*. London: Penguin Books.

Didi-Huberman, G. (2003). *The Invention of Hysteria* (A. Hartz, Trans.). Cambridge, MA: MIT Press.

Doane, M. A. (2003). The close-up: Scale and detail in the cinema. *Differences*, *14*, 89–111.

Dyer, R. (2004). *Heavenly Bodies: Film Stars and Society*. London: Routledge.

Flusser, V. (2014). *Gestures* (N. A. Roth, Trans.). Minneapolis, MN: University of Minnesota Press.

Harrison, J. (1913). *Ancient Art and Ritual*. Montana: Kessinger Publishing.

Kinsey, A., et al. ([1953] 1998). *Sexual Behavior in the Human Female*. Bloomington, IN: Indiana University Press.

Koloski-Ostrow, A. O., & Lyons, C. (Eds.). (1997). *Naked Truths: Women, Sexuality and Gender in Classical Art and Archaeology*. London and New York: Routledge.

McCann, G. (1988). *Marilyn Monroe*. Cambridge: Polity Press.

Michaud, P-A. (2004). *Aby Warburg and the Image in Motion* (S. Hawks, Trans.) New York: Zone Books.

Mulvey, L., 'Fears, Fantasies and the Male Unconscious *or* "You Don't Know What is Happening, Do You, Mr Jones?" [1973], *Visual and Other Pleasures* (Basingstoke: MacMillan Press, 1989), pp. 6–13.

Mulvey, L. (1996). Close-ups and commodities. In *Fetishism and Curiosity* (pp. 40–52). London: British Film Institute.

Mulvey, L. (2006). *Death 24 x a Second: Stillness and the Moving Image*. London: Reaktion Books.

Mulvey, L. (2015). Cinematic gesture: The ghost in the machine. *Journal for Cultural Research*, *19*, 6–14.

Noys, B. (2004). Gestural Cinema? Giorgio Agamben on Film. *Film Philosophy*, *8*(22) ISSN 1466–4615. Available online at www.film-philosophy.com/vol8-2004/n22noys [Accessed 2 March 2015].

Pollock, G. (2013). *After-affects I After-images: Trauma and Aesthetic Transformation in the Virtual Feminist Museum*. Manchester: Manchester University Press.

Rollyson, C. E. (1966). *Marilyn Monroe: A Life of the Actress*. London: Hodder and Stoughton.

Spoto, D. (1993). *Marilyn Monroe: The Biography*. New York: Cooper Square Press.

Vogel, M. (2014). *Marilyn Monroe: Her Films, Her Life*. Jefferson, NC: MacFarland & Co.

Warburg, A. (1893). *Sandro Botticellis "Geburt der Venus" und "Frühling": Eine Untersuchung über die Vorstellung von der Antike in der italienische Frührenaissance*. Hamburg and Leipzig: Leopold Voss.

Warburg, A. (1999). Botticelli's *Birth of Venus* and *Spring*. In K. W. Forster (Trans). D. Britt (Ed.), *Aby Warburg: The Renewal of Pagan Antiquity* (pp. 89–156, 405–430). Los Angeles: Getty Institute.

Warburg, A. (2003). *Der Bilder-Atlas Mnemosyne*. Berlin: Akademie Verlag GmBH.

Zolotov, M. ([1960] 1990). *Marilyn Monroe*. New York: Harper & Row.

The time of gesture in cinema and its ethics

Elizabeth Cowie

School of Arts, The University of Kent, Canterbury, UK

This essay explores the ethical and gesture in film, developing from Giorgio Agamben's two ideas of gesture – of the movement that gesture constitutes, transforming the photographic into the cinematic; and what is pointed to as the feeling, or ethical stance that the gesture instantiates. In representation – whether literary or audio-visual, live or recorded, the time and timeliness of gesture as both the action of a moment, and the movement it constitutes, demands a reading, a recognition, that spurs understanding but also opens a gap in meaning. Gesture involves movement, an action in time, but it also appears as a *moment of action*, and not as a continuing movement, thus the moment of the gesture becomes stilled in its time of action as a communication. A gesture is a kind of event, crystallising meaning at a moment, while opening up to something *next*. Time here is therefore the time of the action itself, seconds or minutes, the stilling of that natural time in the moment of recognition by the observer or spectator of the action and its (potential) meaning, and the opening of implication of a time-to-be, a becoming inaugurated but not caused by the gesture. Agamben's gesture is anti-realist, in his philosophy of ethics as the gestural as undertaking and supporting and hence of responsibility. It is the enigmatic, undecidable quality of gesture in Atom Egoyan's *Exotica* that will be the focus of this essay. Gesture here is an action that carries the burden of responsibility in which the subject neither makes something nor enacts something.

"Gesture rather than image is the cinematic element" Giorgio Agamben (1993, p. 138)

"What happens when I touch her?" asks Francis in *Exotica* (Dir. Atom Egoyan, Canada, 1994)

To consider gesture in film is to be brought to think about the performance of an action as a movement that introduces a change. Gesture is thus an act in relation to an object or person, that communicates: it is *expressive*, whether intended as such or not. Gesture is also an action, in a movement of the arm, or the hand, or the eye; or as a moment, poised or posed, stilled.[1] Gesture directs – pointing, deictic – the observer either inward, to the expressing embodied performer of the gesture, or outwards, from the performer to her action in the world.

The gestures of the body are as central to the actor's performance as the tone and timbre of her voice as she articulates her lines. "Gesture", François Delsarte proclaims, "is the direct agent of the heart. It is the fit manifestation of feeling" and as such "it is the spirit, of which speech is merely the letter" (1995, p. 188). (While Artaud called the actor "an athlete of the heart", and that "One must grant the actor a kind of affective musculature which corresponds to the physical localizations of feelings". (Artaud, 1995, p. 15)). Embodied, and of the body and not of thought, gesture is the performing of the body as a living being in specific time and space and social context.[2]

Our faces communicate, yet our bodily expressions are not straightforwardly readable, for is the expression a smile, or a grimace? Is the laugh an expression of merriment, or terror? The irruption of a laugh which is incongruous – that is, out of sympathy with its context – is both very common and disturbing to those who hear it, becoming read as a levity which denigrates the response of pain, and sadness that is experienced and recognised by others as appropriate. The body responds here not to symbolic reality and conventional readability, but to a real which is outside signification. Not merely the Great War and the trenches of Flanders and France, but the subject's being at the service of the other who desires its annihilation. For the hysteric, seen the documentary film, *War Neuroses* 1917, Netley and 1918 Seale Hayne Hospitals (filmed by Pathé, under the direction of Dr Arthur Hurst, UK), gesture is distinct from simply bodily movement such as walking and talking, instead it is a particular *way* of walking or talking that is marked in some manner, and thereby gains a significance other than its physicality, for the gesture is not motivated by injury but by trauma. Caught by the camera, as spectators (re)viewing such gestures, we come up against a real that is unreadable, as Douglas Gordon perhaps recognised when he appropriated the "found footage" of the case of one soldier diagnosed with "hysterical pseudo-pseudophypertrophic muscular paralysis", that constitutes his video loop 10 ms–1 (1994), which refers to the speed at which an object falls under the pull of gravity.[3]

The time of the performed gesture

It is through gesture that we perform ourselves, or an actor embodies a character, but such gestures are both expressive of the whole yet consist of separated parts and moments – a mouth grimacing, a hand twitching, a languorous stride. In representation – whether literary or audio-visual, live or recorded, the time and timeliness of gesture as both the action of a moment, and the movement it constitutes, demands a reading, a recognition, that spurs understanding while opening a gap in the movement of the narrative and thus is excessive to the narrative.

Gesture invokes movement, an action in time, but it also appears as a *moment of action*, and not continuous movement, thus the moment of the gesture becomes stilled in its communication, its time of action. In the notion of the pregnant or significant moment in his discussion of the classical sculpture of the Trojan priest, Laocöon, G. E. Lessing articulated an understanding of movement in stillness as, John Stezaker suggests, "an expanded moment, rather than as an interruptive one [. . .] which allows an unfolding within the image" (2006, p. 125). Lessing writes, "The longer we gaze, the more must our imagination add; and the more our imagination adds, the more we must believe we see" (1853, p. 17). The stilled action of sculpture signifies a future in which the movement of a gesture begun but held would be – or could be – realised. The arrested flow in the image presents a being forever halted before its becoming, which is nevertheless present because it is imaginable in a possible future time. The moment held is both preserved and also lost to time. A gesture is a kind of event, crystallising meaning at a moment, while opening up to something *next*. Time here is the time – seconds or minutes – of the action itself and, in the stilling of that natural time in the flash of recognition by the observer or spectator of the action now, and of its (potential) meaning, there is the opening of an implication of a time-to-be. This is a becoming not of the gesture completed, but of the understanding of the possible after that follows the before of the gesture.

Gestures are acts of communicability but without a code, thus they may set in train a process of reading, of interpretation. It is the enigmatic quality of gesture in Egoyan's *Exotica* and the demands of interpretation that is the focus of this essay, epitomised by the image which the film cuts to after the scenes of his ritual with Christina, of Francis in a washroom cubicle, pulling on a roll of toilet paper and wrapping it around his hand. It is to Agamben's idea of gesture that I will now turn, to explore how it may help in understanding the ethical of gesture in the film.

The idea of gesture in Agamben

Giorgio Agamben discusses gesture in relation to language and – most saliently here – to cinema, in his claim that cinema is gesture not image.[4] He cites the twentieth-century critic Max Kommerell's claim that "speech is originary gesture, from which all individual gestures derive", and that poetic verse is essentially gesture. But Agamben comments that,

> If this is true, if speech is originary gesture, then what is at issue in gesture is not so much a prelinguistic content as, so to speak, the other side of language, its *speechless* dwelling in language. And the more human beings have language, the stronger the unsayable weighs them down, to the point that in the poet, the speaking being with the most words, "the making of references and signs is worn out, and something harsh is born – violence toward speech". (Agamben 1999, p. 78; quoting Kommerell, 1933, p. 42)

Indeed, Agamben writes, "Gesture is always the gesture of being at a loss in language: it is always a "gag" (1999, p. 78), as an act in the place of speech but whose end, import, is the impossibility of speech. In this, it is not the meaningfulness, the communication, that the gesture may enact or enable – express – but on the contrary a non or not-yet meaning, a potentiality of meaning (hence his discussion of Kafka's "Oklahoma Nature Theatre", 1999, p. 80) Poetry for Agamben is "a hesitation between sound and meaning", and "cinema, or at least a certain kind of cinema", is a "prolonged hesitation between image and meaning" (2000, p. 317).

Agamben argues that "Cinema leads images back into the realm of gesture" (1993, p. 139) and he draws on Deleuze's view that film images are neither "timeless postures" nor "static sections of movement", but "moving sections", images themselves in motion – Deleuze's "moving pictures". "It is not an archetype, but nor is it something outside history: rather it is a cut which itself is mobile, an image-movement charged with a dynamic tension" (2002, p. 314). For Deleuze, movement is not a supplement to the still images but is immediately given, such that cinema is the system "which reproduces movement by relating it to the any-instant-whatever" (1986, p. 6). What we may view as privileged instants in film as a moment of crystallisation, such as in the films of Sergei Eisenstein, are such only subsequent to being already any-instant-whatevers. Cinema is not the celluloid's strip of photograms but the movement enacted by the projection apparatus that enables our phenomenological experience of the "movies". Agamben extends Deleuze's analysis to propose both an ethics and an aesthetic of the stilled-into-movement that for Agamben is gesture.

Every image, Agamben writes, has two opposed possibilities, as image stilled, and as movement beyond the stilling – recalling my earlier reference to Lessing in my discussion of stillness and movement in the image. Stilled, Agamben argues that the gesture in the image is effaced in reification that I would also call a fetishisation – "in magical isolation" – as memory re-found. As movement beyond the stilling the image remains gestural – dynamic, referring out to the motion that continues or is implied and which corresponds to "the image flashed in the epiphany of involuntary memory", referring "beyond itself, towards a whole of which it is part" (1993, p. 139). Here Agamben is drawing on the work of Walter Benjamin and his concept of a "dialectical image" – an image charged with history, from which we obtain historical experience. Benjamin, writing of "the notion of a present which is not a transition, but in which time stands still and has come to a stop", pointed to the importance of stilling – an interval – in the movement of time as action. He argues,

> Materialist historiography [...] is based on a constructive principle. Thinking involves not only the flow of thoughts, but their arrest as well. Where thinking suddenly stops in a configuration pregnant with tensions, it gives that configuration a shock, by which it crystallises into a monad. (1969, pp. 262–265)

For Benjamin this enables what he terms the blasting open of the continuum of history, that is, of historical time as a movement of cause and effect. The historical object appears in a new setting, described more recently by Andrew Benjamin as "the explosive 'now-time,' the instantiation of the present by montage" (2000, p. 236).

For, in *The Arcades Project,* Walter Benjamin writes that,

> It is not that what is past casts its light on what is present, or what is present its light on what is past: rather, image is that wherein what has been comes together in a flash with the now to form a constellation. (1999, pp. 463–464)

Agamben argues that "paintings are not immobile images, but stills charged with movement, stills from a film that is missing" (2002, p. 314). Gesture is thus an aesthetic of the stilled-into-movement, for which Agamben's central example is cinema as "images charged with movement". Image here is the thought as well as the seen, and the stilling, and thus interruption, produces the image as "gesture", and opens the possibility of seeing, thinking, anew. Agamben sees montage as the "specific character of cinema" through which such a dialectical image is made manifest. It is in repetition and stoppage that "the two transcendental conditions of montage" are found – exemplified in Debord's films, as in those of Godard. Referring to the work of Kierkegaard, Nietzsche, Heidegger and Deleuze, he characterises repetition not as a return to the same, but to what was, such that it "restores the possibility of what was, renders it possible anew; it's almost a paradox. To repeat something is to make it possible anew" (1994b, pp. 315–316 "Difference"). Stoppage pulls the image (word) "out of the flux of meaning", exhibiting it as such, producing "a hesitation between image and meaning" (1999, pp. 316–317). Here Agamben is close to Deleuze's account of the time-image as arising through montage, in the "irrational" cut, or interval, (1989, p. 214) and of course is privileging an avant-garde and political cinema.

Gesture as ethics

For Agamben, gesture is a "speechless dwelling in language" (1999, p. 78), and thus an unspoken, a not-yet spoken, or not possible to speak, that demands to be read yet can never the fully articulated in language. He argues, however, that modern society has lost its gestures as the unspeakable in a psychology of moral character expression inaugurated by Honoré de Balzac in the nineteenth century (1993, p. 135).[5]

> But an epoch that has lost its gestures is, by the same token, obsessed by them; for men from whom all authenticity has been taken, gesture becomes destiny. And the more gestures lost their ease under the pressure of unknown powers, the more life became indecipherable. And once the simplest and most everyday gestures had become as foreign as the gesticulations of marionettes, humanity – whose very bodily existence had already become sacred to the degree that it had made itself impenetrable – was ready for the massacre. (1999, p. 83)

What is lost is gesture is an act of communicability, becoming instead an expressivity of emotion or sensibility as access to a knowable truth of the person, or character, which is as such an illusion. Agamben's concept of gesture is instead anti-realist, it does not depend on conventions of interpretation, of verisimilitude; its central importance is not as an expression of the individual subject, but as an act of communicating communicability in a being for another, as a "being-in-language". "However", he continues, "because being-in-language is not something that could be said in sentences, the gesture is essentially always a gesture of not being able to figure something out in language" (2000, p. 59). It is in this communicating communicability that, Agamben argues, "gesture opens the sphere of *ethos* as the most fitting sphere of human action" (1993, p. 140) The gesture introduces a stilling that nevertheless opens communicability but without an already articulated end purpose: "The *gesture is the exhibition of a mediality: it is the process of making a means visible as such*. It allows the emergence of the being-in-a-medium of human beings and thus it opens the ethical dimension for them" (2000, p. 58 Italics in original).

He sees in cinema, the new medium of the twentieth century, however, that: "a society that has lost its gestures seeks to re-appropriate what it has lost while simultaneously recording that loss" (1993, p. 137). Agamben thus identifies gesture with film, and argues that "Because cinema has its centre in gesture and not in the image, it belongs essentially to the realm of ethics and politics (and not simply to that of aesthetics)" (2000, p. 55). Politics, Agamben states in his concluding sentence to his essay in *Means Without Ends*, is "the sphere of pure means, that is, of the absolute and complete gesturality of human beings" (2000, p. 60), and later in the book, that "politics is the sphere neither of an end in itself nor of means subordinated to an end; rather, it is the sphere of a pure mediality without end intended as the field of human action and of human thought" (2000, p. 117). Agamben here draws on Foucault's critique of discursive power and biopolitics, defining instead a concept of politics that can arise outside of the already-given of dominant discursive structures.

Central here for Agamben is his differentiation between producing or making which is a means to a given end other than itself, and action, *praxis*, which is "an end without means" (2000, p. 57), and what he terms a third type of action, in which the subject neither makes something nor enacts something, that he draws from the Roman scholar, Marcus Terentius Varro who inscribes gesture – the Latin *gerere*, from which gesture derives, meaning to conduct oneself (se gerere), to carry or to bear – in action. Theatre provides Varro's examples of the first two actions, namely the writer who makes, who produces the play, but does not act it, whereas the actor acts the play but does not make it. Varro points to a third, through the term *res gerere*, that refers to governance, or managing, by those invested in power, who "takes charge, in other words carries the burden of it" (Cited by Agamben 1993, p. 140).[6] Gesture here is an action of bearing responsibility and thus ethical.

Within a film, the three aspects of gesture Agamben discusses – stilling-into-movement, opening communicability, supporting – can be found both in the actions of characters within shots, and in the editing, in the deploying of a "stilling", that is, a shot of stillness in the moving images as a moment of action held in the unfolding of its real-time of event, as well as the return to, or repetition of images that he finds in the films of Debord. But in addition, the film in its entirety is a "gesture" that is ethical. Gestures address, they figure an interlocutor, whether present or not. Film as such always gestures to its viewer; it only exists in the time of its projection that produces from the stilled image cinema's movement. It is the gestures represented within *Exotica*, as well as the gesture the film constitutes, presents, that I now want to explore.

Exotica

For *Exotica's* director, Atom Egoyan, film viewing is very much an engaged activity, though not one that is always conscious. He comments that,

> To me, the highest aim of any film is to enter so completely into the subconscious of the viewer that there are moments and scenes and gestures which can be generated by the spectator's imagination. That becomes part of the film they're playing in their mind, and I hope the film has enough space to allow that type of exchange.(1995, p. 50)

The film's title is the name of a nightclub, where much of the action takes place, that offers male entertainment – strippers, and tabledancing with its prohibition on touching by the customers, while the deep velvet tones of Eric as the master of ceremonies draws the listener to imagine the delights to be – voyeuristically – enjoyed. *Exotica's* narrative is highly elliptical, in delaying or giving only partial information about characters' back stories, and eliding knowledge of their motives. It unfolds in a present time of indeterminate duration of days or weeks, taking place in just a few locations, but the film crosscuts, indeed jumps, between these as well as to two different past places through subjective flashbacks that are ambiguously motivated, in a repeated return to two scenes in the past.

Egoyan has spoken of drawing on the notion of counterpoint in music within his narrative structures, developing "a theme and certain voices that articulate that theme by playing with it and creating tensions between two disparate tracks, which are ultimately reflecting or mirroring a common concern" (1993, p. 47). This counterpoint is realised on the one hand through accidental interconnections between characters that implicate them in each others' relations of desire, and on the other hand through parallel editing, the use of flashbacks that return to the same scene, with slight differences, producing a doubling, exchange and interchange between characters and their actions.

The film opens with such a counterpoint, as the camera explores the "Exotica" club, tracking and panning across customers and dancers, ending with a voice-over as a sound bridge to the next scene that presents not the protagonist, Francis, but pet shop owner Thomas. Passing through airport customs, he is seen through a two-way mirror as the customs inspector, already heard in voice-over, continues to address his colleague, Ian: "You have to convince yourself that this person has something hidden that you have to find. You check his bags, but it's his face, his *gestures*, that you are really watching". Here is the examining gaze of the law, but also that of the voyeur, and of narrative desire as such in the wish to uncover the truth of what, and why, for which the person's *performance*, his *gestures*, are the expressive truth of the person. It is not what is hidden, however, but what is on the surface that we must attend to, for Egoyan's film confounds attempts to read the gestures as expressive, instead engaging us in the ambiguities of proper and improper desire in *Exotica,* figured in the actions and expressions of characters – their gestural performance. It is the role of gesture in communicating communicability, and the gesture that indicates an unspeakable, that my discussion seeks to explore, in order to argue that the film presents an ethics of desire.

Central to the film is mourning, loss and trauma, "played" in the ritual Francis enacts with Christina at the club as she dances for him, and which is brutally ended when he is lured by Eric to touch Christina, thus becoming banished from the club and from the repetition of the ritual. The central enigma of the film is the nature of Francis' obsession with Christina and how this ritual satisfies it. Her dancing stages unsatisfiable desire, of the object as forbidden – is this what is at stake for Francis? Moreover what is Christina's involvement? For she too appears invested in the ritual between them.

Christina dances dressed as a young schoolgirl complete with satchel, moving salaciously as she slowly strips to the ironic lyrics of Leonard Cohen's (1998) song, *Everybody Knows*, that provides another recurring counterpoint across the film. Joining Francis at his table, her provocative dance for him is, we will learn, an established ritual encounter. Francis leaves while Eric – the mc and Christina's former lover – is heard saying "What is it about a schoolgirl that gives her special innocence? Is it the way that they gaze at you?" as Christina looks up at him. The following jump-cut – to a sunlit field that fills the screen until slowly people appear over the distant hill – is not clearly marked as her subjective memory until we learn from later cutaways to this scene that it is a flashback to the search for Francis' missing daughter, Lisa, and also where Christina and Eric first met and will discover Lisa's body, as Eric reveals to Francis in the penultimate sequence. This flashback is a single shot, without camera movement, lasting 40s, an image stilled. The film cuts back to Francis, so that Christina's remembering becomes associated with Francis, who is now seen standing in a washroom stall, breathing heavily. His intense response is ambiguous: how should we read what we see in his face, his manner? Does his apparent anguish arise from desire repressed in response to the obvious sexual invitation of Christina's performance as seducing schoolgirl?

Each time he visits "Exotica", Francis brings his niece, Tracey, to practise her piano and flute in his home, and pays her, introducing a further question of her role in this ritual, as this scene is inter-cut with the second performance of Francis' ritual with Christina, firstly as he sits watching Christina on stage, then secondly, in the washroom. The ambiguity of the ritual is made more complex when the distraught-looking Francis tells Christina he's thinking: "what would happen if someone ever hurt you?" When she replies, "How could anyone hurt me?", he responds, "If I'm not there to protect you", but she rejoins "You'll always be there to protect me". Francis, apparently speaking of a past traumatic event, asks: "Why would somebody want to do something like that? How could somebody even think of doing something like that?" But is he addressing Christina, or himself and his own desire that is not only paedophiliac but also incestuous? For as he enters the men's room again, we are introduced to his daughter Lisa by way of a cut to his niece Tracey at his home looking at the many photographs of his wife and daughter. Tracey's look then becomes replaced by the film's, as we see video footage of Lisa playing the piano, with her mother beside her, laughing and smiling, as her mother puts her hand over the camera lens. Francis now appears as a devoted father and husband but the next shot returns us to him, still in the washroom stall, breathing heavily.

The event that motivates Eric to lure Francis to touch Christina, thus changing the stable world of these characters, is not shown directly but must be inferred as a response to the change in the emotional triangle he participates in with Christina and her new lover, Zoe who is also the club's owner. Involved here is both heterosexual and homosexual desire, but also maternal, and perhaps paternal love, when we see first Eric gently touch Zoe's distended belly, then later Christina's caress that is followed by Zoe's passionate kiss. Eric has lost Christina to Zoe, and he will lose his unborn child to their relationship, while he also loses Christina's respect and friendship when she discovers his paternity-contract with Zoe, who may thereby, too, have lost Christina's love. What, then, of Eric's desire? It soothed him to see Christina and Francis' ritual, Eric says after he has destroyed it. Is his revenge against Francis, or Christina? What is the role of this ritual, with its problematic reference to paedophilia, and thus to the death of Lisa at the hands of a child molester? Opposed here is the proper parental love for a child, and perverse and deadly desire, but which do we associate Francis with? And what is Christina's investment in the ritual?

In the third and final ritual, Francis is seated at a balcony table, his gaze averted while Christina – removing her stockings and undoing her blouse – gazes at him as Francis declares "How could anyone hurt you? Take you away from me? How could anyone?" Rising to sit astride him in a palpably erotic gesture, Christina leans forward as if she might kiss him, but her lips skim past his as she drops her head to end resting on his shoulder (Figure 1). The reverse-field cut to a rapid panning shot reveals Francis leaving, matched in the next shot by Eric, watching at his MC station, who turns and leaves. A counterpoint is introduced as the film inter-cuts to Thomas in his apartment with Ian (the customs officer), as they become sexually intimate, the explosive force of their burgeoning relationship figured in the thunderstorm heard in the distance. The cut-back reveals Francis in the washroom stall pulling off a long strip of white toilet paper he wraps around his hand in a gesture that is both a bandage and a cleansing, as we again hear a clap of thunder, but here it portends a quite different climax. Eric now

Figure 1. The third and final ritual between Christina and Francis, she leans forward as if she might kiss him.

139

enters the men's room, passing the urinals to halt by a washbasin in whose mirror he's seen reflected, opposite the door to Francis's stall, which he now bangs on. Using a fake accent, Eric begins his seduction of Francis, tempting him to touch Christina. What he voices may also be what we have been thinking: "she seems to have a bit of a thing for you, doesn't she?", observing that their conversation is not "what I would call usual … You get pretty intense, my friend".

A drum, pounding like a heartbeat, is heard as shots of Eric alternate with close-ups of Francis, his expression suggesting that he is trying to control his emotions as he calmly replies, "You're not supposed to touch". "Yes, but she is into it, believe me", answers Eric as he walks around – one might say strutting – brushing back a lock of hair, performing his part, *enjoying* his scenario of revenge; a Faustian devil that knows Francis' thoughts. Indeed, Eric appears to float above Francis' head in two shots where the camera's high-angle reveals him in frame, seen behind the filigree ironwork of the grill above the stall door, much like the devil in religious paintings (Figure 2). Francis asks "How do you know?" Eric's reply, "Everybody knows", recalling Cohen's song, "Trust me […] Just a little touch. Nothing too drastic. Then you will get the full experience, my friend. And you will love it, you will love it". Are not his words expressing what we might believe is Francis' true desire? "What happens when I touch her?", Francis demands, and the film cuts to the video footage seen earlier of his wife and daughter together at the piano (Figure 3), their joyous laughter heard together with the club music and a thunder clap, and Francis repeats "What happens?"

In the next shot Christina is again dancing for Francis but he is looking down, his fingers held together in a gesture of contemplation, or prayer. A brief cutaway reveals Eric standing watching them, then we see Francis – still without looking at her – place his palm upon Christina's belly, repeating Eric's gesture earlier when he touched Zoe's swollen belly to feel the growing child. The pace and tone now change to violence as the camera cuts and pans fast to Eric, as it earlier has panned to follow Francis, running to Francis and, pulling him away to the exit, throwing him down the stairs.

In the film's third act, Francis commences a counter-action, having blackmailed Thomas to perform in his place while he listens via an audio wire. Having audited

Figure 2. Francis in the washroom stall, Eric seen above and behind him, as Francis repeats "What will happen if I touch her?"

Figure 3. The video image of Francis' wife and daughter shown at the end of the film as he records them laughing happily, seen earlier as flashbacks to an ambiguous image.

Thomas's accounts, Francis offers to conceal the evidence of Thomas' illegal importing of protected bird's eggs. Christina tells Thomas of Francis' tragedy, that Francis himself was suspected of Lisa's murder and although cleared, remained deeply affected. Christina then introduces a new enigma, never fully resolved, when she explains their ritual, saying "Well, we've always had this understanding. I mean, I need him for certain things, and he needs me for certain things […] I was doing things for him and he's done things for me […]."

Thomas is persuaded by Frances to return and touch Christina in order to draw Eric outside, where Francis intends to shoot him. In the club Zoe now introduces Christina, watching her as intently as Eric had, thereby occupying his place in relation to Christina but without his rivalrous identification with Francis. Inter-cut, we see the now-sacked Eric surprise Francis outside the club, and tell him that it was he, with Christina, who found Lisa's body in the field – shown in flashback. Jealousy, with its homoerotic overtones, becomes replaced by a brotherly – homocentric – embrace by Francis.

Francis' ritual with Christina can now be understood not as repressed desire but as a form of incomplete mourning by a father for his dead child. Incomplete because the loss is marked by trauma, namely, his inability to protect her from a sexual desire he must repeatedly enact his indifference to. Such a reading would release us from our implication in a position of desire in apprehending Christina as the woman-child offering herself sexually – a desire to be or to have her. But if Francis traumatically repeats his inability to prevent Lisa's lostness in his ritual with Christina, why is he drawn by Eric's seductive cajoling to touch her? And has our narrative desire been dashed, or fulfilled?

Nevertheless, why does Francis touch her? Narratively, he must – in order to be thrown out, while his action appears to resolve the narrative question the ritual has posed: he does desire the child/woman. Christina's assertion to Zoe and Eric, however, that Francis didn't want to touch her, contradicts this reading. Is he seduced by Eric's claim, echoing the refrain from Cohen's song, "Everybody knows […]" – and thereby also its ironies – that "she" wants it, that is, Francis' desire? If so, what is his desire?

For when Francis touches Christina, he does this by placing his hand on her belly, reprising Eric's gesture earlier, when touching Zoe's belly, swollen in pregnancy with his child. These two gestures contrast with the third touching by Thomas, when – acting in Francis' place – he puts his hand on Christina's thigh, a gesture of heterosexual desire that is a masquerade, for his story in the film is of discovering homosexual love. In understanding that Thomas' gesture is not what it seems, we may infer that this is also true of Francis' touching of Christina. If associated with Eric's touching, however, Frances' gesture evokes the child-to-be within the figure of the maternal, and thus a masculine desire in relation to the mother of his child, which was the flashback that precedes his touching over which Francis repeated, "What happens?" Christina's performative gesture in the club "Exotica" is as child/woman, but in their ritual, for Francis she is the daughter he does not touch; in touching her, she is not as Lisa, his daughter, but rather his wife – whose desire he seeks, and whose loss he re-enacts, indeed doubly lost in her affair with his brother, and her subsequent death in a car accident which left his brother crippled.

We usually question our first readings, Slavoj Žižek suggests, believing that meaning only discloses itself in a second reading but this, he argues, is a defence formation against the shock of the first reading. (2004, p. 286). What shocked in our initial reading was not just Francis' apparent paedophilic desire, but rather and more importantly his *ritual of submission* to its prohibition, making apparent the illusion of "if only", namely that, as Žižek notes – writing of courtly love – without such a hindrance the object of desire would be directly accessible (1994, p. 92). In his embrace of Eric, however, Francis enables the reassuring second reading that he does indeed, *not* desire his daughter, for his gesture is a response to Eric's revelation of his role, with Christina, in finding Lisa. It is an ethical gesture within the film, opening communicability between the characters. But what, in Eric's revelation, motivates Francis' response? It is, I suggest, Eric's jealousy of the intimate relation Francis has with the adult Christina, whom Eric desires but has lost. There is, in the embrace then, an identification, an equivalence, in which the "proper" desire of Eric for the adult woman, Christina, corresponds to a "proper" desire on the part of Francis, namely for the adult woman Christina here stands in for. Yet the suddenness, indeed abruptness, of their embrace, makes it appear under-motivated, thereby questioning this re-assuring reading. The film's ethical gesture is in this opening of communicability which is held, stilled. Meanwhile Francis' transgression in touching Christina has opened us to the intolerable knowledge of what Lacan describes as the unattainability of the desired object, as always-lost, which his embrace of Eric – if read as identificatory – reiterates, in a gesture that speaks the unspeakable, but as a "gag", in a stopping of speech. It is a "gagging" in Agamben's terms, for within the film it produces a hesitation between the image of the embrace, and its meaning that is irresolvable.

The ritual, the gesture, between Francis and Christina, however, involves not touching, the emotional kernel of which is a father repeatedly enacting not that he does not desire daughter, but his inability to protect her from another man's desire – a desire that is figured via a displacement, namely in the image of Christina's seductiveness. The expressive gesture here for this – mental – action is Francis's visible distress but which instead becomes readable as repressed desire.

It is Christina's story we now follow when, as Thomas touches her, a brief flashback to the finding of Lisa is followed by Christina gently removing Thomas' hand from her thigh and folding it closed, she gives it back to him. This is closely watched by Zoe – as Eric, but also and importantly as her mother, used to – from the private observatory, of a joyously smiling Christina. The inter-cut close-ups of Zoe's face, rather than the jealous anxiety of Eric, suggest curiosity – mirroring our own as spectators, and we may understand Christina's gesture and smile as a closure to the role the ritual has performed for her, in a process of repair, in an opening out to the world anew.[7] If so, what is the importance here of the same-sex desire of these three characters, Zoe, Christina and Thomas? Certainly it is a desire that in the film is not marked by violence.

Egoyan's cinema is gestural in his deployment of the flashback because in it the images, and their narrative, are fixed in a past time *before* that, introduced into the present or now time of the film's action presage an *after* in the future of the film's action. *Exotica*, cutting to the video of Francis' wife and daughter, connects Christina to his tragedy in a flashback unmotivated by a character's look. The next shot shows Francis filming them before answering the door to a younger, plainer Christina arriving to babysit Lisa. The next shot shows Francis later driving Christina home, talking proudly of Lisa's achievements, but then he says that Lisa thinks Christina's unhappy at home, and that, if she should want to talk about things "you know that I'm here, okay?" Christina does not respond, instead, as Francis pays her, Christina tells him how much she enjoys these drives home, and Francis replies, "So do I".

The film closes with Christina walking up the path to her "unhappy home", turning us away from the masculine traumas of loss of Francis and Eric and their redemptive embrace, to the film's real, in the sense that Lacan proposed, of an unrepresentable in the experience of trauma of a different girl child, Christina, and her story that is untold, unredeemed (Figure 4). Christina's performance at the "Exotica" club, as Emma Wilson poignantly articulates, realises the "forbidden, disallowed image of the daughter" (2009, p. 83) as a subtext of desire that she also addresses to herself, reflexively performing the image of a seductiveness projected upon her by another, the perpetrator of the implied abuse experienced within her own family. For this film, Egoyan has spoken of having drawn upon the understanding he gained from his involvement with a girlfriend who was being abused, of "how somebody who is abused makes a parody of their own sexual identity as a means of trying to convince themselves that that part of themselves which has been destroyed is somehow not as vital as it is" (1995, p. 48)

Figure 4. The film's final shot, of Christina walking up to the front door of her home.

If in touching Christina Frances seeks to know "what happens", it is as reassurance that Christina's performance is truly a masquerade, for only as such does she make Lisa live again as his innocent daughter. What Francis "does" for Christina is not the repression of desire in a submission to the external prohibition that her father may have failed to observe, but an ethical act that is also a gift of love, signified in the traumatic re-enactment of his inability to protect his daughter, performed with Christina as Lisa, whereby Christina is recognised as the girl child that should be protected, but wasn't. Christina's is the story the film does not show but which we must conjure for ourselves, yet what Egoyan offers us for this act of magical thinking involves us in the very ambivalence of our desire. Through *Exotica*'s gestures something is endured and supported that engages the ethical, and political of desiring.

Acknowledgements

The development of my theoretical discussion of gesture in this essay draws on my analysis of *Exotica* in "Mourning, Loss and Trauma, and the Ambiguities of Proper and Improper Desire in *Exotica* (1994)", in *Film Moments*, eds. Tom Brown and James Walters, London: Palgrave/BFI, 2010.

Notes

1. The OED tells us that "gesture" as an intransitive verb, means to make or use gestures, to gesticulate, and as a transitive verb, to express by gestures; to accompany with or emphasise by gestures. As a noun, it refers to the manner of carrying the body: bearing, carriage, deportment (more fully, *gesture of the body*), but that, in a more restricted sense, it is the movement of the body or any part of it in such a way that the movement is expressive of thought or feeling. A gesture, then, may express good will, or anger.
2. Maurice Merleau-Ponty, for example, writes: In reality, we have already introduced consciousness, and what we have designated under the name of life was already consciousness of life. The concept is only the interior of nature, says Hegel. And already it seemed to us that the notion of a living body could not be grasped without the unity of signification, which distinguishes a gesture from a sum of movements (1963, pp.161–162).
3. The soldier walks with a severely arched back that he is unable to bend, and hence he cannot lie down without falling. Gordon refilmed and slowed the man's painstaking and deliberate movements, both echoing the work of Marey and Muybridge and undermining it, for this movement that is endlessly repeated can never reveal a scientific truth of the body. Instead, it engages the real of the body but no longer through the particularity of its specific historical context, for the 1919 film shows the soldier cured – able to bend his back normally. Gordon's work is part of the collection of the Tate Modern in London.
4. Agamben also discusses painting, sculpture, theatre and dance in developing his concept of gesture, but language and film figure pre-eminently.
5. Agamben contrasts Balzac's view of gesture as "only an expression of moral character" with the careful identification and description, but not interpretation, of involuntary gestures and tics in 1886 by Gilles de la Tourette, the syndrome to which he gave his name. From thousands of such cases observed from 1885, it almost totally disappears from records until Oliver Sacks, in 1971 in New York, observes what he recognises as three cases of Tourettism, and it is now, again, a well-documented syndrome. For Agamben this demonstrates the way in which gesture as such, and its communicability, have been lost (Agamben, 2000).
6. Agamben further extends the role of gesture in his thinking to philosophy, as well as politics, that is, to how we think ourselves in the world: "For politics is the sphere of the full, absolute gesturality of human beings, and it has no name other than its Greek pseudonym, which is barely uttered here: philosophy". (1999, p. 85).
7. A related, but much more extensive, reading of the face, is given by Joan Copjec her discussion of King Vidor's film *Stella Dallas* (1937, USA) (2002, pp. 118–131).

References

Agamben, G. (1993). Notes on gesture. In *Infancy and history: The destruction of experience*. (L. Heron, Trans.). London: Verso.
Agamben, G. (1999). Kommerell, or on gesture. In *Potentialities: Collected essays in philosophy* (pp. 77–85). Stanford, CA: Stanford University Press.
Agamben, G. (2000). Notes on gesture. In *Means without end*. (V. Binetti & C. Casarino, Trans.). Minneapolis, MN: University of Minnesota Press.
Agamben, G. (2002). Difference and repetition: On Guy Debord's films. In E. McDonough, (Ed.), *Guy Debord and the Situationist International: Texts and documents*. (pp. 314–319). Cambridge, Mass and London: October Books and MIT Press.
Artaud, A. (1995). Athlete of the heart. In T. Cole & H. K. Chinoy (Eds.), *Actors on acting* (4th ed.), (pp. 234–235). New York, NY: Three Rivers Press/Random House.
Benjamin, A. (2000). Time and task: Benjamin and Heidegger showing the present. In A. Benjamin & P. Osborne (Eds.), *Walter Benjamin's philosophy: Destruction and experience* (pp. 216–245). London: Clinamen.
Benjamin, W. (1969). Theses on the philosophy of history. In T. Cole & H. K. Chinoy (Eds.), *Illuminations*. (pp. 262–265). (H. Zohn, Trans.). New York, NY: Schocken Books.
Benjamin, W. (1999). *The arcades project*. (H. Eiland & K. McLaughlin, Trans.). Cambridge: Harvard University Press.
Cohen, L. 1988. Everybody Knows. Retrieved August 2, 2013, from http://www.lyricsfreak.com/l/leonard+cohen/everybody+knows_20082809.html
Copjec, J. (2002). *Imagine there's no woman*. Cambridge, MA: MIT Press.
Deleuze, G. (1986). *Cinema 1: The movement-image*. (H. Tomlinson & B. Habberjam, Trans.). Minneapolis: University of Minnesota Press.
Deleuze, G. (1989). *Cinema 2: The time image*. (H. Tomlinson & R. Galeta, Trans.). Minneapolis: University of Minnesota Press.
Deleuze, G., & Guattari, F. (1994). *Difference and repetition*. (P. Patton, Trans.). New York, NY: Columbia University Press.
Delsarte, F. (1995, September 26). Elements of the Delsarte system. In T. Cole & H. K. Chinnoy (Eds.), *Actors on acting* (Vol. 188, 4th ed., pp. 187–190). New York, NY: Three Rivers Press/Random House.
Egoyan, A. (1993). *Speaking parts*. Toronto: Coach House Press.
Egoyan, A. (1995). *Exotica*, script and interviews, Toronto: Coach House Press, 50.
Kommerell, M. (1933). *Jean Paul*. Frankfurt am Main: Klostermann.
Lessing, G. E. (1853). *Laocöon*. (E. C. Beasley, Trans.). London: Longman.
Merleau-Ponty, M. (1963). *The structure of behavior*. (A. L. Fisher, Trans.). Boston, MA: Beacon Press.
Stezaker, J. (2006). The film still and its double: Reflections on the "found" film-Still. In D. Green & J. Lowry (Eds.), *Stillness and time: Photography and the moving image*. (pp. 113–127). Brighton: Photoworks and Photoforum, University of Brighton.
Wilson, E. (2009). *Atom Egoyan*. Champaign: University of Illinois.
Žižek, S. (1994). *The metastases of enjoyment: Six essays on woman and causality*. London: Verso.
Žižek, S. (2004). The foreign gaze which sees too much. In A. Egoyan & I. Balfour (Eds.), *Subtitles: On the foreignness of film* (pp. 280–308). Cambridge, MA: MIT Press.

'The exchange of two fantasies and the contact of two epidermises': gestures of touch in *Gattaca* (1997), *The Talented Mr. Ripley* (1999) and *The Piano* (1993)

Naomi Segal

Department of European Cultures and Languages, University of London, London, UK

Touch in film can communicate the success or failure of desire. The social contact of two epidermises – as defined by Chamfort in 1796 – is often mediate or indirect. Theorised by Sartre and Merleau-Ponty, the caress is the inverse of the haptic grasp. In this essay I look at two versions of the caressive gesture, found in Jane Campion's *The Piano*, Andrew Niccol's *Gattaca* and Anthony Minghella's *The Talented Mr Ripley*. In no case is this simply the action of sexual desire, though it may also be that. In each of the films, these gestures are born not so much out of the wish to *have* as the wish to *be*. In *The Piano*, the non-haptic caress turns over, using the back of the hand to touch the other – the husband, the child, the piano, the sea – and this is part of the release of the protagonist Ada from the autistic 'egg' in which she is initially enclosed. In *Gattaca* and *The Talented Mr Ripley*, the desire to be the more successful other is expressed in two related ways: by the touch of the face on a garment and in the visible blending of two faces into one.

> Love, as it exists in Society, is nothing more than the exchange of two fantasies and the contact of two epidermises. Chamfort, 1796[1]

The recent introduction of the concept of the "haptic" in cinema looks not at

> technologies that attempt to reproduce the sense of smell (for example, Odorama) or touch (for example, the Power Glove) – in effect, movement-image strategies for evoking smell and touch – [but at] how audiovisual media evoke these other senses within their own constraints

(Marks, 2000, p. 131). It works against the dominance of the optic as primary filmic sense, not by pretending to overcome or supersede it but by looking at what it does other than present or represent things to our eyes. In a similar way, this essay looks at scenes and images in which, in three films of the 1990s, the cinematic gesture communicates certain mediate kinds of touch.

I want to begin by proposing two versions of the caress that are the opposite of haptic, in that they avoid grasping, gripping or any other kind of acquisition.[2] Here is a paragraph by Merleau-Ponty in his posthumous *Le Visible et l'invisible* (1964), which appears unexpectedly in the middle of a discussion of the "solipsistic illusion" of the bodied subject:

For the first time, the body no longer couples with the world, it intertwines with another body, applying itself carefully to it with its whole expanse, tirelessly sculpting with its hands the strange statue which, in its turn, gives everything it receives, cut off from the world and its aims, occupied with the sole fascination of floating in Being together with another life, making itself the outside of its inside and the inside of its outside. And then at once, movement, touch and vision, applied to the other and to themselves, head back to their source and, in the patient, silent work of desire, commence the paradox of expression. (Merleau-Ponty, 1964, p. 187)

What is perhaps most striking in this passage are two key images: caressing the body of the other described as the "careful" creation of a "strange statue" which is, at the same time, the beginnings of a paradoxical attempt at "expression". I will return to these images in relation to *The Piano*.

And here is Sartre in *L'Être et le néant*:

Everyone is disappointed by that famous saying: '[love is] the contact of two epidermises'. Love is not meant to be mere contact; it seems that only man can reduce it to a contact, and when that happens it loses its true meaning. The caress is not a simple floating touch: it is a *fashioning*. When I caress another person, I create their flesh by my caress, with my fingers. [...] By means of pleasure, the caress is able to create the body of the other both for them and for myself as a *touched* passivity, in the sense that my body becomes flesh in order to touch their body with its own passivity – in caressing itself against it rather than caressing it. This is why the gestures of lovemaking have a languor that one might almost call studied: it is not so much that we *take hold of* a part of the other's body but that we *bring* our own body up against the body of the other. Not so much pushing or touching, in an active sense, but *placing up against*. [...] By *realizing* the other's incarnation, the caress uncovers my own incarnation to me. [...] I make the other person taste my flesh through their own flesh in order to make them feel themselves being flesh. In this way *possession* is revealed as a *double reciprocal incarnation*. (Sartre, 1943, pp. 430–431, italics Sartre's)

In this essay I am going to look at two versions of the caressive gesture, as they are found in Jane Campion's *The Piano* (1993), Andrew Niccol's *Gattaca* (1997) and Anthony Minghella's *The Talented Mr Ripley* (1999). In no case is this simply the action of sexual desire, though it may also be that. As we shall see, the gesture is born not so much out of the wish to *have* as the wish to *be*. In *The Piano*, the non-haptic caress turns over, using the back of the hand to touch the other – the husband, the child, the piano, the sea – and this is part of the release of the protagonist Ada from the autistic "egg" in which she is initially enclosed. In *Gattaca* and *The Talented Mr Ripley*, the desire to be the more successful other is expressed in two related ways: by the touch of the face on a garment and the visible blending of two faces into one.

In an interview of 1983, Didier Anzieu talks of the way the psychoanalyst may avoid the demand of touch in the analytic setting: "one can touch with the voice" (1991, p. 75). He goes on:

In everyday language we talk of 'getting in touch with someone' or 'having good contact' with them. This shows that the earliest version of contact was actually tactile, and then it was metaphorically transposed to the other sense organs and sensorial fields. What seems to me specifically analytical is to draw on these sense organs and sensorial fields in order to find verbal equivalents of those primal exchanges that introduce the nursling to the world of signifiers, but which have to be abandoned afterwards if the child is to develop. (1991, p.75)

What happens in *The Piano* reverses and subverts this principle: touch stands in for the voice. As in Merleau-Ponty, the caress in this film is an aestheticising act, but one that changes the "strange statue" that Ada has been along with her piano, into sentient flesh. This pygmalionesque process comes about, I'd like to suggest, both by her being caressed and by her own caressing.

In the opening scene, a high-pitched woman's voice speaks lines that we sense are audible only to her and us: "the voice you hear is not my speaking voice but my mind's voice", she says, "I have not spoken since I was six years old". It is not clear that the hazy vertical stripes of reddish light are fingers until we see the reverse shot: a wedding-ringed hand with one dark eye looking out. Preparing to leave Scotland, the protagonist tends to her sleeping daughter, from whom she cuts a roller-skate – echoed later in the shoe she loses off to save herself from drowning – and then turns to her piano:

> in the dim light she begins to play strongly. Her face strains, she is utterly involved, unaware of her own strange guttural sounds that form an eerie accompaniment to the music.

> An old maid in night-dress looks in. abruptly the woman stops playing. The emotion leaves her face, it whitens and seems solid like a wall. (Campion, 1993, p. 10)

The guttural noises are omitted in the film, but the air of concentration and the "wall" are very clear. That wall is what Anzieu would call Ada's psychic skin ([1985], 1995). Annie Anzieu describes such silence in autistic mutes: "nothing emerges from [them] but nothing goes in either; their body is rather like an egg in motion. It seems as though they use this imaginary shell to protect an essential inner core" (Anzieu, 1989, p.129). Ada is not autistic but she has made an autistic choice, "not a handicap but a strategy" (Campion cited in Pryor, 1993, p. 25). All the characters think of her silence in the Victorian terms of an exorbitant "will". This impulse will itself gradually be undone as another "fashioning" or "incarnation" takes its place.

If the voice is a normalising emissary, Ada chooses two ways to replace its function. The first is her daughter (Segal, 1997), the second is the piano; both are also objects of intense intimacy and both are mediated by the hand. As we have already seen, when we watch Ada playing her piano we witness something that is inward-turned, involving all her senses together. The piano stands in for its owner's body and is an image of her relation to something of herself that does not form words. It is all the more essential as a means of communication between Ada and Baines because he cannot read so she cannot write.

Hands feature in most of the scenes of *The Piano*, not just when we hear the music. They flail and catch as Ada and Flora are uncomfortably transported onto the beach. They play, inseparably stroking and communicating, as the mother tells her daughter a story. They hold a portrait, a message, they need scrubbing, they dress and undress, they dictate rebuffs; they shadow-mime threat and carry out violence; they cover a mouth to indicate shock or frame a face viewing itself; they measure out a bargain or turn pages; a hand held in an audience may suggest marital intimacy (though Ada removes her ring to play the piano but not to make love); hands touch and caress.

What I am looking at here, though, is a particular image that occurs at a number of significant points in *The Piano* and, I suggest, punctuates (without explanation) Ada's progress from enclosure to emancipation – the caress of the back of the hand. Ada's key objects are four: the piano, the child, the man and the sea. Before taking each of these in turn, I want to discuss the importance of the back of the hand. Rilke complained to Gide that the German language has a word for the back of the hand but no word for the palm:

> At the most, we can say 'Handflächen': the flat [*plaine*] of the hand', he cried. 'Imagine calling the inside of the hand a 'plain'! Whereas 'Handrücken' is used all the time. That's what they think about, the back of the hand, a surface with no interest, no personality, no sensuality, no softness, by contrast to the palm, which is warm, caressive, soft, and expresses all the mystery of the individual! (Gide, 1924, p.61)

From the point of view of this film, he is entirely wrong. In a late publication, Eve Sedgwick wrote: "to touch is always already to reach out, to fondle, to heft, to tap or to enfold" (Sedgwick, 2003, p. 14), but I disagree with her too. The touch of the back of a hand suggests the fingers in their least haptic, most patient mode; it is the obverse of grasping and very much what Sartre has in mind when he writes of the "languor" of the caress that is "not so much pushing or touching, in an active sense, but *placing up against*" (Sartre, 1943, p. 431).

Let's begin with the caress of the piano. Between Ada and Baines her back has been the object of attention from the start; this has been his way to reach the woman making music who turns away towards her own playing – not, I think, because this is what refuses him nor because it exposes her "vulnerable spine" (Dyson, 1995, p. 271) but because this inward-turning gesture is what is most fascinating about her. When, with the return of the piano, Ada loses this scenario, she discovers it is something she cannot do without. In the screenplay,

> she starts with wholehearted feeling, her eyes closed, but before long […] a reflex has her glance across her left shoulder and she pauses in her playing. Disquieted, she starts again and again she looks away. She stops, confused, unable to go on, unable to get up, one hand on the lid and one on the piano keys. (Campion, 1993, p. 80)

At this point, then, Ada perceives that it is not enough to enjoy the piano without the participation of another; she needs to be the object of a desiring gaze. This scene of playing is briefer in the film. We see Ada gaze without warmth at the piano while chewing a forkful of food; go over to it; place her napkin carelessly on it, and then pass the back of her hand across the keys, first one way and then the other. She starts to play, looks behind her, again runs the back of her fingers over the unsatisfying keys (Figure 1).

This gesture has occurred once earlier on. With Baines kissing her shoulders and neck as she lies warily beside him, we watch her expression change from the backward-consciousness of him to a forward concern with the piano. He stops, she gets up, goes to the piano and runs the back of her hand along the keys – then he shuts the lid so that she has to pull her hand away, and with tears in her eyes, puts on her jacket and leaves. In these scenes, the non-haptic, non-active relation of the fingers' back to the piano stands at the turning-point between two ways of living for Ada. The piano, like Baines, always faces her, offering itself front-on. By touching it through the back of her hand, she moves away from its prosthetic role in her address to herself and begins, uncertainly, to address herself to the other.

The second object that Ada touches with the back of her hand is her daughter. We see the girl take this initiative first, lying in bed laughing, caressing her mother's cheek

Figure 1. *The Piano* (Campion, 1993) Ada's hand caressing the piano keys.

with the back of her fingers while the latter signs to her the story of her relationship with Flora's father. Once, we see the back of Ada's hand on Flora: barricaded in Stewart's house, they are asleep together and the mother passes the back of her hand across the child's nightdress and hair until this wakes her and she moves on to her husband, in the scene we shall look at in a moment. The same placing, mother and daughter with hand-backs on each other's chest and neck, finds them asleep on the morning that Stewart decides to take down the planks. If it stands for anything, I suppose it is for innocence – which is the challenge we also take into the next example, Ada's caressing of her husband's body.

When an almost sleepwalking Ada comes to his bed to caress him (having been, we surmise, shocked to find herself reaching for Flora while dreaming of Baines), it is his skin that she focuses on, caressing it carefully and seemingly tenderly, running the back of her hand across and around his face, turning it in his open palm. Campion's stage directions here focus more on a strange equivalence of childlike qualities: Stewart "looks up into her face like a child after a bad dream, fearful and trusting" (Campion, 1993, p. 89) but then "childlike she stops and kisses the soft skin of his belly. [...] Ada seems removed from Stewart as if she had a separate curiosity of her own" (Campion, 1993, pp. 89–90).

In the second scene, he is lying on his front. Ada has her eyes closed. She places first the front, then the back of her hand on his buttocks. When he leaps up, saying "Why can't I touch you? Don't you like me?", she just "looks back, moved by his helplessness, but distanced, as if it has nothing to do with her" (Campion, 1993, p. 93). What is interesting here is the dedication and glow of this desire redirected onto an unloved body and simply "curious" and detached. It is as much a surprise to see Stewart bathed in golden light as to see Baines draping a pink lace cloth in his hut, so dominant have the shades of blue been in this film.

It is with these shades of blue that my last example is concerned. Ada is seated in the long boat that is carrying her, her lover, daughter, possessions and piano to Nelson. Suddenly she signs to the child that the piano must be thrown in the sea: "she doesn't want it; she says it's spoiled". At Ada's insistence Baines agrees. She strokes the water with the back of her hand – once, twice, as if preparing it or herself; then gazes at it. A moment later, she steps into the coiled rope and is pulled down with the piano.

Once again the director attributes her protagonist's action to "curiosity" (Campion, 1993, p. 121), this time "fatal [...], odd and undisciplined". Moments later, of course, Ada chooses life and enters into the unexpected happy ending that many viewers cannot forgive. But my question is: why the back-of-the-hand caress at exactly this point? Is it because she is bidding a complicated and ambivalent farewell to the whole skin of that world in which she was consensual with herself, the "egg in motion" of her autistic enclosure, which is no longer in season now and the piano must be abandoned for good?

When Gide looked at a photo of Pierre Herbart, a handsome young friend of Cocteau's whom he met in 1927, he said "I really think he has the physique that I would most like to inhabit" (Van Rysselberghe, 1974, p. 205). We need to distinguish this fantasy of entry inside the other from a notion of sexual penetration. In *Gattaca* and *The Talented Mr Ripley*, the skin of the other is not so much the object as the context for desire, the imagined pleasure of being rather than having. This is the desire to live as another person, don their appearance, in order to do something we cannot do in any other way.

Here, for example, is a governess finding herself literally in the shoes of her admired employer:

A strange thing about those shoes was the way in which, when she was wearing them, Mrs Brock, who was a heavy treader by nature, planted her feet and walked with the same long steps as Lady Grizel, and stood in the same careless, rather flighty way. A lovely sort of fantasy possessed Mrs Brock as she moved in this new pretty way, this confident way. Part of herself became Lady Grizel – she absorbed Lady Grizel and breathed her out into the air around herself, and the air around was a far less lonely place in consequence. (Keane [1981] 2001, pp. 20–21)

As we shall see in the examples that follow, the donning of a false self like a shoe or a second skin can prove, though seductive and difficult to slough off again ultimately suicidal.[3] Thus Musset's eponymous Lorenzaccio, after years of acting the part of companion in corruption to the duke his cousin whom he wishes to assassinate, recognises with despair that "vice used to be a garment – now it has become stuck to my skin" ([1834] 1976, p. 118). The original purpose that motivated disguise is no longer there "inside" the gestures and actions he has aped too well – indeed, this mimicry seems to prove that he never can have been the innocent he thought. An act of futile murder is, after this realisation, "all that remains of my virtue" (Musset [1834] 1976, p. 119).

Whether motivated by "virtue", curiosity or a more sinister end, the desire that assumes the costume of another's identity will always find it difficult to remove – as painful as the psychical tearing of the infant's fantasy of a "common skin" with the mother (Anzieu [1985] 1995, p. 85*ff*). In these two films, a male protagonist takes on the bodily existence of another for reasons of combined envy and desire, and with varying mitigations of success, haunted by crime. Like the puppetry motif developed in *Being John Malkovich* (2000), this raises questions not only within the fiction but also extra-diegetically – not least because of the interesting coincidence that the object of

151

desire of both Vincent Freeman [Ethan Hawke] and Tom Ripley [Matt Damon] is played by Jude Law. The main questions are two: by what gestures does the protagonist tries to appropriate the outer body of the other and how do the visual, gestural resources of cinema make it possible for internal and external viewers to see one face become another? To stay with the puppet metaphor for a moment: when puppets dance or John Malkovich imitates a puppet dancing – or when Matt or Ethan pretend to be Jude, or for that matter Jude Law pretends to be Dickie Greenleaf or Jerome Eugene Morrow – what "possesses" what, body or "soul"? Is the exterior mastered by something contained inside it, or does the container shape and control its contents? Is the relationship between appearance and self as labile as acting, dancing or fantasy seem to make it? Why did the late 1990s have a particular obsession with the exchangeability of skins?

Gattaca is a dystopia set in "the not-too-distant future"; it represents a time when both society and the individual are rigidly policed by a system of bodily screening. The eponymous space station is spelled with the four letters of DNA, G-A-T-C – and these are shown in the opening titles in their dazzling permutations on an identity screen: above the genome, we see the name "Morrow, Jerome", and above the name, in large capitals, the word "VALID". The face in the image is a blend of the faces of actors Ethan Hawke and Jude Law. The film's theme is a study of the forensic use of body elements – inner stuff converted into readable evidence – masquerading as a triumph of masculine aspiration over the limitations of the body. In order to reach the stars, Vincent Freeman has to lodge his "dreams" in a better body. His ambition needs Jerome Eugene Morrow's frame to function in.

Vincent is the elder of two brothers. The product of love in the back seat of a car, he is what is known as a "god-child", despised for being assumed rather than chosen: his genes carry a likely early death, whereas his younger brother has the carefully selected genes that make him a "valid". The epithet "in-valid" follows Vincent everywhere but most especially into Gattaca where, his father has warned him, "the only way you'll see the inside of a spaceship is if you're cleaning it". Cleaning is the work of keeping in order surfaces he wants to penetrate. To enter, you press a fingertip against a reader that takes a drop of blood and judges you with the buzz of a red or green light. The most intimate stuff from depth or surface – a smear of blood, a drop of urine, a single hair or flake of loose skin – acts as an index of worth. If such body bits are read as markers of self, how are they to be controlled in such a way that "you can", in the terms of the American dream, "be whoever you want to be". Inner and outer space is the large context for this, and the story is that of the "inner self" (soul, love, aspiration, a myth of personal being) becoming outer (physical appearance, the arbitrary limits of birth in this new aristocracy). In order to get off "this ball of dirt" (Eugene's phrase), Vincent has to appear to be someone else, and that someone is Jerome Eugene Morrow. Vincent and Eugene use the body for an economic transaction in which advantage proves spurious in competition with desire.

There are two versions of this desire. The first works on the surface of the body, exchanging the shameful and dangerous debris of the self for the valuable detritus of the perfect other. The wheelchair-bound Eugene despaired of life because he never was – of course – quite perfect enough: he waves a silver medal bitterly in Vincent's face, saying "Jerome Morrow was never meant to be one step down on the podium" and dies in the closing frames still clutching the medal. It is true that we expect him to disappear once Vincent goes away, because his function is to supply, not to demand. But I wonder exactly why this is; for they are not hydraulically exchangeable according to the fraternal equation "Is that the only way you can succeed: to see me fail?" Nor do they – to turn to the second mode of gestural desire – exactly blend either, despite the identity picture that puzzles the investigator. Let us examine the key instances of this "double reciprocal incarnation". First, there is a photograph beside which Vincent himself gawps comically (Figure 2).

Second, seen in the opening sequence and later, is the handsome, iron-jawed, face-labelled "Jerome Morrow – Valid" as he gazes out at us from a screen, while, we recall, the pre-metamorphosis Vincent ("In-Valid") who offered a silly half-smile, glasses on nose, unconvincing.

Vincent is weedy, Eugene is seedy, but their combination Jerome is steely, a new being, permanently on the *qui-vive* and, finally, let through for reasons combining his own greed and another man's sentimentality, and the audience is encouraged – "There is no gene for the human spirit", insists the poster – to applaud him. However, the process of borrowing body detritus is never complete: Vincent never starts "growing" Eugene's body parts of his own accord. This is most definitely not a cyborg fantasy. Body and technology, for all the intentions of the civilisation the film represents, never do work together; they are always inimical. So Vincent never gets a transplant or transfusion of Eugene, he has to renew the process laboriously day by day – this is *Groundhog Day*, not *The Fly*. It is the laboriousness and labour of the process that is the moral basis of the tale: masculine aspiration is no easier than feminine housework, both are reproductive, apparently purposeless repetition, the mountain never conquered, until suddenly it is, and you are no longer Sisyphus/Prometheus but the eagle. The lesson is that you really will only see the inside of a spaceship by cleaning it, and by cleaning

Figure 2.   *Gattaca* (Niccol, 1997) Vincent to Jerome.

153

yourself, over and over again everyday. But then, one might wish to ask: what is the point of seeing the inside of a spaceship?

The second reason takes us into an extra-diegetic area. I want to suggest that it is the non-identity of the two men for the audience that provides part of the effect of the film's myth. Intra-diegetically, the disguise, although always provisional, is successful. "You look so right together I want to double my fee", says black market agent German. "We don't look anything alike", Vincent replies. "It's close enough", says German; "when was the last time anyone looked at a photograph?" Both their eye colour and their accents are different, yet it is understood that with the prosthetic adjustments this will not matter: "He's a foreigner" – "They don't care where you were born: just how". And it doesn't. Bit by bit the identity swap "takes" place. When Vincent wants to give up, Eugene retorts angrily: "You still don't understand, do you? When they look at you they don't see you, they only see me".

Do we as an audience come to accept it as reasonable that Vincent/Ethan Hawke is taken for Eugene/Jude Law? This question arises again in relation to *The Talented Mr Ripley*, in which again Jude Law plays the body to be assumed. Having acted Lord Alfred Douglas the same year in Brian Gilbert's *Wilde* (1997), Law established himself as the quintessential beautiful Englishman – an Englishman capable of playing Americans as well, as other films show. In *Gattaca*, his English accent is preserved. When the two men are first seen side by side, it is not true to say, as the early screenplay did, that "we are struck by the similarity of Eugene's face to Jerome's", and again we must assume that Niccol chose to present us with this challenge. When an audience watches an actor playing a part, what difference does it make that Ethan Hawke has taken over from Jude Law the task of playing a character squatting inside the latter's body?

If, ultimately, we see what we want to know, we virtually invent the blended face of the neo-Jerome Morrow, which neither we nor the characters in the fiction have ever actually perceived outside a photo-fit. It appears that Eugene/Jerome accepts this logic, for he disposes of himself as the credits roll – down with the rubbish, like a golden Gregor Samsa. Or rather, he knows he has not been blended but replaced, and perhaps this is what makes him so sure of being redundant. In my other example, the Jude Law character has no such choice.

In *The Talented Mr Ripley*, again, we find two very different faces – and voices, and bodily styles – blended into one. At one point, we see Dickie Greenleaf show his passport to an unconvinced American Express official, insisting: "It is me, it's an old picture". Later, Tom Ripley twice uses the same passport photo to identify himself as the now-disappeared Dickie; the officials look down, then, up, then smile in recognition. Enough people mistrust Tom to put him in permanent danger, but by the end of the film they are either dead or disbelieved. And this is because this fairytale is altogether less forensic than *Gattaca*. Whether, as in the earlier case, we wish the upstart to succeed – and Minghella's Ripley is much more poignant than Highsmith's, for a variety of reasons – what is certain is that we are as seduced by the magic of Ripley's imitations as he is by the magic of what Dickie possesses: two fetishisms work through each other.

By contrast to the two protagonist/actors in René Clément's *Plein Soleil* (1960), Tom/Matt and Dickie/Jude are physically un-alike. But there are several moments when we see an image by which their faces appear so close as to cross and combine. The first occurs during a visit to a jazz club. Dickie invites an initially reluctant Tom to join him and another singer on stage. Briefly and joyfully, their two faces form one. The second, as we shall see in a moment, occurs when – and because – this idyll is ending.

Tom's desire for entry into the charmed space of others' pleasure is a combination of jealousy and avidity, as we shall see in a moment. When Dickie rejects him, it is at a record store where Dickie's and Freddie's heads bend together, in a closed glass booth, over a common headset. And of course it is Freddie, a grotesque version of Dickie's drawling superiority, who later, in Rome, defines the failure of Tom to convince in his assumption of Dickie's style and identity, with the single damning epithet "bourgeois".

In Rome, Tom Ripley assumes dead Dickie's name and style. He does this by a more conventional version of the bodily fetishism of *Gattaca*: he takes up the external objects – clothing, gait, furniture, décor – that he once coveted. Dickie was always casually but elegantly dressed, Tom eager and uncomfortable in his knitted lime-green trucks or corduroy jacket.[4] To cite Minghella once again, touching the objects is nourishment to Tom, poring caressively over Dickie's leather case of cufflinks and rings, "drinking in" or "eating up" the aesthetic of Dickie's world, a world of gleaming surfaces. Indeed it was with the deceptively glamorous surface of a garment that the whole process began: Ripley was mistaken for a Princeton graduate, and thus Dickie's peer, because he borrowed someone's jacket in which to accompany "Lullaby for Cain" in the opening scene. With Dickie gone, he can use his money to enter that world. In the novel, returning to Mongibello after killing Dickie Tom had an ecstatic moment when he thought of all the pleasures that lay before him now with Dickie's money, other beds, tables, seas, ships, suitcases, shirts, years of freedom and years of pleasure. Then he turned the light out and put his head down and almost at once fell asleep, happy, content and utterly confident, as he had never been before in his life. (Highsmith [1955] 1999, p. 97).

In the film, as we have seen, Tom appropriates the objects first by gazing and touching. But this is not only with his fingertips: in two key scenes, he touches with his face. The first occurs in a train, bringing together my two versions of gesture in this film. The two young men are sitting side by side in a closed railway carriage; Dickie seems to be asleep. Knowing this is the end of the "blissful" (Minghella DVD commentary) period of their friendship and unable to resist, Tom bends towards Dickie – or, specifically, towards the lapel of his silk jacket – and lays not his fingers (after hesitating) but his face on it – lips, nose, cheek (Figure 3).[5]

The conductor knocks on the window, and both heads move; then, looking beyond Dickie at their joint reflection in the window, Tom sees what he longs for: their two selves united (Figure 4).

With his eyes still closed, cruel Dickie asks: "Why do you do that thing with your neck?", breaking not only the spell but Tom's ability to hope with his body. Thus, in this brief moment on the train, the last journey they will take together except to death, both gestures coalesce and then fall apart.

From here on Tom can desire only to be Dickie, not to have him or to be with him. Being taken for the other replaces that desynchronicity of touch and image that is possible (if frustrating) while the beloved exists; once he does not, wholly new possibilities arise. We saw Tom hand over Dickie's passport photo and be accepted with an obsequious smile; later, as suspicion and detection close in on him, just before he leaves for Venice, two images show his separation from the brief fantasy of living Dickie's life: first he scratches the face out of the passport, and then, reflected in the glowing wood of the piano, his face comes apart like unjoined twins. This marks, as Minghella comments, "the end of the joy being Dickie Greenleaf and now [he goes] back to the punishment of being Tom Ripley".

Figure 3. *The Talented Mr Ripley* (Minghella, 1999) Tom touches Dickie's lapel.

Figure 4. *The Talented Mr Ripley* (Minghella, 1999) Tom and Dickie's reflections merge.

The shape of the narrative, indeed, follows the progress of Tom's gestural desire. First, he "catches" voices, musical tastes and handwriting, thereby also catching the attention of Dickie in what Minghella calls "impressions to impress". Later he desires both the man and his appurtenances: the objects, the manner, the glow. These could be accessed by touch or by an imitation that blurs into a blending – but only after Dickie is materially dead: only then he can be reincarnated in the beliefs of others, including (almost) Tom's own. Finally, Tom separates from this and his nemesis comes – again, in a boat – when, once again and for the last time before returning "to the basement", he lays his face on a garment: the sweater of the unsuspecting Peter, whom he is at the same time murdering.

The non-haptic caress that we see enacted by Tom's face or the back of Ada's hand is always elegiac. It cannot "possess", in either sense. It does not grasp, not only because all caress is perforce a "placing up against", but also because it recognises the approximation of desire, which is always only a borrowing of the other's surface. It is provisional. Thus the mediate touch just before Tom strangles Peter or Ada places her foot in the coil of rope carrying her piano to the ocean's bed, is itself a winding-about of what cannot be held.

And to return, finally, to the question of film: what do we get out of watching fictional people look at Vincent or Tom and see Eugene or Dickie – or, more accurately, looking at Ethan or Matt and seeing Jude? I would like to suggest that it is something of the same quasi-mathematical problem that we face when putting *Gattaca* and *Ripley* together and asking whether this is supplementation or replacement. For all they dwell avidly on the other's surface, Vincent and Tom are cannibals: their object must perish by their greed; desire may borrow but replacement is theft. But what goes on for us, the audience, extra-diegetically? As I have suggested earlier, in seeing someone believe that there is no Jude Law except occupied by Matt or Ethan, we are doing nothing so very different from seeing him occupied by Eugene or Dickie. The pleasure of seeing others believe is connected to our own pleasure in suspending disbelief. But in cinematic gesture another dimension is added. What characters and actors have in common is that they are materially there: they can touch. We of course, cannot reach into the film world, deny fictionality and touch them. All we can do is make believe.

Acknowledgements

Elements of this essay have appeared in my *Consensuality*. All translations from French are my own and reference is to the original text.

Notes

1. This, the 359th of Chamfort's *Maximes et pensées* is a familiar notion in French culture; it is cited not only by Sartre in this quotation but also, for example, in Gide 1911, p. 61 and Anzieu, 1995, p. 32.
2. In relation to the use of the term "haptic": Rodaway, 1997 uses the term for the full range of the sense of touch (pp. 41–60) and Marks, 2000 defines it as "the combination of tactile, kinaesthetic and proprioceptive functions" which she associates in video with "the caressing look" p. 2 and p. 8). But, leaning on its etymology in the Greek for "fasten" or "grasp" and its current usage in the science of cyber-touching (see Castañeda, 2001), I prefer to keep to a narrower definition that distinguishes it, as does Sartre, from the "studied languor" of the caress, which does not lay hold of anything.
3. Though they may resemble them somewhat, my examples and my topic are very different from either masquerade, as represented in Joan Riviere's "Womanliness as Masquerade"

article of 1929 or performativity, as theorised by Judith Butler in 1990 and subsequently transposed by other theorists to performance studies, etc. If we take Riviere's analysis of the assumption by career women of "feminine" costume and gesture as a sub-set of Butler's analysis of the daily work of gender, these are ritual and quasi-enforced processes that act in a continuous way, creating individual personality within a social regime. The examples I cite from *Gattaca* and *The Talented Mr Ripley*, like the similar acts in *Being John Malkovich* (1999), are momentary expediencies assumed for motives of personal gain, pleasure or ambition.

4. Curiously, in Highsmith's novel, it is Dickie who wears the corduroy jacket, a reminder of how anachronistic glamour can be.

5. *The Talented Mr Ripley* (Minghella, 1999). Minghella's audio commentary is on DVD released by Miramax in 2000.

References

Anzieu, A. ([1977] 1989). De la chair au verbe: mutisme et bégaiement'. In D. Anzieu, B. Gibello, R. Gori, A. Anzieu, B. Barrau, M. Mathieu, & W. R. Bion (Eds.), *Psychanalyse et langage* (pp. 103–131). Paris: Dunod.

Anzieu, D. (1991). *Une Peau pour les pensées: Entretiens avec Gilbert Tarrab*. Paris: Apsygée.

Anzieu, D. ([1985] 1995). *Le Moi-peau*. Paris: Dunod.

Butler, J. (1990). *Gender trouble*. New York, NY: Routledge.

Campion, J. (1993). *The Piano screenplay*. London: Bloomsbury.

Campion, J. (Director). (1993). *The piano*. Australia: CiBy.

Castañeda, C. (2001). Robotic skin: The future of touch? In S. Ahmed, & J. Stacey (Eds.), *Thinking through the skin* (pp. 223–236). London: Routledge.

Chamfort, Sébastien-Roch, N. ([1796] 1923). *Maximes et pensées*. Paris: Éditions G. Crès.

Clément, R. (Director). (1960). *Plein soleil*. France: Robert and Raymond Hakim.

Dyson, L. (1995). The return of the repressed? Whiteness, femininity and colonialism in The Piano. *Screen, 36*, 267–276.

Gide, A. (1924). *Incidences*. Paris: Gallimard.

Gilbert, B. (Director). (1997). *Wilde*. BBC Films.

Highsmith, P. ([1955] 1999). *The Talented Mr. Ripley*. London: Vintage.

Jonze, S. (Director). (1999). *Being John Malkovich*. Universal Studios.

Keane, M. ([1981] 2001). *Good behaviour*. London: Virago.

Marks, L. U. (2000). *The skin of the film*. Durham: Duke University Press.

Merleau-Ponty, M. (1964). *Le Visible et l'invisible*. Paris: Gallimard.

Minghella, A. (Director). (1999). *The talented Mr. Ripley*. Miramax and Paramount.

Musset, A. de ([1834] 1976). *Lorenzaccio*. Paris: Bordas.

Niccol, A. (Director). (1997). *Gattaca*. Columbia Pictures.

Pryor, I. (1993). Interview with Jane Campion. *Onfilm, 10*, 25.

Rodaway, P. (1997). *Sensuous geographies*. London: Routledge.

Sartre, J. P. (1943). *L'Être et le néant*. Paris: Gallimard.

Sedgwick, E. K. (2003). *Touching feeling*. Durham: Duke University Press.

Segal, N. (1997). The fatal attraction of *The Piano*. In N. White, & N. Segal (Eds.), *Scarlet letters* (pp. 199–211). London: Macmillan.

Segal, N. (2009). *Consensuality: Didier Anzieu, gender and the sense of touch*. Amsterdam: Rodopi.

Van Rysselberghe, M. (1974). *Les Cahiers de la Petite Dame Cahiers André Gide* (Vol. 5). Paris: Gallimard.

Waters, M. (Director). (2003). *Freaky friday*. Buena Vista.

A mark on the Canvas

Carol Mayo Jenkins

Department of Theatre, College of Arts and Sciences, University of Tennessee, Knoxville, TN, USA

This essay considers the meaning and importance of gesture on stage and screen. It analyses how gesture is used by actors as a means to advance narrative and to communicate feeling. Drawing on her own experiences in theatre and television, Jenkins addresses the crucial, critically instructive differences that exist between how an actor approaches gesture in on-camera acting and in acting on stage. The essay also reflects on how Jenkins's training, particularly with Yat Malmgren, has influenced her outlook on gesture which she perceives as a vital dimension to the actor's craft.

Contemplating the subject of gesture in theatre and film acting, I find I must first clarify the parameters of the term "gesture". The Oxford English Dictionary definition is: "a movement of part of the body, especially a hand or the head, to express an idea or meaning". That is quite clear, but here's another: "any body movement (including facial expressions), which accompanies or replaces speech". I prefer this second definition, because I feel that, for the actor, any movement at all – no matter how small – is a note played on the instrument and therefore key to the performance.

An actor has three tools – the voice, the body and the mind. This correlates to the audience's perception – what they hear, what they see and what they think. Perception varies, of course, in all three areas, but the actor must hone his skills carefully to project exactly the meaning he wishes to convey with clarity and the requisite power. Feelings – emotion – arise, both in the actor and the audience, as a result of the successful deployment of these three skills.

It is a disturbing truth that in the theatre our audiences do not listen as intently as in the past. We have been conditioned, first by film, then television, then the Internet, to rely more upon what we see than what we hear to gather information or to be entertained. Falling chandeliers (*Phantom of the Opera*), landing helicopters (*Miss Saigon*) and flying bodies (*Spider-Man*), are some of the more spectacular attempts of theatre to offer experience visceral enough to lure audiences. Certainly, film is a more visual than auditory medium – after all, the original name of the invention was "moving pictures".

In the theatre, we spend a great deal of time training our actors NOT to gesture. Extraneous flapping about of the hands and arms in space only muddles the picture, so the audience cannot discern what is going on with the actor. ANY movement in space must be generated by the character's intention, the actor's need to communicate a specific truth of the moment. The movement, or gesture, will come from the actor's response to a circumstance, through a body trained to precisely reflect the actor's impulse. Training of the actor's body takes many forms, but the essential goal of all, I believe, is to develop the inner core of awareness and create release, strength and flexibility so that the body can respond freely and immediately to the actor's impulse. This is a lifetime's work, of course, and requires constant maintenance. However, that is the goal – the actor's instrument is like a clean canvas upon which he may draw any character he wishes and defines that character by shape, sound, and – of course – gesture.

The actor's job, simply put, is to tell a story. In the beginning, we have the writer's words – not only the words we speak, but often quite poetic stage directions or, in film, descriptions of action. Our job is to bring those words to life. For speaking the author's words, we train our voices with rigorous physicality as we do our bodies, to open areas of resonance, to strengthen breath support and to be as responsive to our thought as our bodies are to our impulse. We choose pitch, rate and volume in the same manner that we choose gesture in order to bring our story to life.

Some may opine that gesture is more important for the stage actor as the audience sees the entire body all the time, while in film the actor is often in close-up or even off camera. This, in my view, is nonsense. The actor's use of gesture is certainly as compelling in film as in theatre; it is, however, very different.

I remember seeing Arianne Mnouchkine's extraordinary Théâtre de Soleil and marvelling at the extreme physicality of her company. They were speaking French; I could not follow the words at all, but I knew exactly what was going on all the time because of the clarity of their gesture. The actor playing Hotspur in *Henry IV* was so angry and frustrated in the "My Lord, I did deny no prisoners" speech that, around "God save the mark!" I expect, he simply flipped over backwards and continued his harangue the moment his feet hit the floor. It was as stunning an evocation of that character in that scene as I have ever witnessed. Helene Weigle's silent scream in *Mother Courage and Her Children* (Dirs. Peter Palitzsch and Manfred Wekwerth, East Germany, 1961) is another legendary example of an actor finding in a gesture more than words could possibly convey.

There is, of course, an entire language of gesture that we all recognize – the hands up to ward off danger or pain; the dropped head to signify shame or sorrow; and the collapsed torso conveying fatigue or lack of will. François Delsarte, in the nineteenth century, created an enormously complex science of gesture, posture, facial expressions and physical attitudes, in order to project to an audience the character's exact emotional state. But then, later, Stanislavsky proposed an entirely different way of working – that the actor must, through imaginary given circumstances and his own experience, truly recreate what the character is going through, and his body – if well trained – will respond with authentic posture and gesture. This "Method" has become the hallmark of our modern acting, in one form or another, although the quest to find the perfect gesture – the one physical attitude or phrase that will most tellingly communicate our story – is always in the actor's mind.

I had the great good fortune to study for three years, in the 1960s, with Yat Malmgren at the Drama Centre, London. Yat and his associate, Christopher Fettes, led us through a rigorous training combining the movement analysis of Rudolf Laban, the theory of psychological types of Carl Jung and the work of Constantine Stanislavsky (Jung, 1971; Laban, 1960; Stanislavsky, 1968). The complexity of this training is at the heart of my work to this day. I remember Yat speaking often of "shadow moves", simply the movement of the eyes in film, the slightest shift of which could define a moment. I think I didn't really understand at the time, but years later his words came back to me when I began work on the television series, *Fame* (1982–1987). I had done a few things on film before, but I quickly realized that I needed much more knowledge to deal with the camera. I went to our cinematographer and asked for help. He was very willing to teach me, but he insisted that I go to "dailies" to watch the scenes we had shot the day before. "No one knows your work better than you" he said. "You know what you want; you know how to get it".

It was great advice. Painful as it was, watching myself began to work like bio-feedback. The habits I hated disappeared; the glass wall between me and the camera came down. It took a very long time for me to trust that I could "do" so little, that the camera would read my thoughts, and that the "shadow moves" I was not even aware of were telling my story. This, to me, is the most important use of gesture in film. Eventually, one learns the art of this gesture. If the eyes are the windows to the soul, so the actor's soul is laid bare to the camera through his eyes in a scene. Sometimes, the gesture is minuscule; most often, its impact is huge. As with all gesture, the "shadow moves" will come from the purity of the actor's involvement in the scene, the clarity of his intention and the discipline of his craft.

At least 30 years ago, I saw a Japanese film called *The Naked Island* (Dir. Kaneto Shindō, Japan, 1960). It was an unforgettable experience. A man and his wife live and farm on an island which has no water. Their plot is on a hillside, each row descending from the one above. Every day they must load heavy water jugs onto their small boat and row to the mainland, where they fill the jugs with precious water and row home. They then carefully eke out just the right amount to each row until their supply is exhausted. They eat a small meal, sleep, and the next day repeat the process. It is back-breaking work, repetitive and endless. They never speak. There is no dialogue at all in the two-hour film. The rhythm of their life, of their work, is established. There is no need for words; they communicate by action. One day, the woman's foot slips on the hillside and she drops the heavy jug; the water spills down, uselessly flooding a row. The man approaches her, watching the water flow away. He hits the woman, knocking her to the ground. They are both motionless. After a time, the woman gets up, fetches another jug, and they resume the rhythm of their work. It has been 30 years – I don't remember the looks that may have passed between them, I don't remember details of their day. I only remember the beauty of the simplicity of their story, the symphony of their movement and the huge emotional impact of its disruption. This is the power of gesture – in film or in theatre – when it is so clean and specific, when it indeed becomes art.

A few years ago, I saw the great Quebecois theatre artist, Robert LePage, in his *The Blue Dragon*. The play began with LePage on stage with an artist's pad and brush, making strokes of calligraphy. Each time his brush marked the paper, it was simultaneously shown on a great blank screen before the audience. "Ah, yes", I thought. "This is the actor's art – the mark upon the canvas. The shape, the gesture, the one clear image that defines the character and tells the audience "You recognize me. Here is my story". Again, it is a lifetime's work.

References

Jung, C. (1971). *Psychological types*. Princeton: Princeton University Press.
Laban, R. (1960). *The mastery of movement* (2nd ed.). London: MacDonald & Evans.
Stanislavsky, C. (1968). *Creating a role*. London: Mentor.

Index